William Goldman:
The Reluctant
Storyteller

About the Author

Londoner Sean Egan has contributed to, among others, *Billboard, Book Collector, Classic Rock, Record Collector, Tennis World, Total Film, Uncut,* and RollingStone.com. He has written or edited twenty-three books, including works on The Beatles, The Rolling Stones, Bob Dylan, Manchester United Football Club, *Coronation Street,* James Kirkwood, and Tarzan. His critically acclaimed novel *Sick of Being Me* was published in 2003, while his 2008 collection of short stories *Don't Mess with the Best* carried cover endorsements from Booker Prize winners Stanley Middleton and David Storey.

William Goldman:

The Reluctant Storyteller

Sean Egan

BearManor Media

2014

William Goldman: The Reluctant Storyteller

© 2014 Sean Egan

For information, address:

BearManor Media
P. O. Box 71426
Albany, GA 31708

bearmanormedia.com

Typesetting and layout by John Teehan

Published in the USA by BearManor Media

ISBN—1-59393-583-8
978-1-59393-583-2

Table of Contents

Introduction

WILLIAM GOLDMAN IS A RELUCTANT STORYTELLER.
Although he harbored ambitions to be a professional writer from childhood, and persisted with those ambitions in the face of incredible humiliations, the achievement of his goal did not bring about the joy that might have been expected. The reason for this may be as much to do with an absence of self-esteem resulting from his loveless childhood as the lack of encouragement his first writing submissions yielded, but during the entire course of his professional life he seems never to have been able to take the risk of assuming himself to be gifted. He has always characterized the location of his work as his "pit" and likened the process of writing to a miniature prison term.

All of which makes it a startling fact that that he was one of the late twentieth century's most popular storytellers.

Amongst his more than two-dozen motion picture screenplays number such iconic works as *Butch Cassidy and the Sundance Kid, The Stepford Wives, All the President's Men, Marathon Man*, and *A Bridge Too Far*. Although the job is by definition usually uncredited, he is also well-known as a 'script doctor,' somebody whose knowledge about what does and does not work cinematically is so vast that he has been paid large sums to apply his magic touch to already existing screenplays that lack that vital something to make it a box office smash.

This sort of achievement has been the making of the reputation of many. However, there is—remarkably—far more to Goldman than his motion picture-related career. He began life as a novelist. That his sixteen works in that field include *The Temple of Gold, Boys and Girls Together, The Princess Bride*, and *Marathon Man*—respectively an elegant literary novel, a sprawling state-of-the-union address, a post-modern fairytale, and a blood-drenched thriller—indicates the extraordinary breadth of his

1

prose vision. Goldman has also produced a significant body—more than half-a-dozen works—of reportage and journalism. *The Season* is an irreverent but fearsomely well-researched examination of Broadway, which, over four decades since its publication, is still considered by many the definitive work on the subject. In the eighties, *Adventures in the Screen Trade* kicked off Goldman's parallel career as the twinkle-eyed chronicler from a ringside seat of Hollywood vanity and vacillation. It bequeathed the endlessly repeated quote about the movie industry, "Nobody knows anything."

That Goldman has also written plays, musicals, short stories, and children's books demonstrates, yet further, how vigorous and expansive are his creative abilities.

Moreover, he has achieved all of this without ever lunging for the lowest common denominator. Although his body of work has been consumed by millions, he has never let his populism overwhelm a glittering intelligence and penchant for upending expectation.

That extraordinary body of work is examined within these pages.

The main focus of this book is Goldman's prose. For the first time ever, his books are scrutinized at length. Whereas a newspaper review of one of his novels might usually run to a few hundred words, in these pages sometimes five thousand words are spent exploring why a book works or fails.

Some will be surprised by this. It instinctively feels logical that motion pictures should be the main focus of a study of Goldman's oeuvre because, although he has had plenty of million-selling books, movies routinely reach a far wider audience. That the ratios in this book are as they are is for a reason that couldn't be better summarized than by the words of Goldman himself in his book *William Goldman's Story of A Bridge Too Far*: "No one is the author of a film, just as no one is author of any national magazine or big city newspaper. These are group achievements … In a movie, everything overlaps. Unless you are right there, on that spot at that moment, there is just no way of ascertaining what anybody's specific contribution was."

However, while it is easier to attribute responsibility to Goldman for the merits and demerits of his books, to not discuss his movies at all would be absurd: that the body of cinematic work bearing his name is widely-acclaimed proves on some level that he is a screenwriter of profound ability. Accordingly, all of his motion pictures are critiqued, if not to the same extent as his books. Where they are, what has been assessed is what made it to the screen, regardless of the fact of it being, by definition, a vision filtered through the minds and techniques of others. Drafts of Goldman's scripts are stored in the

William Goldman Papers at his *alma mater* Columbia University, but no attempt has been made to analyze these. A mission of contrast-and-compare with regard to the finished motion picture would prove nothing. It would also be hugely onerous: Goldman revealed in *Four Screenplays with Essays* (1997) that there were twenty-one drafts of *Misery* over the course of eighteen months. In any case, such a step would offend against the unwritten agreement between critic and reader whereby the average reader has the ready means by which to relate his conclusions to a critic's.

Similarly, no analysis is proffered of the considerable number of Goldman screenplays that have been commercially published. (Journalist Liz Smith claims that Applause's program of publication of Goldman's scripts constitutes the "largest collection of work ever by a living screenwriter.") These screenplays are simply snapshots in a long production process. That a script is always fluid is reflected in, for instance, the fact that having a song accompany the bicycle frolic in *Butch Cassidy and the Sundance Kid*—one of the film's cornerstones—was not in Goldman's original work but was the idea of director George Roy Hill. Goldman has also admitted that he has tampered with his commercially published scripts, reinserting cherished parts jettisoned in that long production process.

Something with which this book will also not deal, except in passing, is Goldman's uncredited doctoring work. Such works resist analysis as being definably the undiluted product of his consciousness even more than do his produced, credited screenplays. Also not discussed are works written by Goldman that did not see commercial release or production. In addition to being a very deep well, it would again undermine the principle of the critic not being at an advantage.

It should be noted that an analysis and contextualization of everything to which Goldman has ever attached his name is an endeavor guaranteed not to meet the approval of its subject. "Critics are all whores and failures," Goldman says within these pages. This acidly absolutist point of view did not stop Goldman from being kind enough to cooperate with this book by granting the author a series of interviews from 2007 to 2013, quotes from which are dispersed throughout.

Goldman frequently makes comments like, "I don't like my writing," perhaps another reason for his disdain for critical analysis. Yet his cooperation would suggest that he understands that his canon bears examination. This book seeks to explain why it does.

PART I

A Guilty Success

1

> "I think Graham Greene once said, 'an unhappy childhood is a writer's gold mine,' a statement with more than a little wisdom."

So said William Goldman in his 1977 book *William Goldman's Story of A Bridge Too Far* (a slim volume with, it is already evident, a disproportionate number of quotable passages). Goldman is a man who never experienced financial hardship and a writer whose early success meant that he did not benefit from the valuable rites-of-passage that see budding novelists soaking up raw material as they scuffle through their twenties in a series of menial positions to support their writing ambitions. "I've never had a real job. I've only been a writer," says Goldman in a tone of voice that communicates knowledge of the potentially detrimental effect of this fact upon his career. Apart from research and imagination, he has generally only been able to draw upon the experiences and insights accumulated before he obtained what used to be called the age of majority: a solitary, desk-bound and well-rewarded profession is not the kind of thing to create a repository of interesting stories to which the common man can relate. Unfortunately for the young Goldman's sense of self-esteem but fortunately for his writing career, his childhood was as grim as they come, and the experiences and insights gained therefrom gripping stuff.

Goldman was born on August 12, 1931 in, he says, "a small town, not so small anymore but it was when I was growing up, outside Chicago: Highland Park, Illinois." He explains, "My father was a lot older than my mother. He was an alcoholic. He was a brilliant man and profoundly unhappy and, as he got older, the drinking got worse and worse and whatever effect that had on me I can't even begin to tell you, but clearly it had an effect on me … My father was a successful businessman in Chicago. He worked for a large company and he was the vice-president of it. My mother became obsessed that my father would never be made president of the company because it was family-run. So she convinced him to retire, which I don't think he wanted to do, and he went into business with another man. He formed a company and it was successful but his drinking was growing out of control and his partner couldn't deal with [it] anymore, so they closed that company. That was when my father came home to live and he was in his pajamas for the last five years of his life. I was fifteen when he committed suicide. I found his body. I wasn't a good student at this point—everything was going crazy—and I was a junior in high school, I think, and I was writing a paper on wool. That had been the nature of my father's business—he'd been in the clothing business. He helped me on it and I got an 'A.' He was living in the guest room of the house at this point and I was going to go back and show him the 'A' and then I thought, no, I should do my homework first. So I did my homework and then I took the paper with the red 'A' to show it to my father and he had committed suicide and I always thought that I could have saved him obviously if I'd just gone in."

Goldman was already wrestling with an inordinate amount of guilt courtesy of his mother: "My mother was deaf. We're talking the thirties and forties. It's still a huge problem for anyone who's deaf, but back then it was just gigantic. Now they have these miniature hidden things deep inside their ears and they hear wonderfully, but in that time she wore an earpiece and she had a big, big battery that she wore on her chest or shoulder and then she had a really huge battery that she wore on her hip—and even with all of that she couldn't hear very well. I once asked her how she lost her hearing and she said, 'When you were born.' I was about fifteen and I always had that knowledge, which is a terrible thing. And then the week she died she told me the truth, which was that she lost her hearing when my brother was born. He was four years older than I was and he was the favorite in the family."

That elements of the above real-life narrative are spread across Goldman novels spaced as far apart as *Boys and Girls Together* (1964), *Control* (1982), and *The Color of Light* (1984) would seem to confirm the truth of what he said about writers in *Hype & Glory* (1990): "All we really have is our imagination, steadily weakening as we age, and whatever pipeline we can keep open to our childhood."

Big brother James would ultimately be, like Goldman, a successful writer. The fact that the brothers were roommates and writing collaborators as young men suggests that their relationship survived the complications of what Goldman terms their "fucked-up family" reasonably well. However, when he was growing up, the only person whom William Goldman felt cared if he survived was Tomine 'Minnie' Barstad. "She was the Norwegian maid we had," he explains. "She came to work for my family five years before I was born and she stayed there for forty-five or fifty years and she went back up to Minnesota. She was probably the most important person in my life. She cared for me and was very dear. The family was complicated and she was always there for me. She was also a great cook." If that sounds like Barstad assumed the role of surrogate mother, Goldman's dedicating his 1988 sports book *Wait Till Next Year* to her on the grounds that she taught him how to hit a baseball when he was aged around six even suggests something of a substitute father.

Another female who was significant for the young Goldman was one Miss Roginski. Goldman: "She was my teacher in first, second and third grade. She was very important back then. Not as important as Minnie, but there were certain teachers that I had when I was six, seven, eight, nine, ten who liked me and that was a big deal because my family life was very strange." Said teacher's influence has echoed down the years in Goldman's fiction, if in various spellings. There is a murder victim named Belle Roginsky in *No Way to Treat a Lady* (1964), a kindly and inspirational teacher named Miss Roginski in *The Princess Bride* (1973), and a similarly loved teacher named Miss Roginsky in *The Color of Light* (1984). If by the time of his 2000 non-fiction work *Which Lie Did I Tell?* he was now calling her "Rogelski"—an apparent confusion with a Bertha Rogelski who featured in his 1963 short story 'Something Blue'—the weight of Goldman's tributes down the years surely merited clemency.

Goldman says, "I went to Oberlin, which is a small school in Ohio and a wonderful school, and I didn't do very well but I got through it … I graduated at Oberlin in '52 and went in the army for two years 'til '54 and then I went to Columbia and got a masters in English. I had the hours for a doctorate and I thought I would get the PhD. Then I realized I could never get a PhD because I don't speak languages well and you had to have a couple of foreign languages in those years to get a PhD in Columbia …

And then my life was over: I was going to go back to Chicago and take a job in an advertising agency, probably. I desperately wanted to write … I didn't know what to do. I had gotten one job offer, to teach high school in Duluth, Minnesota and I didn't want to do that. I went back home to Highland Park." Goldman started writing what would transpire to be his first published novel on June 25, 1956, not long after completing his Columbia University thesis, *The Comedy of Manners in America*. "I wrote *The Temple of Gold* I think in two weeks. It was a desperate time because I remember thinking, 'I have never been beyond page fifteen, I don't think' and suddenly I was on page fifty, and then page eighty and then whatever and then I had this novel." Beyond that element of being in uncharted territory would seem to have been an additional layer of apprehension, for as he explains, "Nobody thought I had any talent and that was the curse that I carried with me and maybe still do."

Goldman's writing ambitions started quite early but evolved over time. "I wanted to be a sports writer when I was a kid," he says. That urge died in favor of a hankering to tell stories of his own. However, sports and literature would always be intertwined in Goldman's work. In the long term, this would be manifested in him shoehorning sports references into the most unlikely places in his output. In the short term, one of the reasons for his love of Irwin Shaw was that the latter writer's football-orientated short story 'The Eighty-Yard Run' proved that literature could be about subjects about which Goldman cared. Said story appeared in Shaw's 1950 celebrated compendium *Mixed Company*. "He changed my life," claims Goldman. "I was given that book the year it came out and it changed everything. I'd wanted to be a writer and then I read *Mixed Company* and I want to say the first story is 'The Eighty-Yard Run' [it's the second] and I'm a sports nut. It was just this amazing thing and I wasn't the same. I finished the book in like two days and I was not the same ever after. He was my hero. I think my two heroes are Ingmar Bergman, who was for me the greatest screenwriter, and Irwin Shaw. I think Shaw and Fitzgerald are the two most graceful writers we've ever produced. There's very little in Irwin Shaw in the short stories of the early years that doesn't do it for me with just total grace. Never a wrong word in the stories. I just adore him."

Goldman has also publicly expressed the importance to him of Philip Wiley's *Finnley Wren* (read when thirteen or fourteen). He has stated that he considers Graham Greene the greatest novelist in English of the twentieth century. It wasn't only prose that was important to him, either.

He has stated that he started going to the theatre when he was eight and subscribing to *Variety* before he was ten.

Before the advent of the home computer, typing was an uncommon skill. Goldman acquired it in 1951, the summer after his junior year at Oberlin, where he took a modern novel course, teaching himself to navigate the QWERTY keyboard after figuring that it would be a useful proficiency both in terms of his writing ambitions and his desire to avoid being conscripted to fight in the Korean War (people with clerking abilities stayed home). Yet neither this nor his precocious penchant for literature and the stage stood him in good stead in his early storytelling activities. He recalls, "I had taken a writing class at Oberlin and gotten the worst grade in that, gotten the only C. I took a writing class at North Western University and gotten the worst grade in that ... I think I took it at summer school when I was at Oberlin, maybe junior year ... I was at Oberlin with John Kander. Johnny took the short story course at Oberlin College and we were talking in the coffee shop at college one day and he said, 'Well I've got to get back to my room, I've got to write the story for tomorrow.' And I said, 'Shit, you haven't written it yet? I've been working on mine for weeks.' And we turned in our stories and I got a C and he got a B+ and as we walked out of class he saw my grade and he started giggling and said, 'I'm sorry, Billy' ... There was a literary magazine that was published several times a year and I was the fiction editor of it. There were these two brilliant girls—one was the poetry editor, one was the overall editor—and everything was submitted anonymously. I would submit my short stories and they would say, 'Well we can't publish this shit' and I would hear myself concurring. I never got anything published until my first book. No one thought I had the least sign of talent."

Of *The Temple of Gold*, Goldman says, "I didn't know what to do with it and I had met a guy in the army who had an agent. I sent it to the agent and through [him] got Joe McCrindle, a lovely man. He sent it to Knopf, which was then—as now, I guess—the best publishing house we had. They wanted me to double it in length and I didn't know what to do about that ... That's still the most amazing thing I've ever heard any young writer be told. I was able to do it though some kind of madness but, Jesus, it's an insane thing for an editor to say."

By the time Goldman heard the verdict on his artificially lengthened literary effort, he was domiciled in a New York apartment with two other young men. They were a triumvirate of roomies individually destined for great things: one of them was his brother James, the other was his ex-Oberlin classmate John Kander, who anybody who has examined the showbills of musicals like *Cabaret*, *Chicago*, and *New York, New York* will know is one of history's outstanding stage composers. Recalls Goldman, "I got a phone call from my agent's secretary that Knopf had accepted the book. I went into a catatonic state. I didn't know what to do. I just couldn't believe it and I just walked around the apartment alone for an hour or two and I didn't tell anybody. I couldn't... I was just absolutely in a state of shock ... Then Kander came home from wherever ... He was probably coaching young singers or something, and he said, 'What's up?' and I said, 'I heard from Knopf' and he said, 'What did they say?' and I said, 'They're taking it.' He said, 'Oh Billy, that's wonderful. Have you told everybody?' And I said, 'I haven't told anybody' and then he realized the kind of shape I was in and very carefully said, 'Would you like me to help you? We could sit at the desk and you could tell me who you want told and I could dial them.' And that's what we did. I remember calling up friends and Johnny would say, 'Billy's book was taken by Knopf but he's not in very good shape,' and then friends would say, 'Oh God, that's wonderful, Bill' and I would say, 'Thank you very much' and that would be the conversation because I don't think anybody that's had a career as a writer came from further behind the starting line than I did. I mean, Jesus—it's still amazing to me."

2

"A stunning novel of today's angry, rootless, seeking young men and women in a frantic search for fulfillment."

So reads the blurb of the front cover of the 1965 UK Corgi paperback of William Goldman's first published work, *The Temple of Gold*. It was the sort of rhetoric common to the era. "I've no idea why they took it," says Goldman, "but one of the things that happened, there was an interest in publishing books by young writers and I was one of those writers who basically got picked up along with it."

When Knopf first published *The Temple of Gold* on October 14, 1957, only six years had elapsed since the publication of J.D. Salinger's *The Catcher in the Rye*, which epoch-marking classic suggested that the young had something worthwhile to say. Not only was this a radical suggestion

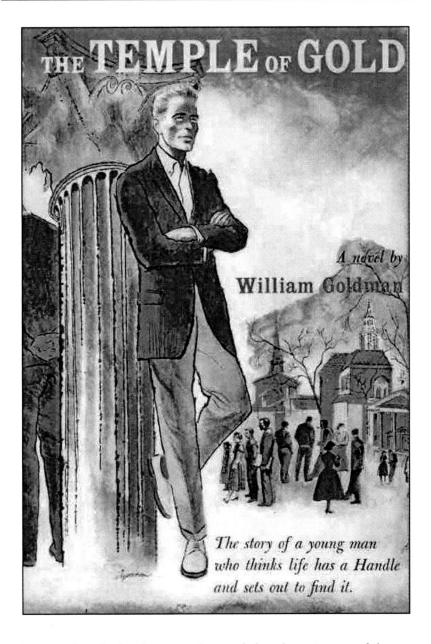

at the time, but the book even submitted that the opinions of the young might be more valid than the conformist and careerist assumptions and values of their 'elders and betters'—ones characterized by its schoolboy protagonist Holden Caulfield as "phoniness." Young perspectives became a literary fashion of the next few seasons, whether rendered in slang- and catchphrase-packed teenage vernacular as in *The Catcher in the Rye* or in a more formal, less colloquial style. Goldman remembers *Bonjour Tristesse* by Françoise Sagan—1954—as being "the big book by young people" of the period, and it's interesting that one of its central characters is named, like the protagonist of *The Temple of Gold*, Raymond. Said perspectives soon spilled over into other areas of culture with the popularity of James Dean in movies and Elvis Presley in music. As a coming-of-age tale, *The Temple of Gold* benefited from this demand for insight into the way the young felt—which, in an era well before the mindsets of young and old began to overlap, was almost a foreign language to the middle aged, particularly the middle aged who ran government and media. However, although it rode a tailwind, the book also achieved publication on merit. *The Temple of Gold* is a remarkably assured work for someone in his mid-twenties.

Raymond Trevitt is known to one and all by his middle name: Euripides, bestowed by his Greek classics expert father, a college professor whose homemaker wife is active in the local PTA and Red Cross. Euripides was raised in Athens, an Illinois town where people leave their doors unlocked. Although smoothly rendered, Euripides's childhood and teen-aged escapades range from uneventful to bland: crises are minor.

Zachary 'Zock' Crowe moves in next door to Euripides's family. He is an ugly but precociously eloquent child with whom Euripides makes instant friends. Euripides hitchhikes with him to Chicago, where they end up watching *Gunga Din*. Euripides and Zock are moved by the symbolic self-sacrifice of the water carrier at its climax, which takes place at the Temple of Gold. (Goldman has repeatedly stated in his writing that he thinks this 1939 movie the greatest of all time.)

Euripides loses his virginity and has a succession of girlfriends. Although they rather merge into one another for the reader, when one of them, Annabelle, dumps him for a college professor named Janes, Euripides goes to pot, drinking endlessly at a local bar. Zock tries to snap him out of his malaise. Euripides rewards him for this by drunkenly causing his death in a car crash. Zock in his dying breath urges Euripides to seek out the Temple of Gold, a metaphor—one which will run through the narrative—for the key to a happy life, or the 'handle.' Euripides joins the army to flee his guilt, where he kills another friend called Ulysses S. Kelly by driving him to suicide in a well-meaning attempt to make him break free of his bullying military father.

This was roughly the location of the original ending. Says Goldman, "The book ends halfway through. Zock dies and then basically he goes to pieces." This would have constituted a worthy, if rather body-strewn, novella. Impressively, there is no feeling of contrivance about what follows. If there is a different timbre to the added material, which takes Euripides to the age of twenty-one and his final departure from his hometown, it feels less a matter of seeing the join than the naturally evolving mindset of someone making the transition from adolescence to adulthood.

The grenade-inflicted suicide of Ulysses gives Euripides a knee injury that gets him demobilized within eight weeks of enlisting. He returns to an Athens where his father has just died, and where everybody feels sorry for his mother for the shame Euripides has brought on the family by killing Zock. (There is no legal comeback for such: as with the suicide of Ulysses, there seems to be no proper inquest, although that may merely be an accurate sign of the less stringent times rather than a plot hole.)

Euripides impulsively gets married to a common prostitute called Terry whom he barely knows. Although it is unsatisfying that Goldman never adequately explains why (we seem expected to accept this as the sort of thing to which young people are driven by the narrow-minded demands of parents and small-town life), Terry is a vividly-drawn character. A vulgar ingénue who wants to better herself but doesn't know how, her dialogue is the best in the book. However, the marriage is clearly doomed: Terry only ever calls her husband by his surname.

Euripides grovels his way back onto the rolls of the school out of which he had flunked and, on his return, begins work for the literary magazine. (That he gets a couple of pieces accepted for publication proves that this book is certainly not autobiography.)

Euripides's mother marries an Englishman. Her wedding day marks the occasion of her son's discovery that his own wife is being unfaithful to him with a teenaged neighbor. Not only does Euripides now not have a wife, but his childhood home is being sold as his mother decides to go and live with her husband in his homeland. Whether this latter fact causes Euripides trauma isn't explored, but when he goes looking for Terry at brothels and runs into an old college friend who has abandoned his intended romantic career as a poet for prosaic army life, it brings him down so badly that he babbles incoherently to a random priest about his guilt over Zock's death and ends up committed (coincidentally or not, the fate that befell Holden Caulfield in *The Catcher in the Rye*). Euripides is allowed to leave after a week. At home, he has a flash of understanding when he realizes that his father had not been the austere tyrant he assumed but a good man who had tried to help him.

Euripides elects to leave Athens but, before he does, pays another visit to the grave of Zock. In a moving scene, he apologizes to his old friend for the fact that he doesn't think the Temple of Gold actually exists and that he is going to stop searching for it.

Something else the departing Trevitt informs his friend's resting place is a line that could have come out of the 1953 Marlon Brando biker movie *The Wild One*: "There's a lot of places I haven't been and I've been here." Yet Euripides is not a rebellious firebrand. Not only is he bourgeois, but where there might be expected self-aggrandizement in his make-up, very often there is self-deprecation and amusement at past immature folly. He is more a 'Crazy Mixed-Up Kid' in the style of James Dean's character in *Rebel Without a Cause* (1955), lashing out almost in spite of, not because of, his economic privilege and relative domestic stability.

In the fifties and sixties, the fashion was to portray and perceive such behavior as not sociopathic but an inverted form of integrity, the sign of a healthily questioning mind. This supposed integrity and the fact that he is funny—possessing a neat line in wisecracks and retorts—does not quite compensate for the fact that Euripides is not very pleasant even over and above the self-absorption of youth. Goldman stops short of *The Catcher in the Rye*'s out-and-out colloquialism but employs a first-person, chatty narrative. It is superficially attractive, a style which makes the protagonist feel like good company. However, it becomes clear after a while that, however amusing Euripides may be as a storyteller, you wouldn't want to live with him. He is consistently, glibly ungrateful for acts of kindness. He is especially offhand with women. A particularly unpleasant incident occurs when Annabelle begs him for some money for an abortion after she has been made pregnant by Professor Janes. They have sex on Zock's grave, but Euripides has no intention of making good on his promise of money in exchange. It's a symbolic but convoluted act of vengeance, Euripides's reasoning being that if Annabelle hadn't dumped him, he would not have spiraled into the alcoholism that ultimately killed Zock.

The quality of *The Temple of Gold*'s dialogue is, as it will always be with Goldman, mixed. Already, he is demonstrating a penchant for unrealistic but entertaining repartee that would become one of his trademarks, a type of dialogue in fact which—perhaps significantly—is far more common in screenwriting than prose work:

"...you're supposed to come to a party at my house a week from Sunday. Two in the afternoon. And wear a necktie:"
"Ridiculous," I answered, hitting a big oak across the ravine. "I won't come."
"My mother may never get over it," Zock said. And then: "What if we forget about the necktie?"
"I might," I told him. "You going to be there?"
"Unfortunately, yes."
"If you can take it," I said. "Then so can I."
"Fine." Zock laughed. "You just won me a double allowance."

The exchange produced at the juncture at which the pair's brawny friend Felix casually holds Zock over his head ("Must you do this?"/ "Sometimes it satisfies me") is simply the stuff of comic books.

Yet Goldman also displays a knack for naturalistic speech, such as Euripides's flustered reaction when Zock is preoccupied preparing for a date: "Who's the girl, Zock? Do I know her? Is she from around here? Who's the girl? You're not really going. You're kidding. Aren't you, Zock? Who's the girl? Naw. There's no girl. You're only kidding."

However, one thing that would never ring true in Goldman fiction is the dialogue of children. Raymond's first meeting with Zock at the age of eight or nine contains some resoundingly false exchanges ("I hear you're an angel"/ "I hear you're not").

Although not a classic, and sometimes tiresome to read because of the way the young tend to be of the impression that their problems are unique to them, in many ways *The Temple of Gold* is actually far classier than most of Goldman's later works. It is a true literary novel, from that title/central theme—which gives it the aura, however superficial or illusory, of being more than simply a sequence of events—on down. Goldman weaves subtle patterns, nudging the reader into comprehension instead of underlining his points. He throws in detail that has the whiff of the symbolism beloved by serious writers, for example, the fact that the bedroom of Terry's teenaged lover was once Zock's bedroom.

There are some nuggets of truly fine writing, one example of which resembles cinema 'undercranking': "I ran along the road that led to Athens. I ran past the bushes and the trees and the lanes and the big highway leading to Chicago. I ran past the college and Patriot's Square. I ran until I saw my bed in front of me and then I lay down, staring up at the cracks in the ceiling or out the window at the sunrise."

Some of the writing is remarkable not just for its technical class but its philosophical maturity: "We are not remembered for what we are, not for an act that portrays us truly, but more often for some little thing, some one-time wonder when we crossed, just for a minute, outside of the natural orbit of our lives."

Despite its quality, *The Temple of Gold* is compromised by exigency. Goldman feebly attempts to shoehorn some sense of the teenage alienation zeitgeist into the book by depicting Euripides's father as fickle in his love for the guppies whose accidental killing by his son infuriates him and by portraying his mother as uncaring about the death of his dog Baxter. The author would have been better advised to use the far more powerful alienation material from his own childhood, but almost none of this finds its way into his text, something quite remarkable considering that debuts are traditionally the most autobiographical works of a novelist's oeuvre. Asked whether he left out this potentially powerful material because he was worried at the time about upsetting his family, Goldman says, "Sure. Must have been." In fact, he defrayed full exploitation of this wretched hinterland until *The Color of Light* three decades later.

A 2001 Ballantine paperback edition of *The Temple of Gold* included as an afterword a first chapter excised by Knopf, although a large chunk of it does appear verbatim in the original published book's text. The rest of the deleted chapter is waffling and seeks to give a false life-affirming rationale to the contents.

Goldman reflects, "When I went home to write that first book, if that book had not been taken—and, God knows, nobody I knew thought it would ever be taken—I never would have written the second book because there was no reason to go on." That Goldman—clearly at that point beaten down by years of rejection—lucked in to a publisher who could apprehend his talent is fortunate for both him and those who have enjoyed his subsequent career.

3

There will be little analysis of his work by Goldman himself in this book. This is principally because Goldman has no understanding of his own work.

"I'm totally instinctive. I don't know what I'm doing. I never have," he says. "I'm always amazed when I can write something. I mean, I haven't written a novel in twenty years and I'm just as amazed that I haven't written a novel in twenty years. I don't know what I'm doing. I wish I did so I could say, 'Ah yes, you see the symbolism here is what James Joyce did there.' That's all bullshit. I'm just trying to tell a story. That's all I ever wanted to be, was a storyteller." He also says, "I [don't] like my writing. I wrote a movie called *Butch Cassidy and the Sundance Kid* and I wrote a novel called *The Princess Bride* and those are the only two things I've ever written, not that I'm proud of, but that I can look at without humiliation."

Some might feel extremely surprised by this statement. After all, going back several decades, Goldman's books, almost without exception, carry a page listing all of his officially credited work: books, motion pictures, play and even the never commercially released musical *A Family Affair.* That unusual policy—far more exhaustive than the standard "Other books by this author you may enjoy" or "Also by 'X' in 'Y' Books"—seems to suggest a contractual stipulation, itself implying great pride in his output. "No, that's just the publishers doing it," Goldman says. "Nothing to do with me."

Consistent with his instinctive approach is the fact that "it's pretty much the case" that he doesn't take notes and that he doesn't inspect his own work either before publication—with the exceptions of a read-through before submission and corrections of proofs and galleys—or after publication, except in instances of adaptation for the screen. He sometimes does not watch even once motion pictures he has scripted. "I haven't looked at some of the stuff probably for fifty years now," he says. "I haven't looked at *Temple of Gold,* so God knows what's in there." This can make him the world's most irritating interviewee. "I don't know," "I don't remember" and "I haven't read it in years" or variants thereof are standard responses to queries about his plots, characters and creative impetuses.

As mentioned, although becoming a writer had always been his dream, Goldman does not obtain pleasure from the act of writing. He reasons, "Going in your pit all day and coming back feeling failed, it's just shit. But that's the nature of the beast … It's one of these things because of the way I began, with nobody ever having any faith in me and nobody thinking I had any talent, which is an easy thing to accept. If you really believe you have no fucking talent, you think you're in on a pass. You always think they're going to find you out. I don't know if other writers think this or not, but I bet a lot of us do. It's, 'Why isn't it better? Why isn't it wonderful? Why is it shit?' I think that's a curse that a lot of us have. I mean, why are there so many fucking drunks and suicides? Why was Hemingway a drunk who killed himself? Shit, could he have asked for more? ... Writers, I think we're all nuts. I don't think there's anybody who walks around saying, 'Oh my God, I wrote this glorious page today' ... How can Fitzgerald be an alcoholic and destroy himself? He was famous when he was like 22, and why wasn't that enough for him? Why were all these guys so miserably unhappy?" Does that mean that he actively dislikes writing? "No. It's just what I do. You go with it and you wish it was better."

One observation he does have of *The Temple of Gold* is, "The book, like most of my books, got crucified in hardcover and was a very, very successful book in paperback. Most of the books that I've written had their success in paperback."

Your Turn To Curtsy, My Turn To Bow was published on September 4, 1958. Goldman recalls that it was written a year after completion of *The Temple of Gold* in less than two weeks. "I had this nutty feeling that, if I really wanted to be considered a writer, I had to write a book a year," Goldman says. "*Your Turn to Curtsy, My Turn To Bow* [is] very short, depressing etc., and I wrote that, I think, in ten days and in the rest of the year I went to the movies. In my hometown, we had one movie theatre which played Hollywood films and Oberlin had some other kind of art films, foreign films, whatever you want to call them. In New York they had all these movie theatres and I hadn't seen anything much. There was a movie theatre on the Upper West Side, no longer there, called the Thalia and it played a foreign double feature every day. Between 42nd Street and The Thalia, I got my movie education. I don't know how many hundreds and hundreds of movies I went to, and then I wrote my second novel."

The narrative of *Your Turn To Curtsy, My Turn To Bow* alternates between first and third person, the latter utilized to indicate the points where narrator Peter Bell is looking back on his seventeen-year-old self from such a distance and changed perspective that it is as though he is viewing a completely different person.

Like the protagonist of *The Temple of Gold*, Peter Bell is the son of a rich father and hails from Athens. He has obtained a summer job at the tautologously titled Camp Blackpine Camp for Boys, where he meets and becomes besotted with a beautiful young woman named Tillie Keck. Working-class Tillie is much less culturally sophisticated than he, even despite the fact that, emotionally, Bell is something of an ingénue. Tillie is very anxious to improve her social standing. Bell's infatuation with her

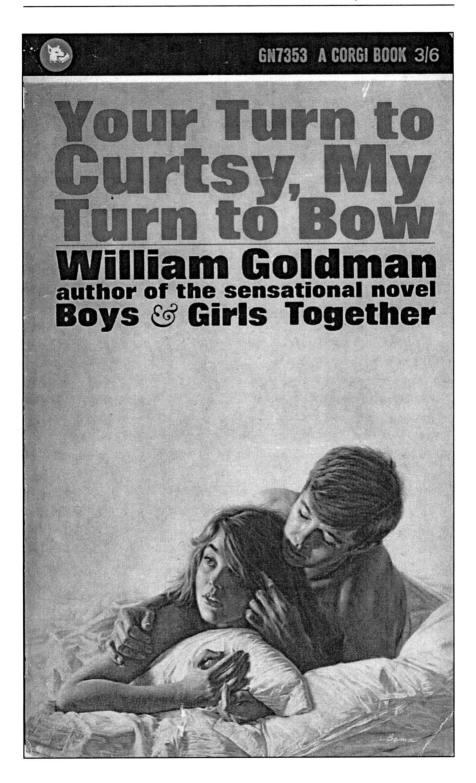

is never quite convincing, Goldman writing of her beauty in such banal and bland terms that he fails to communicate how irrationally attracted a person can be to someone with whom he has nothing in common.

Bell is dismayed to find that one of his overseers at the camp is an archetypal muscle-bound class bully named Granville 'Granny' Kemper. However, he is delighted to discover that joining them will be an older boy named Chad Kimberley, whom he has always idolized for his athletic achievements and good looks. Bell continues to worship Chad even when Chad confides in him about a mental breakdown. Chad's experiences in a sanatorium are relayed to Bell in a dozen uninterrupted pages of dialogue.

Bell finally gets his dream date with Tillie but is devastated to find out afterwards that Granny and his buddies have been placing bets on whether he would manage to "score." (He hasn't, and indeed asked for nothing more than a kiss.) In revealing this, Granny tells Bell that Tillie is a "regular living whore." A distraught Bell retreats into the woods, where he is tracked down by Chad. Chad had tried to get him to agree not to go on the date with Tillie and now explains to Bell that he knew about the betting pool. Asked how he could let him be thus humiliated, Chad says it is because he wanted him to learn a lesson. He then imparts the knowledge that an old man he had met when suffering his breakdown was in fact God and tells Bell he must "follow" him. Bell is naturally skeptical— yet strangely he can see Chad's eyes even though he is standing with his back against the moon.

Bell flees and make his way to Tillie's cabin. Tillie is contemptuous of his disgust over the fact that she prostitutes herself. ("You just got born in the right place. Well, I didn't. I got born in the wrong place but that doesn't mean I got to stay there.") Although they fight, they end up having sex. Bell's shedding of (we presume) his virginity is somewhat spoilt the next morning when he insists on giving an unwilling Tillie money for the encounter.

Bell goes off in search of Chad. Finding him neither in his cabin nor in a woods clearing he knows he frequents, he heads—with a mounting sense of both dread and certainty—to a part of the camp in which stands a wooden cross. To his horror, Chad has nailed his feet and one hand to it. Chad weakly asks Bell to complete the job. Bell gets him down and eventually accompanies a shattered, half-comatose Chad back to their hometown. On the train home, he gets to his knees and throws his arms around Chad's legs, intoning hysterically "I don't care" over and over.

The book ends with a chapter set a decade later in which Bell says, "I don't ask many questions any more" and reveals that Tillie has entered into a cynical marriage with a Bolivian tin heir. Chad, meanwhile, has disappeared off the face of the earth.

The title phrase, employed as a closer but included earlier in the book in a conversation between Bell and Tillie, refers to a dance class Bell attended as a young child when the instruction meant nothing to the mixed-gender pupils who were so young that they didn't know who curtsied and who bowed. This partly sums up the faults of the book. The metaphor sounds meaningful—and shows Goldman throwing the shapes of a serious author in incorporating a literary conceit—but it is trite and semi-coherent.

That Goldman wrote the book in under a fortnight shows: it is not fully developed, either in terms of execution—it reads like a shorthand version waiting to be fleshed out—or concept: there are implications of homosexual attraction between Bell and Chad and hints that Bell might actually be just as delusional as Chad, but these plot strands are so sketchy that we are not quite sure whether we are supposed to infer from them what we do; meanwhile that eerie scene wherein Bell can see Chad's eyes, even though he is standing with his back against the moon, is never explained.

The lack of depth is exacerbated by a complete absence of grittiness. Implausibly, there is no swearing throughout, nor drug-taking (there is a reference to "smoking" in chapter nine but we are not given enough information to even be able to tell whether this is supposed to be ambiguity). It almost feels as though the book is aimed at teenagers or even children. Meanwhile, although there are flashes of brilliantly colloquial dialogue ("That's what let's do," says the inarticulate Tillie), there is also a lot of speech that is unrealistically melodramatic and banal. Additionally, while the themes and the dramatic situations are all potentially highly interesting, they are ineptly handled (Bell is actually given no information by the betting pool to back up the contention that Tillie is a prostitute, yet immediately assumes she is) or not thought through properly (surely, nailing oneself to a cross is physically impossible?).

Goldman's endless bad luck as a writer was clearly unequivocally over, for the fact that *Your Turn To Curtsy, My Turn To Bow* was even published at all is rather puzzling.

4

William Goldman's first published short story appears to be 'The Ice Cream Eat,' which appeared in *Transatlantic Review* no. 2, dated Winter 1959-60, occupying nine of its roughly A5-sized pages.

As with most Goldman short fiction, it echoes and foreshadows his long-form fiction. When Presky, one of its two main characters, says of the central eating contest, "First we got to have some rules," it strikes one as a precursor to the preamble to the kick-in-the-groin scene in *Butch Cassidy and the Sundance Kid* a decade later. The set-up and the staging of the eating contest itself are rather reminiscent of the events surrounding a beer-drinking competition in *The Color of Light* (1984). However, people familiar with the qualities of those works who expect this tale to match their standards will be severely disappointed.

Just about nothing in the story rings true, starting with the fact of the contest itself. The pugnacious Presky and the diminutive, over-sensitive Flynn are drinking partners with a love-hate relationship. As a consequence of their bristling repartee, they wind up agreeing to a head-to-head involving food consumption in Slattery's bar.

> "Talk, talk, talk. All you can do is talk. Hell, my dog can eat more than you can."
> "It's a bet," Presky said, holding out his hand.
> "You're damn right it is," Flynn echoed.

From the above, it's not even clear at first that this is not actually a bet that pits human against human. It's only when Flynn goes home to his pet hound Harlow and ascertains that ice cream is the food he will probably do best at consuming that we realize the nature of the wager. The rest of the story is not so maladroit—merely flat, unconvincing and cartoonish, whether it be the very nature of the competition (at no point does it seem plausible that either of the men would be sufficiently riled to participate in a whimsical contest taking place several days later as opposed to on the spur of the moment, or that more than 100 men would pack the bar to observe, even if there is money to be made from betting on the outcome) or the utterly manufactured result (a draw, after both man and dog cannot bring themselves to attack a sixth pint of ice cream, with a contrived completion-of-character-journey as Presky displays a fondness toward Flynn not hitherto apparent via the act of beating up two bruisers who impugn his friend's pet).

There is another passage of actively bad writing. With the line, "During the rest period, Presky jumped up and down, smiling confidently," Goldman unintentionally achieves the feat of making a human sound like the animal with which he is in competition.

The fact that 'The Ice Cream Eat' was reprinted in *Stories from the Transatlantic Review* (1970, Holt Rinehart)—a hardcover compendium that purported to feature some of the best stories from the magazine's pages over the previous decade—is semi-farcical, especially considering that *Transatlantic Review* had in that period been privileged to publish the likes of Malcolm Bradbury, Joyce Carol Oates, Alan Sillitoe, John Updike, and Sol Yurick. Goldman was an editor at the *Transatlantic Review*. Of his work there, Goldman says, "A friend of mine was the publisher and I don't remember ever being an important figure. I probably did it as a favor to him." Both the original publication and the reprinting of 'The Ice Cream Eat' seem only explainable by the fact that the magazine was returning Goldman's favor.

5

Published on July 14, 1960, *Soldier in the Rain* is the first Goldman novel that feels like the author is not playing to the gallery, the first that gives the impression of being largely autobiographical and—perhaps not coincidentally—the first of real substance.

Any reader coming to it today will immediately be struck by its resemblance, at least superficially, to *Catch-22*. However, it was actually published a year before Joseph Heller's celebrated military satire. It also doesn't really address battle, being set at Camp Scott, Hastingsville, in the American South, far away from the Korean War, which, in any case, is in its dying weeks.

Goldman's caustic and quasi-comedic look at army life is written in the third person, as would be all his subsequent novels. It revolves principally around young Sergeant Eustis Clay, whose brain is constantly whirring with schemes to make his fortune, whether it be lyrics for songs or business ideas. Unfortunately, Clay's lyrics are inane where they are not nonsensical and his entrepreneurial schemes hare-brained. This may sound like a recipe for an endearing character but Clay is also a complete misogynist, one of his favorite games being to grade passing women on a score sheet (few get anything higher than a C, although this doesn't stop Clay bedding as many

females as he can with a contrived boyishness). The thing about which Clay seems to care most in the world is his elderly dog Donald, whose picture he keeps in his room. Superficially cheery, Clay is a troubled soul. He abruptly realizes that he won't be able to cope with the civilian life to which he will soon be eligible for return. He re-enlists, although knows that he will not serve out his new term at Camp Scott, which is being closed down.

Clay has an unlikely friend in the shape of Sergeant Maxwell Slaughter, an older, extremely rotund soldier whose intellectual sophistication masks an unworldliness in other areas (he is almost certainly a virgin). Clay considers himself the "ideas man" and Slaughter the "brains" in their partnership. Although this partnership exists only in Clay's head, Slaughter does seem fond of Clay, even if there is a certain twinkle-eyed mischief in his indulgence of his schemes, both financial and sexual. Slaughter provides a perfect summation of Clay in conversation with another soldier when he says, "He is engaged in a running con game with the world, and since the world has most of the advantages, he feels he has to be devious in order to come out on top."

The only thing the two seem to have in common is the fact that they are on the make. However, this is something they share with a lot of their colleagues. Camp Scott has a considerable internal industry, with soldiers in its vast environs endlessly bartering with the mountains of supplies at their disposal—mattresses, underwear, flak jackets, fans, et al—with the objective of making their tedious lives a little more bearable.

Also coming into the picture is Meltzer, a Private First Class whose essential decency Clay sullies by both initiating him into the female grading game and teaching him the virtues of dishonesty.

The book teeters over into outright comedy at a couple of junctures. The first is when Clay decides to ascertain whether Meltzer is Jewish by checking his head for horns. The second is a scene in which Clay invents a disease called scabosis in order to get back a valued fan from a Captain Magee, into whose possession it has come via the machinations of his enemy Corporal Lenahan: Slaughter confirms the existence of this ailment when smoothly passing himself off as a camp doctor in a telephone conversation with the initially skeptical superior officer. Both scenes are funny, but they also weaken the book slightly, as their quasi-slapstick nature jars with the prevailing naturalism.

Goldman sometimes switches points of view within the same passage, but the absence of delineator is not frequent and, when it does occur, never too jarring or distracting. Goldman's dialogue is excellent and naturalistic throughout, particularly a scene where Meltzer, suddenly woken from sleep, leaps to his feet and demands, "Whazzrong?"

Towards the end of a narrative where scheming and feuding is occasionally shot through with tenderness (Clay tries to alleviate Slaughter's solitary state by fixing him up with a young woman), Clay receives the devastating news from home that Donald has died of old age. He drunkenly tells some people in a bar of the reason for the animal's importance to him. When his parents had decided to migrate west in search of better times, they had been unable to afford to take Clay immediately, so deposited him with an aunt and uncle, purchasing Donald to keep him company until such time as they could afford to send for him. Unfortunately, they never made it west, dying in a car accident en route.

Out of his mind with grief, Clay now gets involved in a fight with a group of four men, which includes his arch enemies Corporal Lenahan and Master Sergeant Priest. Hopelessly outnumbered and outwitted—he absurdly tries a wrestler's drop-kick and is surprised that it doesn't work like it does on TV—he is rescued by Slaughter, who has been tailing him. However, Slaughter suffers a stroke in the process. He dies shortly thereafter, ensuring that Clay has now lost the only other fixture of his life about which he genuinely cares.

The book ends with Clay profanely defying God as he kids himself that he has finally come up with his fortune-making invention: a paddling pool for the back of cars.

It's to be doubted that greatness is within the reach of a novel whose central character is so disagreeable. Goldman, though, says of Clay, "He was sympathetic for me. There was a sergeant who was a villain, but I thought Clay was just a nice affable stoop." He adds, "I'd been in the army. A lot of this stuff is also, as I look back on it, autobiographical."

Despite the dubious characteristics of its protagonist, *Soldier in the Rain* is an enjoyable and sure-footed piece of work.

6

William Goldman's short story 'Da Vinci' was published in *New World Writing* no. 17 in 1960.

The tale—occupying seventeen pages of the A-format paperback-sized volume—concerns a small-town boy called Willy whose father is a barber.

Willy is often used as a guinea pig to ascertain the abilities of his dad's re-cruits. A new employee called H. Bimbaum transpires to possess a sump-tuous artistry with the scissors (hence the title) that is a marked contrast to his cantankerous demeanor. The newcomer becomes the family lodger. Although Willy's father talks shop with him for hours, before long Bimbaum is causing friction in Willy's household because Willy—like the other kids in town—now prefers Bimbaum to cut his hair. Eventually, the wounded father drives Bimbaum out of his shop, using the pretext of the time it takes him to finish haircuts. Bimbaum has the opportunity to save his job but stands by his methodical artistry and refuses to quicken his pace. ("By the time you grow up, the goddamn butchers will own the world," he tells Willy.)

The central character of 'Da Vinci' being a child is bad news from the beginning. That kids' dialogue is perilous territory for Goldman is proven here. "Hurry it up. I'm due back soon," Willy peremptorily says to Bim-baum when he has to interrupt his marbles game to act as guinea pig, an attitude that would have got him a clip round the ear in 1960 let alone the late thirties or early forties timeframe made logical by the retrospective narration. The main problem, however is that the central plot strand is nonsense: the un-elaborate male haircuts of the era could not and did not induce the awe depicted herein ("That's a beautiful haircut. A really beauti-ful haircut"), thus making all the conflicts engendered by Bimbaum's abili-ties impossible. Moreover, even a perfectionist of a barber like Bimbaum would not take ridiculous lengths like 90 minutes to complete his job. The fact that Goldman himself admits he is no stylist means that a story that is basically unrealistic and unbelievable is left with nothing to recommend it.

Nineteen-sixty saw Goldman helping to stage a show on Broadway. No-body outside of the nucleus of the theatre word, however, knew about Goldman's involvement with the musical *Tenderloin*.

It was a doctoring job, theatre (and cinema) parlance for the process whereby a writer or writing team is brought in to improve a script per-ceived to be not up to scratch. Such work is usually not formally credited, a result of the various and sometimes conflicting motivations of script-writers, script doctors, producers and, of course, writers' unions. Gold-man doctored *Tenderloin* in collaboration with his brother James.

Those at this point who might be wondering why a novelist with no produced plays to his name (William) and a playwright with no produced shows to his name (James) were qualified for this job might well have a point. In mitigation, their employment was less arbitrary than it might appear. Goldman: "We'd been writing those other things and somebody must have read it and liked it and we were probably cheap and they asked us to do it." The "other things" to which Goldman refers are the play *Blood, Sweat and Stanley Poole* and the musical *A Family Affair*, scripts of which were, as is standard, in circulation in the theatrical community well before they reached the stage in, respectively, 1961 and 1962. *Tenderloin*'s book (slightly confusing theatre parlance for the script of a musical) was officially credited to George Abbott and Jerome Weidman. Based on a recent novel by Samuel Hopkins Adams, it concerned a clergyman social reformer in the red light district of Manhattan at the turn of the twentieth century.

Tenderloin opened on October 17, 1960 and ran for 216 performances. This may sound respectable enough, but the fact of the large reputations of the people behind it made its relatively short run a flop. As Goldman notes, "It was directed by the great George Abbott and the score was by Bock & Harnick." Goldman could have added that it was coproduced by the very successful Harold Prince. As well as pleasure for Goldman ("It was a great experience for me just watching Mr. Abbott who was the great professional, how he went about his business"), there was also trauma in the project. Goldman later told Richard Andersen, who published a book on his writing, "Now, when you're replaced, it's very wounding, but it happens to everybody, and you leave, but the writer we replaced wouldn't … it was terrifying…" Being replaced by a script doctor would be something that happened to Goldman several times in his future screenwriting career, if in less immediately physical but sometimes no less traumatic terms as involved in *Tenderloin*.

"It's not an important part of my life," Goldman now says of *Tenderloin*, but this would seem to be a symptom of his reluctance to delve into and discuss his past. His assessment in *Which Lie Did I Tell?* (2000) that *Tenderloin* was "one of the great breaks of my career" is surely a more correct perspective. Not only did the *Tenderloin* work forge or cement many of the theatre connections that would help make his later Broadway book *The Season* so well-informed, but it can't have done any harm in the mission of putting his own nascent stage works onto the boards. Moreover, his first taste of the art of doctoring paved the way in the long term for a lucrative—if by definition unlit—byway of his writing career.

7

In the early sixties, James Goldman was experiencing a period of struggle that (discounting the literary frustrations of his schooldays) his little brother had never known and never would. Ultimately, James Goldman would become a celebrated figure. His well-known *The Lion in Winter* first appeared on Broadway in 1966 and was later filmed. He also wrote the book of the musical *Follies* (1971), whose score was provided by Stephen Sondheim, and the screenplay of the post-modern Robin Hood movie *Robin and Marian* (1976). It seems to have been a sense of guilt on the part of Goldman Minor that led to him collaborating with Goldman Major, as well as John Kander.

"They were older than I was, Kander and my brother, and they were the ones who were supposed to succeed and they weren't and I was," says William Goldman. "It terrified me and I wrote a musical with my brother and Kander, *A Family Affair*, which got on, which failed. I don't know why I did it. Here were these two wonderful figures for me and I was doing well and they weren't and I helped them in my own nutty way. Except it didn't work out that way, since everything I tried for the theatre failed." Preceding *A Family Affair* was the Goldman brothers' *Blood, Sweat and Stanley Poole*, William Goldman's only foray into the realm of playwriting for half a century. Goldman says, "We had both been in the army at the same time and it seemed like a decent enough idea and magically we got it on."

Despite the shared and simultaneous military experience, it is quite clear that the raw material that provided the basis for *Blood, Sweat and Stanley Poole* was William's: like *Soldier in the Rain*, its plot backbone revolves around the pilfering of, and trading with, camp supplies on a US army base, even if this backdrop is more overtly comedic than in the prose antecedent.

The camp's internal, illegal market leads to a feud between education officer Captain Mal Malcolm and First Lieutenant Stanley Poole. Poole, a master sergeant, may soon be tumbling back down the ranks due to new army regulations that state that every officer is required to have the equivalent of two years of college study. As someone who freely admits he has no intellectual capacity whatsoever, Poole is glumly contemplating his future. So far, Poole has managed to evade detection over his lack of qualifications, but the

bribery he is able to offer Malcolm in the form of camp supplies abruptly evaporates because he has been apprised of an imminent supply room inspection. Malcolm—whose proceeds have enabled the captain to buy himself a red jaguar convertible—is none too pleased to be informed that goods will no longer be forthcoming from Poole.

Poole, meanwhile, is none too pleased to be told to take under his wing a young private named Oglethorpe, who, although clever, has recently visited a camp psychiatrist over his timidity. However, Oglethorpe transpires to be Poole's savior when—touched by his gruff kindliness toward him—he offers to guide Poole through his examination and preserve his silver star. Savior in more than one way, for Poole cannily/cynically realizes that if he sells Oglethorpe's academic prowess to officers in the same educationally under-qualified boat as him—for camp supplies, naturally—he can then fill the gaping holes in the supply room sufficiently to pass the forthcoming inspection, thus neatly closing off the other threat to his army career. Oglethorpe is willing, and before long a whole classroom of officers who are used to barking orders at his lowly type are sullenly subjecting themselves to Oglethorpe's authority. This in turn creates a new sense of self-respect and confidence in Oglethorpe who—once terrified of rifles—occupies himself getting the manual of arms down pat while his charges hunch over their exercise books.

Come the day of the examination, Poole is elated, knowing he has done more than enough to pass. However, all his hard work and dedication is ripped to pieces by Malcolm who, in an act of petty revenge, fails him. Poole can't lodge a formal complaint, of course, because of the danger of Malcolm exposing his own corruption. Poole must seek justice by other, anonymous means. Eventually a rather elaborate scheme is devised whereby it is decided to wreck Malcolm's precious Jaguar. The plan—involving the cooperation of Military Police and an ambulance driver, all students of Oglethorpe—is intended to culminate in Malcolm becoming so aggravated that he decides to lash out at the nearest convenient target in the most logical way, which target will be Poole and which method will be his dreaded inspection. Malcolm will come a cropper when it turns out that the supply room is now in a position to pass inspection.

However, Malcolm turns out to be *au fait* with the fact that Poole has managed to replenish his supplies. He arranges a different form of punishment, involving the exposure of Poole's failure to make Oglethorpe less mentally fragile by forcing him to perform the manual of arms in front of Colonel Egan, the psychiatrist. However, Malcolm's plan comes unstuck when, in front of Egan, Oglethorpe reveals his newfound confidence in working with arms. The play ends with Egan convinced Malcolm is a psychotic and determined to have him removed from the army. The victory is bitter-sweet, however, for Poole is no longer sure he wants to be a lieutenant anyway, feeling master sergeant—his status for twenty-two years before his promotion—was his correct level. The play ends with Poole symbolically handing one of his lieutenant's bars to Oglethorpe.

There is little structurally wrong with *Blood, Sweat and Stanley Poole*. It has the archetypal 'second act' (by which is meant the completion of a psychological journey on the part of the main character, although technically it has three acts). It also has a reasonably deft twist in its tail. It does however have a large plausibility problem even for a comedy. The manner in which the conspirators cause Malcolm to commit the crucial act of losing his cool and destroying himself is unconvincing. Because of this, the play is entertaining and amusing but doesn't rise above lightweight.

It will seem even more lightweight for those who have read *Soldier in the Rain* and feel they are being served re-heated leftovers. It appears somewhat unwise—even unfair on his brother—for Goldman to have re-used the background and material from a novel. The talky, interior-landscaped medium of a stage play is a limited one in any circumstances but, unless it is spectacularly good, it cannot do anything but come out worse in comparison to the bigger canvass available to a prose counterpart.

Blood, Sweat and Stanley Poole had its first and only preview on October 4, 1961, before opening at the Morosco Theatre the following day. It transferred to the Ambassador Theatre on December 9, one week before it closed, after a total of eighty-four performances. The show did at least have an afterlife insofar as its script was commercially published, and it remains in print to this day.

Goldman is fully aware that getting onto Broadway with your first play is a feat in and of itself (or as he puts it, "The amazing thing was that anybody put the fucking thing on the stage"). However, *Stanley Poole*'s failure was a bruising experience for him, one made all the worse by what he feels is the uniquely vulnerable position occupied by the playwright. "The theatre is so much more brutal than books or movies because you're re-writing up 'til the night before and then the critics come and kill you and you have nothing to protect yourself," he explains. "In a movie or a book, it's usually nine months to a year before they come out and you have time to get away from them. In the theatre it was just that nightmare of working, working, working, trying to make the damn thing better, and then all of a sudden you're killed."

In *Transatlantic Review* No. 8 (cover-dated Winter 1961), Goldman had another short story published, this one titled 'Till the Right Girls Come Along.'

The opening of the eleven-page effort finds a character named Peter Bell half-heartedly attempting suicide with a razor blade. The reason turns out to be that he is torn between his wife Betty Jane and his mistress Natty, a secretary at a publishing house where he is an editor. Feeling guilty both because his wife is blameless and his frustrated secretary is set to leave her job, Peter makes a more serious suicide attempt by swimming out to sea. Although he is stricken by cramp and vomiting, he is saved by the fact of encountering a sandbar. He is washed alive onto shore. The story ends with him back in his domestic routine, musing "if he didn't bother to think, it would be lunch time before he knew it. And lunch meant martinis. And after five or six martinis, he felt he could easily make it through the rest of the day."

Apart from a passage where Betty Jane mysteriously fails to notice Peter's cut wrist, the story combines competent writing with a genuine poignancy. It would stand as the best of Goldman's handful of published short stories were it not for the fact that the well-informed Goldman reader knows that it's not actually a short story but a disguised section of *Boys and Girls Together*—the Goldman novel that would appear three years later. Most of the names have been changed, but the situation, professions, characteristics (including the man's predilection for finding animal shapes on walls), and events appear almost verbatim in that novel in passages featuring Charley Fiske (Goldman dispensed with Peter Bell as his protagonist's name, presumably to avoid confusion over whether it was a sequel to *Your Turn To Curtsy, My Turn To Bow*), his wife Betty Jane, and his mistress Jenny Devers.

Nobody but Goldman's publisher had any way of knowing that at the time, of course, so the story would have been accepted at face value then. Its publication also served a purpose in putting Goldman in the shop window, and a rather prestigious shop window at that: 'Till the Right Girls Come Along' appeared in an issue of *Transatlantic Review* graced by contributions from John Updike and Boris Pasternak.=

8

On January 27, 1962, William Goldman was back on the Great White Way—along with James Goldman and John Kander—for the opening night of *A Family Affair*. The three roommates were pooling their talents in the services of musical comedy.

Richard Seff explains, "I was their agent, the three of them, and we couldn't find a producer once Leland Heyward dropped his option on it. I couldn't find anyone to produce it, so I talked my cousin Andrew into producing it ... He was a lawyer ... *A Family Affair* was one that we had to do very laboriously by literally doing live auditions. Jim couldn't sing a note, Bill can't really sing but John Kander can a little bit, so Kander would play and sing and Bill would sing with him and then I had to get up and sing with them too, so here was the agent playing actor. There were thirty people, fifty people, and we'd raise the thousand dollars one night and two thousand the next and we put together the whole show that way."

The credits on the "Final Production Version" script are: "Book by James and William Goldman; Lyrics by James Goldman and John Kander; Music by John Kander." This differs to the official poster bill credits which simply state that the enterprise is "by James Goldman, John Kander and William Goldman," which is different again to some of the credits that float about on the internet today, which have William Goldman down as the writer of the lyrics, and only that. "We all wrote on that together," says Goldman. "I would not say I was a major contributor to the lyrics, but we all decided the three of us would take the billing." Asked the perhaps stupid, but in the circumstances necessary, question of whether he contributed to the book, Goldman says, "Of course. It was also my idea, as I remember."

A Family Affair is sub-titled *A Wedding in Two Acts* and centers around the preamble to the nuptials of Gerry Siegal and Sally Nathan. What should be a happy time is made misery verging on warfare by Alfie, the orphaned Sally's uncle, and Tilly, the matriarchal figure in Gerry's family. Alfie is insistent on a small wedding while Tilly is adamant on an extravaganza.

With any stage show there is never a definitive version: scripts are constantly changed, especially after previews, plus of course differ-

ent performers provide different ad libs. This reality of fluidity becomes particularly problematic when—as with *A Family Affair*—the playscript is not released commercially. Although even published playscripts are sometimes different to the rehearsal scripts simultaneously in circulation at the theatre, they can at least be cited as the writer's conception of definitive. As well as the "Final Production Version," the William Goldman Papers at Columbia University contain revisions dated December 1960 (i.e., when the show was in tryouts on the road before 'coming in' to Broadway). Although those revisions do not alter the crux of the work (what Goldman habitually refers to as a story's "spine"), there are notable differences, not least the way the wedding is described in much greater detail. Even those aren't necessarily final changes: the revisions still don't include the words "I now pronounce you man and wife" claimed to be the closing line in the official précis.

The show's book is rather effete, all marriage talk, dress selecting, cake-ordering, and genteel familial bickering. It's also, despite its overarching competence, blandly old-fashioned. Partly because of that, there are no belly-laughs. This is humor before people were allowed to talk about the things that are amongst the most funny in life, such as sex and bodily functions. Profanity too is, of course, entirely absent. If the climate of the times had allowed it, this would have almost certainly led to laughter, it being the case that there is little more guaranteed to induce hilarity than the juxtaposition of agonized etiquette and Anglo-Saxon expletive.

Instead, what we get is the tepid like of, "Do they all have to come? Couldn't they elect a representative?" and "Mother, there's no reason to get hysterical. If you'll just use common sense …."/ "Don't you dare talk common sense to me…" Some of the dialogue has had even its once mild funniness drained by changing times, for instance the fact that a daughter in a wedding outfitters complains, "I don't want to get married" and is answered by her mother, "Then what the hell did you propose for?"

As with all musicals, the book could be claimed to be, if not of little importance, then of profoundly less importance than the score. Said score is vibrant and melodic and contains both the life affirming 'Beautiful' and the scabrous and quasi-ribald 'Right Girls.' In some sections, of course, the score is intertwined with the dialogue and it's moderately amusing the way a song called 'Harmony' is juxtaposed with recriminatory exchanges. However, at this end of history, not a single appraisal of the score fails to dismiss it as a prelude to Kander's 'real' career with longstanding lyrical foil Fred Ebb, which took in *Cabaret, Chicago, Kiss of the Spider Woman* et al.

That the script of *A Family Affair* was never commercially published is made all the more curious by the fact that not only did the show have an original cast album but one that marked the milestone of the inaugural use in cast album recording of 35mm magnetic film, which led to, it was claimed by the original sleevenotes, "the most lifelike sound ever achieved."

There are a few of points about *A Family Affair* of interest for long-term (William) Goldman followers. One is that he recycled the character names Betty Jane and Jenny from this work in his prose. Another is that he used the theme and part of the title of the song 'Right Girls' for a short story. The other is that the show at one point employs the conceit of a sports announcer providing an urgent-voiced play-by-play of the rival maneuvers of the Siegals and the Nathans: assuming it was the decision of William Goldman, it's the first example of the way he would shoehorn references to his beloved sports into the most incongruous corners of his oeuvre.

A Family Affair did not feature any household names in its cast, but its Broadway incarnation was helmed by no less a figure than Hal Prince. Already a renowned producer, he was making his debut in a directorial career that would end in legendary status. Although reviews were not all negative—famous critic Walter Kerr's judgment was favorable—it was an indubitable flop. It had a reduced tryout because of poor business, Prince was an emergency replacement for original director Wood Baker, and its Broadway prices had to be reduced. Opening on the Great White Way at the Billy Rose Theatre after five previews, it achieved a lowly sixty-five performances before closing on March 25, 1962.

Seff: "We kept it alive, barely. It earned a living for those nine weeks, but it never made any profit to speak of and to go longer would have meant to take big losses, so it was sensible to close it." He reasons, "When we first heard it, we thought it had great charm. But I think it would have been helped by a director who really understood big musicals and Wood Baker had just had the great success with *Fantastiks*, which was only a few people, in a tiny, tiny theatre, and he did that one imaginatively, but this one he did not do imaginatively and it was very clunky. A lot depends on the director in a musical. He really can make fair material much better and a bad director can take excellent material and make it worse ... Hal Prince took over the direction out of town. He helped it a lot. It got better. It just didn't get good enough."

It was William Goldman's farewell to the stage. Seff says, "He had the play with Jim, *Stanley Poole*, and that was a flop and *Family Affair* was a flop, so who needed Broadway? They get hurt, they really do, in their viscera. He found that books treated him with more respect, so he stuck to books."

When Goldman himself declares, "I would never go back to Broadway," the clear implication is that this is a determination brought about by his unhappy experiences in the locale in the early sixties. Yet Columbia's William Goldman Papers contain the following unproduced plays: *Madonna and Child* (with James Goldman), *Now I Am Six, Something Blue, Nagurski*, and an untitled treatment. They also contain the following unproduced musicals: *Boys and Girls Together* (aka *Magic Town*), *Nagurski, Something Blue, The Man Who Owned Chicago, The Thing of It Is...* (music by Stephen Sondheim), and *The Princess Bride*. Simple mathematics dictates that some, possibly all, of the above playwriting activity occurred after the production of *A Family Affair*. Goldman seems to have mythologized his dispensing with an ambition to succeed on Broadway into an instantaneous, principled absolutism when, in fact, it seems to have been a nuanced, evolutionary process.

Leaving aside the accuracy or otherwise of Goldman's I-quit-they-didn't-fire-me stance, the above list of titles yields interesting nuggets. *Madonna and Child*—which the Goldman brothers also tried to pitch to television—is a similar title to *Madonna with Child*, the name of a play written by a character in Goldman's novel *Boys and Girls Together*. *Something Blue* is the title of a Goldman short story, published in 1963. *Nagurski* was the name of a famous American football player about whose sporting deeds and legend Goldman wrote in both his fiction (*Magic*) and non-fiction (*Wait Till Next Year*). A musical of Goldman's 1973 novel *The Princess Bride* has been percolating for decades.

Asked if the fact that his brother happily continued in the theatre medium implies that he had a thicker skin, Goldman says, "I don't think so. He was always more interested in theatre than I was. Jim wanted to be a playwright." Says Seff of the Goldman brothers: "I think Bill and Jim were two very different people and it was probably sensible not to try to write together again. Also I think different material appealed to them. He did the book to *Follies*, which is kind of a dark book. Jimmy was a dark man. We don't want to get into that—that's another story. Jimmy was really not easy." Not that Seff found William Goldman much easier: "He's kind of a loner and I think he really took what joy he got from this world out of his work."

Asked if he can understand William Goldman being bitter about his Broadway experiences, Seff says, "He shouldn't have been. He was young.

There's nothing wrong with failure when you're young. John Kander had a failure with it too, but he didn't disappear. In fact, his next show was a bigger failure: *Flora the Red Menace*."

There is also a triumph involved in both William Goldman managing to be involved in three Broadway shows in as many years and in *A Family Affair* itself. As Seff points out, "Those three boys were very, very close friends when they were youngsters back in the Midwest. They came to New York with this wonderful idealistic [aim], 'We're gonna write a musical and set Broadway on fire.' Well they did write a musical and I got it onto Broadway which in itself is kind of a miracle because they were all brand new—they'd never been heard of before … They all had very, very luminous careers, which is remarkable: three kids from the Midwest and all three of them became successful."

9

Another Goldman short story appeared in early 1963, this one called 'Something Blue,' which appeared in Vol. 8, No. 4 (cover date April 1963) of *Rogue*. The story's title was sort of appropriate. *Rogue* was a 'stag' magazine, albeit a high-class one: Ian Fleming was one of the writers with whom Goldman shared space in this issue, the publication printing a section of the James Bond creator's travel journalism book *Thrilling Cities*.

Goldman's story—which occupied just over four of *Rogue's* letter-sized pages, excluding the illustrated splash—is not erotica, though, but something that could just as easily have appeared in the pages of *Transatlantic Review*. It depicts Andy Brackett, a rather put-upon middle-aged man who is grappling with his anguish about his wife Jackie's infidelity and the self-loathing that comes with being a prolific writer of formulaic romances. (The source of Andy's professional self-loathing is one for which Goldman, never lucky in placing stories, would possibly have killed.)

The 'something blue' of the title is a kite that has somehow gotten lodged in the branches of a tree in Andy's front yard. After being nagged and mocked by Jackie, he reluctantly retrieves it. Further scornful browbeating sees him knocking on neighbors' doors to ask whether it belongs to a child of the house.

There is one amusing part of the story where "a gigantic negro lady" answers Andy's knock and shortly slams the door in his face with a dismissive, "The lady of the house ain't home." Andy defers shaking his fist at her until he is sure she's gone on the grounds that "she was, after all, bigger than he was and also undoubtedly in better condition." Aside from that, the story is unimpressive. Although Goldman adroitly seeds germane detail, the prose is self-conscious in a way his novels rarely are, peppered with writerly phrases like "the lousy pot would explode on him, scattering brown grounds across the white face of the stove," "falling the five feet like some great clumsy bird," and "plucking poor souls in the very nick of time, guiding them safely past the hungry black brink." Despite his meticulous carving out of such florid fare as that, Goldman pays little attention to more important matters: the pivotal Mrs. Rogelsky is never properly described, "pretty" being about the extent of it.

Mrs. Rogelsky is a resident of one of the houses at which Andy knocks. She admires Andy's writing and they tumble into bed. It transpires that Mrs. Rogelsky's husband is faithless and plays sports on Wednesday and Saturday afternoons, the exact occasions of Andy's wife's infidelities, thus enabling them to hook up on a regular and guilt-free basis.

Andy—who had been puzzled by both the kite's unusual shade of blue and its hyperactivity despite lack of wind—begins to perceive the object as something benignly sentient, a bringer of fortune. When at story's end he releases it into the air, it seems to bow to him before departing. This is either a literary conceit or a tilt at the supernatural, but either way half-baked. It also in no way prevents the story's outcome being as pat as we imagine the climax of one of Andy's romance tales to be.

In November 1963, *Soldier in the Rain* became the first William Goldman novel to make it to the big screen.

It was something of a big deal, being as it was a Blake Edwards production, which featured Steve McQueen, Jackie Gleason, and Tuesday Weld. Admittedly, it was at a point in history when all those names were either on the cusp of or past their heydays rather than resident in them, but at the same time there is nothing second-class about such an array of talent.

Which is not to say the film is anything like a masterpiece. That its black-and-white photography makes it a museum piece today may be unfair, but its mannered dialogue and exaggerated, boggle-eyed acting more justifiably condemns it to the status of antique.

With screenwriting not yet something in Goldman's wheelhouse—or even wildest dreams—the adaptation of his book was handled by Edwards and Maurice Richlin. Says Goldman, "I had never dreamt at that point in my life that I would ever write a screenplay. It was not a thing. Maybe in the thirties you would go to Hollywood and make money and then come back east and write the Great American Novel (which nobody thinks of anymore). But screenwriting was not something that one *did* then."

The Edwards/Richlin screenplay is fairly faithful to the book's plot, if not its timbre: despite the poignancy of the retained deaths of Eustis Clay's dog Donald and Maxwell Slaughter, this is an out-and-out comedy movie. Although Gleason is pretty much a perfect fit as Slaughter, the character's poise is simplistically reduced to the way he is able to procure free bottles of Pepsi via judicious, Fonz-style banging of the dispensing machine in his office. The worst fault is the failure to convey Clay's tragic backstory and why it makes his dog so important to him. (Curiously, the script does ensure to make reference to Goldman's beloved *Gunga Din*.)

McQueen is quite good as Clay and Tuesday Weld very effective as the thin-skinned simpleton Bobby Jo, but neither they, Gleason nor the general high level of craft can save the film from being slightly dull.

Asked whether, when he saw what the scriptwriters had done with his material, he felt he could have done it better, Goldman seems to dissemble: "They made changes. No one says, 'Oh, we are going to fuck up Bill Goldman's book.' Most of this stuff I didn't pay any attention to. I don't know that I've ever seen *Soldier in the Rain*. I must have, because I like Tuesday Wells, but as a rule I don't look at movies I'm involved with and I don't read books that I've written. One does the best one can and that's it."

10

Goldman's preoccupation with three Broadway shows was one of the reasons for the four-year gap between his novels after the publication of *Soldier in the Rain*. Another was writer's block.

Before his Broadway sojourn, Goldman had already embarked on a new book, eventually published as *Boys and Girls Together*, which would transpire to be by far and away his longest work. "I felt—I don't know why—that I should write a long novel," he says. "I spent years writing that fucking thing and my advice to all young writers is never write a long novel. During that time I had stopped to write for Broadway. It meant that I was away from my book for, oh I don't know, a year. When I went back to it, I was blocked, which is I think the worst thing that can ever happen to any of us. I had about 600 typed pages of *Boys and Girls Together* and I was absolutely blocked as to what to do with it." Goldman has estimated that these 600 pages constituted half of the novel.

"I was married by then," he recalls. "There was an article in the New York *Daily News*, a tabloid paper, about the Boston Strangler, which was the big crime in the country then. There was a theory that what if there wasn't one strangler, what if there were two? At that time we were living in a small apartment, our youngest had just been born, and I rented to write. There was a guy who had an ad in the paper. He wanted a roommate and he was only two blocks away, a five-minute walk, so I went up to see him. He had two bedrooms and I said, 'I would like to write while you're at work.' It's a nutty system, but it worked because he was never sick that year and I worked every day in his apartment, and then I'd leave when he came back.

"On my walk up to 88th Street from 86th Street, this thing literally dropped into my head. It was the strangler novel *No Way to Treat a Lady*. I did something I'd never done: I frantically outlined it on a page, and then I didn't know what I was doing so I called up some friends and I told them what had just happened. Because what I was terrified of was I was bullshitting myself and this was just another way to block myself away from getting back to *Boys and Girls Together*, because I had several years worth of work on it done. Everybody said, 'Well, you might be trying to fuck yourself up or you might be able to write this thing, but do it fast.' So I wrote that book. It's a strange-looking book. It's got, I don't know, sixty chapters and some of the chapters are one sentence long. I was doing anything to try and make it seem longer. I wrote it, I think, in a week.

"I had a marvelous editor by this time named Hiram Haydn. He was my editor from *Soldier in the Rain* through *The Princess Bride*, so he was my editor for fifteen years. I adored him … I took it down to Hiram and he said, 'I don't want to publish this. I want you to write *Boys and Girls Together*, so why don't you publish it under another name?' So I did. I published it as Harry Longbaugh, which is the real name of the Sundance Kid, which is of interest only because this was years before I wrote the screenplay but I had obviously started researching that screenplay by 1964. Then I went back and finished *Boys and Girls Together*. It was like agony and it was published also in 1964."

In *No Way to Treat a Lady* (published March 2) a serial killer is stalking the streets of New York, all his victims left naked on the toilet with a kiss drawn in lipstick on their foreheads. The narrative follows him from his first gruesome killing, gradually unveiling information about him as the book progresses, although we do glean from the outset that the killer is extremely plausible and cunning. We learn not too long afterwards that he is highly intelligent and a master of disguise, on one occasion even passing himself off as a heavyset woman. Only towards the end of the book is his identity revealed as society man Kit Gill.

Alternating with the depictions of the killer are chapters involving trainee police detective Moe Brummell, whether as straight narrative or his diary entries. Brummell is haunted by his ugliness, the result of a childhood mishap with hot grease, and irritated by his domineering mother and his successful brother. However, he is a good soul, if somewhat gauche: he is unable to pluck up courage to ask out a young woman named Sarah Stone, who he meets investigating the first murder. She has to—in exasperation—take the initiative.

That the killer begins telephoning Brummell about the murders is the result of an accident: Brummell's name was printed in the papers after the first murder because his superior, who would normally handle the case, was off sick. (Illogically but conveniently for the plot, Brummell doesn't install telephone tracing equipment after the first couple of calls. Moreover, the killer seems confident about making fairly leisurely calls to him from his own house.) The killer begins playing a cat-and-mouse game. However, he endeavors as much as he can to remain civil with the policeman—to such an extent that he is horrified when a murder occurs on an evening he promises Brummell he will not be "naughty." This latter murder is that of a copycat killer, one who subsequently murders another woman. Brummell's incongruous civility doesn't extend, however, to refraining from murdering Sarah Stone, whose death he tries to pass off as the work of the copycat in order to make a confused point to Brummell.

Gill decides to hunt down the copycat killer, whose activities offend against his giant-sized ego. After a street fight between the two killers is stopped by a policeman, Gill—conscious that the authorities now have his and the copycat's names and that if he kills the copycat himself he will therefore be the first suspect—decides to lead Brummell to the imposter. Brummell—already driven to violence by his mother after she tells him she is glad Sarah is dead—turns the tables by allowing the two murderers to kill each other and, in the final scene, exults in Gill's slow, agonized death from knife wounds.

The book's chapters frequently follow the train of thought of characters who will not be seen again, whether they be murder victims or the beat cop who unknowingly captures the two killers. In this, *No Way to Treat a Lady* resembles *Marathon Man* and other amply populated Goldman thrillers written after that 1974 work, although is nowhere near as classy. In fact, *No Way to Treat a Lady* reads very much like a pulp novel. Significantly, and very unusually in publishing, it appeared in softcover first (through Gold Medal Books). (When it did make it into hardcover later the same year, it was via Goldman's usual publisher—Harcourt, Brace & World—and under his real name, an accreditation that has remained ever since.) Although it doesn't dwell on the actual murders, *No Way to Treat a Lady* feels exploitative and unpleasant in the classic tradition of novels published in a day and age where sex was so rare in the media that even its tangential mention was a sure-fire way of selling books; if those books lacked pictures they were less likely to attract the attention of those charged with stopping the distribution of indecency. The scenes of the burgeoning love affair between the detective and Sarah are a touching anomaly in this context, feeling like dispatches from a far better, more warm-hearted book, and it's a pity that they are only present as a way of setting up Brummell's motive for revenge.

One minor point for the defense is that, because at the time serial killers were fairly new to society, what looks like grubbiness today might have seemed to the author a cutting-edge, noble-minded examination of a social concern.

Perhaps full mitigation would have been achieved through good writing. The narrative is not boring—and in some places fairly whistles along—but Goldman doesn't dwell long enough on his characters or settings to provide text that is anything more than functional even by his business-like standards. (Some chapters are only as long as the newspaper headlines reporting the latest atrocity.) The scene in which Brummell tries to strangle his own mother after Sarah's death is clearly intended to make the reader suspect that he has been the murderer all along, but it doesn't inspire any great lurch of the emotions. Having said which, being forced to inhabit the sick and hysterical mind of Kit Gill at any great length would probably not make for a pleasant experience. Which is probably another way of saying that little short of writing genius could salvage this project.

11

Boys and Girls Together started life almost as Goldman's apologia for his success, guilt about which was intertwined with feelings of literary unworthiness.

Says Goldman, "I had come to New York in 1954 to go to graduate school and then, two years later, I was a published novelist and I hadn't expected that. I was a successful young novelist those next few years and it wasn't what I felt was going to happen and I began to realize along about that time that the books where autobiographical. *Soldier in the Rain* was obviously about the army and *Boys and Girls Together* was about the fact that I was in despair because all my friends in New York were fucking up and I was becoming successful and that was the pulse of that book. It was the fact that nobody was making it as I was and I knew I was fraudulent and I knew I'd be found out. It was very hard in those years. It was very hard to be 25 or 7 or 8 and be published when all of your other friends who were writers weren't."

The notion of being "found out" was related to Goldman's business-like prose, which he perceives as lack of technique. "When I say I'm totally instinctive, I don't say, 'Gee, that's swell, aren't I lucky to be totally instinctive?'" he says. "I wish I did know more of what I was doing in those years … I only thought of myself as a storyteller, trying to get through the day … I was making a living as a novelist. I mean, holy shit, if you'd said [that to] anybody who knew me at college, or in graduate school, they would have said, 'Inconceivable.' No way it could have happened. So I didn't know what I was doing. I just knew that it was working."

For his next project, he decided, "I wanted to try and write a great sprawling bitch of a novel." That seems to be Goldman's way of saying that, with *Boys and Girls Together,* he was making a tilt at the Great American Novel. Not only was it panoramic in nature, it was huge in size, 623 pages in its original hardcover edition, where pages are traditionally oversized; the more compact paperback format sometimes necessitated an extra hundred pages. Nothing could better sum up the duality of his feelings about his writing, for, going by what he says, his opus was something about whose quality he would automatically have had doubts. It must have been very painful to have had keen ambition and lack of self-confidence at the same time.

Boys and Girls Together takes its title from its epigraph, which quotes the early twentieth-century song 'The Sidewalks of New York,' but a tru-

er rationale is provided by a comment from one of its main characters, Aaron: "…nobody's *from* New York. They're all from Kansas City or Pittsburgh or Roanoke, Virginia. But they come here. They don't like it, but they don't leave either. Nobody likes it here. You're not supposed to like it here. But you gotta come anyway. It's the place." Through a collection of six main characters and a veritable army of supporting parts, Goldman attempts to depict life—or at least artistic life—in the Big Apple. He doesn't stop there, though. He provides us the various characters' life stories before their (in most cases) relocation to New York City.

The chapters are lengthy—we linger on each character, fully exploring their worlds in protracted sessions rather than flitting between them in small bites. This approach nearly makes the book come unstuck in its opening chapter, a rather nasty one about a rather nasty individual. New Jersey native Aaron Firestone is a bookish and monstrous child who deliberately gets run over—injuring his legs permanently—because he is dissatisfied with the amount of attention he receives. He develops an early hankering to be a writer and decides even then on his *nom de guerre*: Aaron Fire. (The name is comical to English readers, who would pronounce the Christian name "Air-on," thus "Hair On Fire.") When his hated sister gets pregnant and then tries to con one of her squires into thinking the baby is his, Aaron secretly gets a message to the man telling him of the lie. Although this material would have had the mild merit of being unusually frank for its era, its dispiriting, grubby nature is compounded by how cartoonishly written it is. One wonders how many purchasers or lenders gave up at this point.

Walt Kirkaby—scion of the richest family in his hometown of St. Louis—is cut from somewhat more agreeable cloth. Although we see him engaging in childhood play, we are—as in numerous places—then whisked into the backstory of a related character, in this case his father, whose rags-to-riches tale is not just irrelevant but glibly related. In enjoyable contrast is Walt's stalking of an Encyclopedia Britannica salesman he mistakenly suspects to be an infamous gangster, his jealousy of the simple, bagged peanut-butter-and-jelly sandwich lunches of his poor friend Gino, his good-natured sparring with black maid Maudie (who repeatedly tells him he is "d-e-a-d" if he slams the back door) and his realization that he can court popularity by clowning. Maudie—as in many families in this social milieu at this time in history—is essentially a surrogate mother for her employer's children. She feels at least in part based on Minnie Barstad, the inspirational maid from Goldman's own childhood.

Chapter three takes us to Chicago where we are introduced to the couple from hell, Sid and Esther. Sid is a good-looking if rather short wiseguy, Esther a stacked and sassy broad. The tone here is rather inconsistent, lurching from intellectual barrenness to mentions of a "Mozartian meter" of which Sid would have no concept. Also peculiar in light of the book's occasional use of profanity ("shit," "fuck," "piss") is the way Goldman chickens out of mentioning masturbation, using a limp metaphor involving drinking glasses of water.

Chapter four is devoted to Jenny Devers, a hefty native of a Wisconsin town with a population of 206. Towards the end of her idyllic, rustic childhood—in which her best friend Tommy gradually assumes the status of her sweetheart—she develops an ambition to become an actress. As before, the writing lurches between competent to lazy.

The next chapter gives us the wholly uninteresting story of Howard and Rose Scudder written in hack prose. Their romantic intrigues and marital in-fighting are relevant only insofar as they lead to the birth of their son, Branch. The latter is a "sissy," a process helped by Rose dressing him up in her clothes as an act of punishment for playing with the masculinity-draped baseball of her despised and now deceased husband.

Part two begins with a vignette from the childhood of Rudolph Valentino Miller, more commonly, and less laughably, known as Rudy. He is the son of Sid and Esther, who have married after a bristling courtship and a date rape. Sid is now the heir apparent to the family fortune, the rather insalubrious Turk's Delicatessen, run by Esther's decent, sad and gigantically-nosed father. The love between Old Turk and Rudy is touching, although Rudy, like pretty much all children in Goldman's books, is implausibly articulate. Sid and Esther also love Rudy—he is the only thing keeping them together—but in an unhealthily competitive way. Rudy is routinely driven to distraction—and physically to their building's fire escape—by the pressure to please one in preference to the other.

When the old man dies, Sid drives away the customers he is congenitally unable to charm like his father-in-law had. He sees salvation at a Shirley Temple movie: everyone always remarks on how film-star beautiful is Rudy. He literally begs an audition from a movie producer, and locks a reluctant Rudy out on the fire escape until he agrees to attend. However, Rudy stymies this plan by having all of his hair shaved off. Sid, incandescent with rage, beats him savagely. Rudy runs away and the combination of the violence and a fever robs him of a massive amount of his hearing faculties. This could be powerful stuff, but it's not persuasive. Not because the authorities accept Sid's denial of violence and his "family business" explanation for failing to report Rudy's two-week disappearance—such was child protection of the time—but because its doubtful Rudy would have been allowed to go to an audition on his own, more doubtful that a barber would have agreed to shave his head and because the description of his days on the run are superficial, melodramatic and falsely portentous.

When Sid asks a returned Rudy after a pitiful, rambling non-apology if there is anything he can do for him, his son responds, "Die."

At Princeton, Aaron is a high-flier but tormented. He double-dates in a strenuous attempt to convince himself he is not one of the homosexuals he despises. Over at Oberlin College (an appearance for Goldman's own *alma mater*), Walt is having a predictably less tormented time, even though his theatre production aspirations and romantic life have their hiccups. His sniping relationship with Blake, his starchy lover (if that is what one is to call a girl whose claim of having a diaphragm he wouldn't know whether or not is a bluff), features dialogue that is zesty and funny but in no way real. (Blake: "Sometimes I'm so cute and unbelievably adorably attractive I just can't stand myself.") Meanwhile, while fellow Oberlinian Branch Scudder might be painfully taciturn, when he takes over production of Walt's revue, he is discernibly more efficient and intuitive in the role.

Freshly graduated from Princeton, Aaron is writing a book of short stories. His writing career is infuriatingly put on hold when he is drafted, his high intellect deemed to cancel out his weak legs. He detests his new army colleagues. When Goldman runs through them—salami-munching Jews, finger-snapping Negros, sullen Puerto Ricans—and then has Aaron think, "You are clichés … Every bloodless one of you," the reader's reaction is, "Er, they certainly are, Mr. Goldman." Nonetheless, there is some verisimilitude and power in this section, probably courtesy of Goldman's own experiences: he always wrote well about army life.

Aaron is seduced by his superior Sergeant Terry. He then finds fellow conscriptee Branch Scudder is also of what he has come to admit is his persuasion. As the latter is a rich kid and able to lavish him with gifts and luxury, he brutally dispenses with Terry. He exults in the indignities to which Branch is prepared to submit at his hands.

Part Three opens with nineteen-year-old Jenny Devers arriving in Manhattan to seek her thespian fortune. Although still hefty, she is also attractive and large-bosomed. Potentially an opportunity to provide an interesting backwoods ingénue's perspective on the Big Apple, the chapter never comes close to achieving that level courtesy of cartoon lines such as the ones Jenny speaks to a taxi driver she finds suspicious: "New? Oh no, I'm a veteran traveller. I happen to have been here thirty-five times."

Sid meanwhile has made his fortune through—successively—wartime black marketing, an automobile agency, and insurance. Although financially comfortable, he and Esther crave a social acceptance denied Jews. When he realizes that the wife of a man who runs a country club has the hots for his now teenaged son, Sid pressurizes Rudy to accept her advances. Rudy—weary after a lifetime of such manipulation—flares up at the woman, who makes a false attempted rape allegation in retaliation. Sid dutifully punishes Rudy with his belt to placate the country club couple.

A demobilized Branch is still wrestling with his sexuality. He can't resist visiting a bar in his hometown rumored to be a meeting point for "fags." He prepares to pick up a man he finds attractive but not at all likeable, before being apprised of the fact that he is an undercover cop. While that scene powerfully captures the paranoia, loneliness and torment of gay life of the era, the rest of this chapter is flabby, the scenes in which Branch tries to convince himself he can be happy in the family real estate business at least twice as long as they need be and unfortunately soporific in their attempt to portray soporificness.

Engaged in secretarial work at a publishing company while studying acting, Jenny begins an affair with her boss, a married editor named Charley Fiske. The narrative segues in and out of flashbacks to Charley's poverty-stricken childhood. That the flashbacks are quite moving doesn't prevent the reader wondering whether, halfway through the book, we really need another new character with an attendant backstory. Said backstory's greater importance to the author than the reader seems to be confirmed by an unnecessary passage devoted to Charley's schooldays football heroics.

In addition to contrived references to sports, something else that Goldman has rarely been able to resist—and increasingly so as the years wore on—is the 'reversal,' or, more colloquially, the 'switcheroo': undermining the reader's expectations via a sucker punch of a revelation. Such is provided with Charley, whose backstory features him meeting a woman at a party who it is obvious is the wife on whom he is now cheating with Jenny. Except it turns out that their elaborately detailed courtship foundered when he was intimidated by the party woman's family wealth, which means that his wife is someone else entirely.

Walt meanwhile has suffered a mild mental crack-up after being abandoned by Blake, whom he married. Walt uses his crisis to spur himself into action, turning his back on his birthright and moving permanently to New York to find the artistic fulfillment that the family firm cannot confer.

Aaron is already in the Big Apple, having been released by the military for reasons related to his sexuality. He has resumed his writing career, although is motivated more by mammon than literary ambition in penning *Autumn Wells*, an erotically-charged melodrama. Aaron bluffs his way into the office of publishing giant Dave Boardman, whom he tells will be passing up a great find if he sends him away. "You have intrigued me, Fire," says Boardman in the sort of response that—symptomatic of this narrative—is never heard in real life but often on the cinema screen. Convinced that Boardman's agreement to read his manuscript is the harbinger of riches, Aaron makes his move to New York permanent. However, his plans for what he will do with his advance are shattered at a lunch where the publishing giant will concede only that he has potential. His fleeing of the restaurant after Boardman's rejection is pantomime stuff: Goldman has the other diners laughing at Aaron's distress. Not even in New York is a cross-section of human beings of such uniform callousness to be found.

Jenny is beginning to make demands on Charley, namely that he stays with her an entire night. They split up and agree to be friends. Then—reversal—they sleep together again. When wife Betty Jane gives Charley a fright by calling Jenny when he is in bed with her, this would-be intriguing plot turn doesn't surmount the total unlikelihood of a woman being in possession of her husband's secretary's home telephone number. Jenny now begins to demand that Charley choose her over his wife.

Chapter Eighteen is the most powerful part of the book. Aaron picks up an apparently effeminate youth, who turns out to be somebody who acts like a "swish" in order to "roll queers." Shaken by his brutal battering and what he feels to be the seediness of his life, Aaron applies to the Institute for Free Therapy for some psychological treatment. He first has to jump the hurdle of an assessment interview with one Dr. Gunther, who gradually chisels out of him that he has been doing nothing but working in a cab and seeing movies in the three years since the devastating rejection of *Autumn Wells*, that he is a sadist but at the same time perennially seeking to degrade himself and that he has been rattled by a chance meeting with Branch Scudder, whose "whore" he fears once again becoming. Of the latter, he says, "I need the clinic because I'm not strong enough, I don't think, to resist it by myself…" Aaron is faced with a nerve-wracking two-week wait before a decision is made on his application. As he swelters in a dizzying heatwave, he is terrified that Branch will call before Gunther. To save his sanity, he begins writing for the first time since his rejection by Boardman. He is delighted by the story he devises but when Gunther rings with the news that, "They don't want any homosexuals this year," he destroys it. He receives one of the wrong-number calls he occasionally gets for restaurant Chateau de Lille and, adopting a French accent, has fun with the caller, who says she will ask her friend if the menu of intestine with orange sauce is acceptable. When the phone rings again and he answers "Chateau de Lille," it is not the prospective diner but Branch, who mutters an apology about dialing the wrong number and hangs up, reducing Aaron to hysterics. When Branch rings back, Aaron plays cat-and-mouse with him in a telephonic microcosm of the abusive, mercenary relationship he knows he is about to re-embrace. There is no serious flaw in a rollercoaster ride of what feels like a chapter from a more honest, less glib and less flabby *Boys and Girls Together*.

Someone else with whom Branch has had a chance encounter in New York is Walt Kirkaby, currently going out with a woman called Tony. Walt and Tony's half-fond, half-barbed exchanges remind us that we have seen this sort of inter-gender banter from other couples several other times, including Walt and Blake. It certainly doesn't benefit from coming hot on the heels of the latest installment of the endless tango of recrimination between Charley and Jenny. Walt tells Tony the story of how ex-wife Branch cuckolded him in front of his face and with advance warning. The pathos of this occurrence is twice removed, firstly by being rendered in dialogue and secondly because it's recalled merely as a device to get Tony into bed, although these factors are less responsible for its interminability than insipid writing.

Tony declines the seduction because, although twenty-five, she is pure. The dramatic revelation of her *virgo intacta* status is puzzling, because it was mentioned only a few pages previously. We are then told through Tony's interior dialogue that in fact she isn't a virgin—and the heart sinks at the realization that we are being whisked into another backstory, this one particularly yawn-inducing because her good-girl self-image is predicated on a dialogue from her childhood with her father about elves. "Brownies were little elves that helped the shoemaker, who was a nice man, a craftsman too, but his wife was very sick, his children very small, so he had to spend all of his time taking care of his family, cleaning and tidying, and that left little time for shoemaking, and his business got worse and worse until there was almost no money at all…" This section reads like a precursor to *The Princess Bride*, not just because of the fairytale style but due to sickening tweeness purveyed in prose as stodgy as clay.

Speaking of unnecessary flashbacks, Betty Jane's revelation to a friend that she thinks Charley is sleeping with his secretary leads to a scene in which the moment of her and Charley's first meeting is diligently mapped on the assumption that anyone cares a fig. Betty Jane now has a revenge affair. Meanwhile, Jenny has been censured by her childhood sweetheart and notional fiancée Tommy, who is appalled by the cliché of a secretary fresh to New York having an affair with her boss. ("He's never gonna marry you! He's got too good a deal going for him the way it is!") Charley and Jenny's back-and-forth over when he is going to leave his wife certainly feels like cliché, even if there is a power to the scene in which Jenny finally loses patience and rings Betty Jane herself, only to have the phone grabbed off her by Charley.

It has been revealed that Charley is the editor who rescued Rudy Miller's novella about his grandfather, *The Nose is for Laughing*, from the slush pile, convincing Dave Boardman (the same man who turned down Aaron's book) to publish it. The novella didn't sell well, but created a friendship between Charley and Rudy. Charley turns to Rudy for advice as the complications of his affair deepen.

Aaron decides to write a play to fulfill/exploit Branch's production ambitions, basing it on his own sister's failed pregnancy deception, although throwing in some deformity and lesbianism to spice it up. The play proves his undoing, for, at a party, Branch spots Rudy—despite his hearing aids, as beautiful in adulthood as he had been as a boy—and decides he must bring him close to him by casting him in what Aaron christens *Madonna with Child*. The fact that Charley and Betty Jane attend aforesaid party together is another reversal: previously we had seen Charley successively split up with Betty Jane and Jenny, the latter losing interest in him when he was no longer unattainable. It later transpires that both women made up with Charley on the same day he dumped them..

In contrast to Aaron's pride in his work, Branch considers *Madonna with Child* execrable but that's not the reason he plays on Aaron's fear of another *Autumn Wells*-like rejection to persuade him to change the central deformity from a club foot to deafness. Once the rewrites are done and Branch has persuaded Rudy to come aboard, Branch callously dispenses with the man to whom he has so long been in thrall. Aaron hatches a revenge plot involving exposing Branch's sexuality to his puritan and purse-string-holding mother.

Branch persuades Walt—still hankering to be a director—to renew their stage partnership from college days. Cut off by his mother—courtesy of Aaron—Branch doesn't in fact have backing for the play. He admits to Walt that he has roped him in because of his wealth. Walt is not so irritated or lacking ambition that he won't agree to put up the money, even if his take on the quality of *Madonna with Child* amounts only to, "… goddamit, I can make it work!"

Jenny Devers is cast as *Madonna with Child*'s female lead. Rudy has persuaded Branch to engineer Jenny's casting because he is assisting her in a plot to break free of Charley and, specifically, the job that keeps Charley and Jenny in close proximity. When Charley confronts Rudy about this, he can't really bring himself to be angry. Instead, he is concerned about his friend. An utterly world-weary Rudy is showing signs of psychosis. The damage done by his childhood is the reason he accepted the central role in the play: he will do anything for a quiet life. He reveals that objects speak to him asking, "Have you had enough?" This is not particularly convincing considering how well-adjusted—not to mention smart-alecky—Rudy had seemed in his previous scene with Charley. Rudy's statement that he thinks the show will end in "catastrophe" and his assertion that several of the principals are as damaged as him is manipulative portentousness: Goldman is clearly moving the chess pieces into position in preparation for a shattering end-game.

Goldman's drawing of the preparations for the show's preview day is convincing apart from the absence of rewriting. As that preview day approaches, as a function of their stories having dovetailed, the narrative does now flit between characters. In a chat with Jenny, Aaron reveals his insecurities: if the play flops it will—on top of the failure of his novel—prove wrong all the assumptions of superiority on which he had predicated his life. Instead of leaving it at that, Goldman proceeds to turn pathos to bathos by having Aaron say he will have to "initiate general suffering" if *Madonna with Child* falls flat.

That crucial day brings an unexpected pair of visitors for Rudy: Sid and Esther, whom he hasn't seen in the decade that followed him fleeing the family home after the belt punishment. Sid doesn't exactly apologize for it but says it was "a terrible mistake" and that he knows it was prompted by a lie. However, Sid's intentions to "set my house in order" have their limits: he wants Rudy to help persuade Esther to go into an institution. While Rudy finds his mother is confused and fragile, he also sees that Sid is less motivated by her well-being than the unencumbered pursuit of an extra-marital romance—with the woman whose lies years ago led to the assault with the belt. Goldman communicates Esther's fragility via the technique of her saying "Oh," followed by the line "Rudy picked up her purse." This is a neat device the first time, but it is used over and over. By now, we are so worn down by this sort of mechanical technique that we are even beginning to wearily accept it as less of a fault than the denoting of the book's simplistic parameters. Yet Goldman then surprises us by coming up with a conceit that does work: Rudy gets on a carousel with his mother and finds its cacophony and circularity perfectly reflect his tormented mind.

Chapter twenty-five is where the world falls apart for every character. Branch doesn't even attend the preview, making an excuse about needing to arrange the party for the cast and crew at his apartment but in reality devastated by the arrival of his mother, whose shock at his 'condition' has made her balloon in size. Aaron and Sid provide the remainder of the holocaust.

The play's author is devastated by the overheard in-depth dismissal of his play by Tony, whom Walt has sneaked into the preview. As good as his word, he moves around the party casually initiating suffering. He pseudo-guilelessly remarks to Branch's mother that the psychic link between Branch and Rudy is "unnatural."("You mean uncanny," stammers Rose.) He summons Charley to the party even though he knows Jenny is trying to keep out of his orbit. And he destroys Tony's lie about saving herself—and hence her gold-digging designs on Walt—by revealing that she regularly put out for an old friend of his; he had been on a double-date with her back in college.

Meanwhile, in another exception to the presentation of his psychosis in pulpy style, Rudy—pursued for an answer about committing his mother by his relentless father—finds the room warping and turning and staring at him to ask if now he's had enough. The answer is yes, and he throws himself off the fire escape. Cruelly, he finds he is still alive. He crawls back up to the party. He locates his father and instructs him, "DIE!" before doing just that himself. Which itself causes Branch to have a breakdown.

Charley and Jenny walk home together. They have agreed they won't be seeing each other anymore, but as Jenny has just found out that Tommy, her childhood sweetheart, is about to enter a shotgun wedding to someone else and as Aaron has made clear he is invoking the clause in his contract that allows him to close the play, she doesn't have many options about changing her life.

Cut to Aaron, now acting as servant-cum-rent-boy for famous writer Stagpole, who he met at the preview party. Brutal sadist Stagpole tells Aaron an anecdote about a cattle market for young boys he had once witnessed in the East. The boys' fate is to be "used up" until they "disappear." As he tortures Aaron, Stagpole states, "By the time that I am done with you, there will be nothing left. I… will… use… you… up, believe me, trust me, trust my skill. *I am a master.*" Aaron thinks of fleeing but, although Stagpole is cruel, he also spoils him with finery and rich food. "Aaron entered into agony" is the last line of a depressing and distasteful final chapter.

In 1964, *Boys and Girls Together* would have had a sense of quality by default because of the way it gleamed with modernity, especially in its portrayal of homosexuals as rounded human beings instead of freaks or comedy turns. Now, it's a snapshot of a bygone time, one where many young women well past the age of consent valued their virginity, "out of your trick [sic] head" was in the lexicon, "helluva" and "goddamit" were considered by many to be swear words, sodomy was illegal, gays were "swishes," writers pounded out their intended masterpieces on typewriters, people heated pans of water to make instant coffee and Jews were denied entry to country clubs. Although such a snapshot is historically interesting, Goldman can hardly take credit for it—he was committing the prosaic, even unavoidable, act of depicting things as they were. More importantly, without that Now factor, the book loses a considerable part of its validity.

That we never feel New York City's seething, honking, hyperactive texture is indicative. Goldman doesn't go in for description beyond a perfunctory or shallow level. Ditto for characterization. Goldman rarely paints emotions comprehensively. Nor, except in flashes, does he go in for truthfulness rather than effect. This sketchiness and flashiness frequently go with a whistle-stop pace, none of which is designed to produce resonance and gravitas.

This is a dialogue-led book. Sometimes pages go by with nary a line attribution or piece of linking text. If the dialogue were high-quality, this wouldn't matter: these passages could have the same impact as a published stage play. Unfortunately, where the dialogue is not merely poor it is often painfully writerly/stagey/cinematic. Women rummage in purses to disguise their emotions and when asked, "What are you searching for?" reply, "Nothing. I'm just hiding." When a character realizes that another character is waiting for him to say something, she remarks, "You're waiting for me to say something." When Charley starts to call Jenny's name and then stops himself, he thinks, "There had been altogether too much last-minute calling of names lately. It was a device he had always disliked, especially in movies." When a character is about to raise a hand, a cab appears and the character says, "Just like in the movies." It being the case that he is in publishing, Charley's closed-captioning of his own actions is thematically halfway justifiable, but when he and Jenny prepare for sex and a blank line is followed by him saying, "A little while later ... Three little dots," the reference to artifice is buffoonishly self-conscious rather than cleverly post-modern and, like the others listed, conveys the impression of the characters moving stiffly on pulleys operated by the author.

This all reaches its nadir when Tommy, riding in a canoe with Jenny, tells her he wants a privacy even greater than the one conferred by the wide open landscape. He tips the craft over so that they end up conversing in the air pocket under the canoe—a device straight out of a screwball romance flick. Similar cinematic stylization is evident in Aaron's preternatural coolness, him able to rattle an upright dinner party host he has not previously met with a, "Mort, for crissakes, how the hell are ya?"

Some of the dialogue is pseudo-poetic and pseudo meaningful:

> "...Nothing matters."
> Branch turned him around. "You mean everything matters."
> "Yes," Rudy nodded. "That too."

Some of it is florid in its declamatory, know-it-all style:

> "Oh, Charles, if I could manufacture enough Instant Pity I could likely save the world, but it's hard to come by and I had this little bit left only, and as I was walking to the subway stop to meet you this ancient, wretched, leprous cripple hobbled up to me and said, 'Help me, help me, my wife has cancer, my daughter leukemia, my son just ran off with a shiksa, my mother heard the news and went insane and the shock of that killed my father on the spot and on top of everything else my piles are acting up.' Could there be a sadder story, Charles? I doubt it, but I didn't weep. I just whipped out my last smidgen

of Instant Pity and I gave it to him and said, 'Take this, just add air,' and he downed it, and do you know that inside five seconds not only was he chipper but his piles were gone."

Some of the dialogue is the sort of pseudo-philosophy bad writers insist people seasoned in their profession come out with at will, such as Stagpole's advice to Jenny about a perfect day:

"...we all get to pick our day. But we only get one pick ... And the worst thing in the world Jenny, the saddest thing, is to choose the wrong day. You've got to pick a day that won't go bad on you; if you do, you'll have no place to run."

Typical of the book's phony profundity is the fact that Goldman has a room laughing at the rhyme involved in "Tsk, tsk, Mrs. Fiske," when there is no such rhyme: the dental click sound of disapproval is pronounced "tut."

And then some of the dialogue is simply garbage: "I feel it only fair to tell you that my boy friend is fantastically jealous. Of course, he's sort of small, but capable of frenzies, nonetheless." These particular lines are all the more risible because Goldman puts them in the mouth of a teenager.

Goldman frequently has his characters explain their rationales with grave soliloquies about past events in their lives. One begins to groan at the likes of, "One time, back in Ohio, there was this dress I hated..." aware that it is a preamble to another homily of self-justification.

This is all so unnecessary, because Goldman reveals in places he can do so much better:

"It only got uglier and uglier. Just before I got this part, the week before, Charley and I got invited out as a couple. This editor, Archie, he had a place and so, I guess out of desperation, Charley asked could he use it and Archie was delighted. We fooled him for so long, he just loved it that we were sneaking around. He thought it was funny, us sneaking around and all the time pretending to be so moral and upright. He used to ride me about it in the office. Leave little notes for me, things like that. Then, the week before I got this part, Archie invited Charley and me out as a couple."

That's not great dialogue, but it is unshowy and believable. In small bursts, Goldman even provides dialogue that sings: "'It so happens,' Walt shouted, hurrying alongside, 'it so happens—slow down, dammit—that I am one helluva neat guy.'" When Rudy tells Sid that he once had a book published, part of Sid's response is, "I read *Exodus*. You read *Exodus*? Terrific." As well as being idiomatic, it perfectly summarizes Sid's self-absorption and philistinism.

The problems are not restricted to the dialogue, however. There are acres of dead prose: unnecessary and therefore pointless-feeling explorations of the lives of minor characters, groan-inducing real-time descriptions of mundane activities and reams of empty authorial waffle. In the latter category is this:

> "For though Walt had spoken to Imogene but once (eight words), been close to her that-one-time only, it was enough. He knew. There was something about her. Something. An air, an aura, a way. She was a mystery. Open and sweet, yet a mystery. Not mysterious, therefore mysterious, therefore glamorous, for mystery without glamour is like love without like: false; much trumpeted, but false; much avowed, yet false; pledged, sworn, promised, still, and always false; false, nothing more."

This sigh-making vacuity makes it feel like Goldman is being paid by the word.

In short, the writing is rarely something to savor and while the breathlessness and plot turns can, in the book's better parts, keep the reader turning the page, a second reading—when the plot details are already known—is dismayingly less rewarding.

There is no denying that the narrative of *Boys and Girls Together* possesses an increasing vitality as it finds its feet somewhere around forty percent of the way in, but the manuscript needed judicious (for which read considerable) editing to make it a substantial (for which read less tedious and less trashy) work. As it is, one has to resist the temptation to give up on the book before reaching the good stuff, and even that good stuff remains interspersed with banality and superficiality.

Perhaps Goldman isn't cut out for prose of such an extended length. He rarely wrote a novel even half as long again. Certainly one is struck several times at the end of an uncharacteristically fine chapter or section whose ending happens to possess the flavor of a resolution that if some of the better parts of this book were shuffled and their characters' names altered, they could help form a far preferable (and more slender) book, namely a collection of quality, all-American short stories in the vein of Goldman's beloved Irwin Shaw.

"My editor, who was like my father figure, was a genuine intellectual," says Goldman of Hiram Haydn. "He was the leading editor in America. He was the publisher of *The American Scholar*, which was the magazine of the Phi Beta Kappas, which is the brilliant people who get good grades in college. He was a very distinguished figure. Hiram thought *Boys and Girls Together* was going to establish me as a serious American novelist—and it got crucified. It just got very, very badly reviewed because people thought I was more popular than I was. I've never been particularly well-liked by the critics as a novelist. I remember it was so depressing. I hate critics. Critics are all whores and failures and you can put that in capital letters if you want because I say it all the time and I've written it and I believe it. It's a terrible job, being a critic."

Take with a pinch of salt Goldman's claims of uniformly terrible reviews. Publishers have never had any difficulty in honestly extracting superlatives from reviews for use on his paperback covers. In the case of *Boys and Girls Together*, they could—and did—quote the *Cleveland Plain Dealer* ("an unforgettable novel of life in our time"), the *Los Angeles Times* ("the novel of the year ... a superb, brilliant evocation") and the *San Francisco Chronicle* ("has life, power, beauty and truth"). In any event, Goldman could afford to shrug off the fact that his new book was not unanimously praised and certainly didn't achieve Haydn's ambition of establishing him as a "serious American novelist." In terms of its advance and its sales, *Boys and Girls Together* sent Goldman into the stratosphere.

Despite his early success, Goldman's books had not so far set the world on fire. He might have had three novels published before he was thirty, but they were not bestsellers. As Richard Seff notes, "In those days it was easier for a young writer to get a publisher. It wouldn't be today. They were not huge bestsellers and these days publishers seem to keep one eye on the bottom line." Moreover, although Goldman's flurry of Broadway work from a standing start is also superficially impressive, all those projects were even less obviously portents of future glory.

In other words, Goldman's career could have sputtered to a halt around this point, handy ancillary revenue like the movie rights of *Soldier in the Rain* notwithstanding. Asked if he was worried about the precariousness of his position in the late fifties and early sixties, Goldman says,

"I was so stunned that any of this happened ... No one thought I had any talent and I believed them, so when this madness happened I was staggered and thrilled... Not really. I was so shocked, I wasn't nervous. I mean, of course I was nervous. Probably Robert Louis Stevenson was nervous. Hemingway was probably nervous. It goes with the territory."

Hiram Haydn's insistence that Goldman publish *No Way to Treat a Lady* under a pseudonym was partly because he was an editor who dealt with literary novels and didn't understand thrillers, but also because he thought such a book would damage Goldman's name if it appeared before his supposed opus. Leaving aside the fact that *Boys and Girls Together* is in its own way no less aesthetically crass than *No Way to Treat a Lady*, Haydn's ambitions for a big splash for it were more than fulfilled. When the manuscript was finally delivered to his agent, Haydn found publishers biting his hand off. Goldman: "I think I got ten thousand dollars for my first novel and five thousand dollars for my second—which indicates what a huge success the first one was—and the third one probably another five, and then my memory is that I got a hundred thousand dollars for *Boys and Girls Together* as an advance. I don't know if *Soldier in the Rain* had sold to the movies or whatever happened, but there were a bunch of people who wanted *Boys and Girls Together*." That bunch of people was not restricted to publishing houses: upon its publication, the public turned out to covet the novel in vast numbers, or as Goldman later put it, "...that summer, *Boys and Girls Together* was *the* beach book in paperback."

■

PART II

Stumbling Into Hollywood

1

The inspiration or displacement activity, or combination of both, that constituted his novel *No Way to Treat a Lady* had unexpected but ultimately seismic ramifications in Goldman's career.

The first was that he had provided himself with a rough template for the type of thriller he would begin turning out in 1974 with *Marathon Man*. The other was that it handed him a wholly unexpected admission into the realm of screenwriting, at which he became arguably more successful than novel-writing.

Goldman found himself approached by Cliff Robertson, a middlingly successful motion picture actor of the era, who had somehow gotten hold of *No Way to Treat a Lady* prior to its publication. "He knew somebody who I knew and he came to see me in my apartment and he said, 'I read your screen treatment,'" recalls Goldman. "I didn't know what the fuck he was talking about. He meant he had read *No Way to Treat a Lady* with all those chapters and he thought I had written a screen treatment." A screen treatment is a sort of shorthand version of a proper screenplay, designed to communicate the broad idea of a project while deferring the conjuring of fine detail. Goldman: "He said, 'I would like you to make a screenplay out of this short story

I've optioned.' Because his career… He's a fine, fine actor, but he never got the movie roles of the television movies he starred in." The short story in question was *Flowers for Algernon* by Daniel Keyes, a science fiction tale about a man who artificially boosts his intelligence. It had already been adapted for the small screen in 1961 in the form of *The Two Worlds of Charlie Gordon*, in which Robertson had starred. Goldman: "I said, 'Well, I'll read the story and tell you if I think I can do it.' I remember saying to my wonderful ex-wife Ilene, 'I don't know what a screenplay looks like.' I was 33 years old, I'd never seen a screenplay. I remember going down to Times Square in the middle of the night—and you didn't want to be in Times Square in the middle of the night—and there were a couple of bookstores that were open and I remember saying to the poor fuck whose job it was to work all night in a Times Square bookstore, 'Have you got anything on screenwriting?' and he sort of gestured and I went over. There was one book on it. So I bought the book and took it home and I realized I couldn't write in that form … I remember looking at the format with that capital 'INT. BILL PICKS UP THE PHONE'—I could not write in that format because I'm always trying to tell stories … I knew that it stopped your eye and the whole thing about my writing has always been to try and keep you going, keep you going. So I wrote the screenplay for Robertson in the form that I've basically written all my screenplays in." Goldman's screenplays are a hybrid of the conventional movie script format and something more to his own convenience: he uses the phrase "Cut to"—traditionally employed in screenplays to signify a new scene— almost as a replacement for the "he saids" in his novels and as a rhythmic device to control the reader's vision. "It's not the same but that's not because I intended to do something revolutionary," he reasons. "It's because I realized that I would be inept if I [tried] to write in what was then the proper format." That to his knowledge no studio has ever refused to read his scripts because of his idiosyncratic technique may be less a function of studio broadmindedness than the vast profits his movie work has tended to generate.

The manner in which Goldman had landed the gig was farcical enough, but there was another turn of events suffused with bizarre irony. Robertson had replaced Englishman Rex Harrison in the lead role in a movie being made in Europe ultimately titled *Masquerade*. Robertson nominated Goldman for the necessary task of Americanizing his character's dialogue. At this point Robertson hadn't read the *Flowers for Algernon* screenplay he had commissioned. When he did, following Goldman's work on *Masquerade*, Robertson considered it to be unsatisfactory and rejected it. "Well it was shocking," says Goldman. "He read it and fired me and hired Stirling Silliphant, who [won] Robertson the Oscar. He was very smart to fire me." Goldman has stated that Stirling Silliphant's screenplay for what was re-titled *Charly* (1968) had not "a scintilla" of his original *Flowers for Algernon* script. By that time, though, Goldman's dismissal had long since ceased to matter.

Goldman has done three types of work for motion pictures: screenwriter, script doctor, and a more nebulous role with no formal title but that can best be summarized as "consultant." *Masquerade* fits into the middle category. Unusually for a doctoring job, he receives credit, a co-screenwriting billing with Michael Relph (although, possibly due to the very specific nature of this particular doctoring job, there is neither an ampersand or an "and" linking the two men's names). As Relph was also the producer, this bespeaks a certain generosity and integrity on Relph's part. Asked if he was surprised by receiving a credit, Goldman responds, "Yeah, I think I was."

Released in April 1965 (UK cinemas), *Masquerade* is based on the 1955 novel *Castle Minerva* by Victor Canning. Although the re-casting of an American in the lead role after the departure of Harrison disguises it to some extent, this picture was actually intended to muscle in on the massively profitable and then-novel James Bond territory. The debt owed to OO7 by this tongue-in-cheek drama featuring a man of action with a line in glib quips is acknowledged at one point when a character shows another a copy of a paperback of *Goldfinger*. This film should be so lucky to be mistaken for an entry in the vastly entertaining, Sean Connery-led Bond franchise.

David Frazer (Robertson) is persuaded temporarily out of retirement by the British Foreign Office to keep safe Prince Jamil of Ramaut (Christopher Witty) during the three weeks before his ascension to the throne on his fourteenth birthday. As competing nations are anxious that the prince sign oil deals with them, he is a very valuable young man. Several parties—freelance and official—have their sights set on abducting and/ or eliminating him. That some of said parties are ostensibly on the side of the good guys at the picture's beginning gives it a veneer of topicality; irreverent acknowledgment of base human motives in the British ruling class had rarely been depicted in cinema. Just about all of the characters un-intriguingly double- and even triple-cross one another as the plot careens toward an utterly unexciting climax on a rope bridge.

An all-star cast that includes Cliff Robertson, John Le Mesurier, and Jack Hawkins ensures a certain standard of professionalism, but *Masquerade* is resoundingly poor and now antiquated—the type of thing that disappeared along with full-length second features. Although it technically did not have that status, its many B-movie qualities include back projection, leaden-footed direction (by Basil Dearden), an overactive, shrill soundtrack, formulaic devices (Frazer turns off the lights in a room to gain an advantage in fisticuffs), and self-indulgence (at one point Robertson says directly to the camera, "Somebody up there hates me").

It's difficult to assess the quality of Goldman's contribution to the project. He states in *Adventures in the Screen Trade* "…most of what I did was what I'd been hired to do: fuss with the dialogue." However, in the same book, he claims responsibility for a scene wherein an imprisoned Frazer goes to great lengths to obtain a set of keys hanging from a hook, only to realize, when his task is accomplished at great pain to himself, that they're the wrong keys. (Goldman cited this as "the first reversal I ever wrote." Presumably he means it was his first screen switcheroo: the years-in-the-writing *Boys and Girls Together* had shedloads of them.) In Americanizing Robertson's dialogue, Goldman does reasonably well, although even there he seems to have left intact some British expressions, which sit oddly in an American's mouth: e.g., "belt you," "mucked it up."

Either way, *Masquerade* will feature on nobody's list of memorable movies—except perhaps that of a certain then-young writer. As Goldman says, "Essentially, it's what got me into the movie business."

2

"I never dreamt I was going to get in the movie business and I went back to writing novels," says Goldman of the immediate aftermath of *Flowers for Algernon/Masquerade*. Once again, serendipity played a part in a career he had never intended.

Goldman had a meeting with producer Eliott Kastner, who had recently optioned *Boys and Girls Together*. Although the screenplay to this film was not slated to be written by Goldman, the two men happened to get chatting about other potential projects. Goldman: "He said, 'I want to do a movie with balls.' That was a direct quote. I said, 'Read some Ross

Macdonald,' who was a fabulous novelist, I thought. He called me and said, 'I love them, find one that you want to make a movie out of.' So I did. I think it was the first one, *The Moving Target*."

Goldman wrote the *Moving Target* screenplay on spec. However, when it was accepted, his fee was $80,000, not far off that astronomical sum he had received for *Boys and Girls Together*, which had had a far longer and infinitely more difficult gestation. As if that wasn't enough, Goldman secured an extraordinary stroke of luck that ensured his script could barge its way past all the other pre-production projects in Hollywood. He recalls, "Paul Newman had just been doing a period drama in Europe in which he had to wear costume. I think he felt it wasn't what he should have been doing. When he was given *Harper*, it's very American, it's *film noir*, or whatever it is. I went up to Connecticut with the producer and we met with Newman and he said that he would do it. We're driving back to the city and the producer said, 'You don't know what just happened to you. You just jumped past all the shit.' Because Paul Newman was a giant star and when Paul Newman said he would do a movie, most of the time, if it was not an amazingly expensive period piece, that movie got made."

The title of *The Moving Target* was changed for its movie adaptation along with its main character's name. Different reasons have been given for the switch from Lew Archer to Lew Harper. One story (told by Goldman) has it that contractual reasons forbade the use of the name Archer. Another (not necessarily conflicting) version states that Newman insisted on *Harper* because he had had luck with movies whose titles began with the letter "h."

Harper, released February 23, 1966, is in the private dick tradition that started with the 'hardboiled' crime novels of Dashiell Hammett and Raymond Chandler in the 1930s and their even more famous film adaptations. As it is very generic, it's pre-ordained that Harper is a loner, broke, smarter than the police, and doesn't suffer fools gladly. Almost as inevitable is that he is hired to track down a missing person. His client is Elaine Sampson (Lauren Bacall, herself a familiar face from movie adaptations of Marlowe novels), whose wealthy and dissolute husband disappeared a day previously. Harper soon finds deep levels of intrigue, crime and violence beyond that mundane vanishing act. All of this very familiar turf is compounded by Harper making progress on the trail by finding in a corpse's pocket a book of matches bearing the name of a sleazy bar. Or course, as the private eye movies had been moribund now for two decades, there was a defense of 'homage' for such creaking devices, but this is of little comfort to the bored viewer.

Leaving aside how confusing the red herrings, dead ends, and unexpected developments are, the film is generally plausible, apart from a couple of things. One is the naïveté of the deputy sheriff (Martin West) of the community in which Harper is digging for leads. A scene in a men's room where Harper suggests to the gawky deputy that he hang around here because it's a hotbed of information, followed by the deputy looking expectantly at the walls, is goofball comedy that is completely incongruous in such a *noir* context. A jarring note for different reasons is Harper's insolence to the Chief of Police, ranging from simple sarcasm to patting, almost slapping, him on the cheek. This is schoolboy fantasy; in real life, Harper would find himself unable to nurse his black eye for the handcuffs around his wrists.

The suffocating generic feel would not be such a problem were it possible to warm to anybody in this movie. Goldman, in a commentary in a DVD release of this film, opined that although Harper is no saint—illustrated by the way he sleeps with his estranged wife (played by Janet Leigh—this is truly a star-studded cast) only to then callously puncture her hopes for a reunion—he is somebody whom the audience nevertheless likes. Not so. They may like Paul Newman—whom Goldman found utterly professional and pleasant during his visits to the set—but Harper, the man, is simply reminiscent of a gnarled old tree, made twisted, hardened and unlovely not by elements beyond his control but by the self-inflicted wretchedness of his life.

His one virtue is that he is not as nasty as the movie's other characters, who are all murderous, grasping, or vicious, even the ones who initially appear harmless. Harper's friend Albert Graves (Arthur Hill)—Mrs. Sampson's lawyer—seems like a loveable old boob but murders Sampson. Alan Traggert (Robert Wagner) at first seems like a nice kid but turns out to be up to his neck in the criminal shenanigans.

That those shenanigans are bewildering may be, for some, a yardstick of clever plotting, but the fact that nobody can fully understand *Harper's* labyrinthine developments on first viewing exposes ostensible depth as unnecessary obfuscation. Another criticism that can be leveled, if not at the screenwriter, is that the casting of Shelley Winters as Fay Estabrook verges on cruelty. The latter is a formerly glamorous movie star gone to fat—a career trajectory that can be said to apply to Winters.

There are several things in the film's plus column. The major one is Newman. Courtesy of his incredible, and in no way feminine, beauty, his blue eyes and what can only be described as his poise, he is a mesmerizing screen presence—the archetypal actor whom the camera loves. Also to the film's credit is its refusal to glamorize violence, as evinced by the utter grisliness of the moment when Harper brains a villain with a metal object, and Harper's evident horror when he causes the same man to plunge to his death.

"I was totally ignorant and I did it and it got taken and it got accepted by a major star and it was a hit," summarizes Goldman of *Harper*. "You can't have a better start to your movie career than that." Except perhaps winning your first major award for that work. *Harper* garnered Goldman the Mystery Writers of America's Edgar Allan Poe Award for Best Motion Picture. However, Goldman says, "I don't know when I knew I won it. I never pay attention to that."

Goldman wrote a further screenplay revolving around the Archer/Harper character but was shortly the victim of another type of disappointment pervasive in the movie industry. In an almost perfect reversal of his good luck in getting *Harper* off the ground, his adaptation of the Macdonald novel *The Chill* was not put into production because Newman declined to repeat the role. Newman did eventually return to the Harper character in the 1975 movie *The Drowning Pool*, but Goldman was not involved. There were probably no hard feelings, for by then Goldman and Newman had a bond stemming from their mutual involvement in a movie project that was successful almost beyond credibility.

Post-*Harper*, Goldman was firmly ensconced as a screenwriter. It is a career that brought him great riches and great acclaim (a further 'Edgar'; two Academy Awards; two Writers Guild screenplay awards; Lifetime Achievement awards from the Writers Guild of America, the Writers' Guild of Great Britain, and the National Board of Review of Motion Pictures). Yet it is a career about which he has remained ambivalent, some might even suggest churlish. Despite his never having convinced himself of his prose gifts, he has always been almost dewy-eyed in gratitude at the fact that he has been able to pursue a career as a novelist. In contrast, he says, "I don't mean to piss on screenwriting, but I don't know that fulfilling is the word you would use." He said something similar to Richard Andersen: "...as a general rule, screenwriting is not something about which

I care a great deal."

It seems an illogical contrast in outlook: after all, he appears to have loved movies most of his life no less than he loved books. Moreover, although the physical act of writing for the screen is a functional process—the finished film can be art, but the screenplay is not—one doesn't have to be too cruel to observe that Goldman's prose style is also pretty utilitarian.

"If I were to say what were the two most unusual things that young writers might be intrigued by today, I was totally shunned until I wrote my first novel and then I had never seen a screenplay until I was 33 years old," says Goldman. "There are screenwriters now whose careers are finished when they're 33. I remember when I first heard of the existence of film schools, I felt, 'What's the punch line? Why would anybody want to go to a film school? What can you learn in a film school?' And then all these film school kids exploded and now it's what people do." Although—like everybody else in that era—formally unschooled in the medium, Goldman notes, "Clearly I had a facility for screenwriting. You could argue that I had a facility for novel-writing too, I don't know, but I would have thought I was just going to keep on writing novels. I never dreamt I would write movies."

The fact of having stumbled his way into the industry, though, doesn't explain his indifference to, if not the industry, then his role in it. His reasoning seems to be along the lines of prose having an inherently greater integrity insofar as it springs from a place more personal than screenplays. He observes, "When I write a novel for the most part, I just was writing these things out of whatever impulse I had. I never had a contract to write a novel 'til at least twenty years into my quote-quote career as a novelist. I was just writing these things and they would get published."

Additionally, he has an issue with the fact that novels are completely in the control of the author, the occasional pitiless sub-editor and proofreader notwithstanding, and movies are not. "It's always collaborative," Goldman says of motion pictures. "When you write a novel or a piece of non-fiction it's your baby, but when you write a movie… You can get lucky. I got really lucky in *Butch Cassidy*, had a great director, George Roy Hill, who liked it and did a phenomenal job of delivering the screenplay and we didn't change much, and he put in some wonderful stuff of his own, but that's a crapshoot." His opinion on the lack of full creative control inherent in being a screenwriter is, "It's terrible." He adds, "One of the reasons most screenwriters become directors, if they can, [is] because they're going fucking nuts having directors screw up their work." However, Goldman has been caught in a quandary in that respect: "I never wanted to be a director. I don't understand actors. I don't have a lot of friends who are actors. They're different humans from the rest of us and, if you're a director, you have to deal with them. I wouldn't know how to do it. Whatever visual sense I had is not something I would trust."

Another problem experienced by the screenwriter, virtually unknown to the novelist, is 'turnaround hell;' that situation of stasis where a movie script has been written but for whose shooting a green light is awaited, and one dependent on things maddeningly unrelated to the creative process such as finance, politics, and whim. Goldman has experienced this sort of thing many times since the example of *The Chill* mentioned above. Below is an alphabetical list of unproduced Goldman screenplays that are known about because Goldman has spoken or written about them, because third parties have spoken or written about them, or because a copy exists in the William Goldman Papers at Columbia University.

> *The Chill*
> *Damages*
> *Flora Quick, Dead or Alive*
> *Good Old Charley Gordon (Flowers for Algernon)*
> *Grand Hotel*
> *In The Spring the War Ended*
> *Low Fives*
> *The National Pastime*
> *Rescue! (On Wings of Eagles)*
> *Papillon*
> *Piano Man (Father's Day)*
> *The Right Stuff*
> *The Sea Kings*
> *The Ski Bum (Hot Shot)*
> *Singing Out Loud*
> *That's Life (The Thing of It Is...)*

These projects never saw fruition (or, in some cases, never saw fruition with a Goldman script) for a variety of reasons.

Grand Hotel was a project on which Goldman worked twice and ultimately abandoned when he discovered there was a picture in preparation that he felt overlapped with his one, thus draining his motivation, which was partly predicated on it being a unique proposition. *The Thing of It Is...*

is a project on which he worked twice at the turn of the seventies. He deliberately sabotaged the first version by demanding payment after finding himself in what he felt the iniquitous situation of being forced out of a picture written by him and based on his own novel. The project was revived a year later, but the second version was abandoned after problems arose in the casting of the lead actors, some of them related to overweening vanity.

Sometimes Goldman pictures have crashed and burned at the last minute. His late sixties screenplay for an adaptation of the Steven Linakis novel *In The Spring The War Ended* was accepted, he felt, enthusiastically by 20th Century Fox, but the project was then shelved by the studio because it was worried a nominally anti-war film would scupper Pentagon cooperation with their forthcoming military biopic *Patton*.

Some turnaround hell situations have ultimately been resolved. The movie *The Princess Bride* finally reached the cinema screens a decade-and-a-half after Goldman completed the screenplay.

Although Goldman was paid for all the work he did even when a picture did not get made—surprisingly, he has written that Hollywood is quite an honest industry in this regard—most would imagine that repeatedly investing time, energy, and emotion into work only to find it buried is a recipe for heartbreak. Yet this seems to be one of the few facets of the movie industry by which Goldman is not vexed. "It's not my problem," he shrugs. "It's not our job. In other words, if somebody wants to hire me, that's their decision. Just like it's my decision to say yes or no."

He also got paid when scripts of his were deemed unsatisfactory. Sometimes a movie reaches the screen in ways wildly different to what he anticipated or, more to the point, wanted. In others words, he has not only doctored scripts but had his scripts doctored. Goldman thinks he was the original writer on *Papillon*, but says the last line of the picture released in 1973 is all that remains of his three drafts across six months, unless he can claim credit for the fact that it was his decision to end the narrative where it does, dispensing with the events in the concluding couple of hundred pages of the book. Either way, so minimal was his contribution to the final product deemed to be that, as per union rules, the writing credit went to others, in this case Dalton Trumbo and Lorenzo Semple, Jr. Only if a screenwriter's contribution is deemed by the Writers Guild of America to exceed thirty-three percent (fifty percent for an original screenplay) is he ceded partial credit.

On some movies, Goldman retained writing credit but still had to endure what one might imagine to be the indignity of having his work (in the studio's or director's eyes) improved. Yet quotes included later in this text indicate that Goldman was relatively sanguine about his script for *The Stepford Wives* being substantially altered. *Maverick* bears his sole credit but he admitted in *Which Lie Did I Tell?* that Gary Ross was brought in to do another draft of a crucial scene and that "I wasn't even remotely upset—I didn't have it in me for another go." Similarly, Robert Towne rewrote the finale of *Marathon Man* and, although he disagreed with the result, Goldman admitted that it worked for the audience.

Goldman's supposed lack of ego about his screenwriting work is open to question. He was devastated by events relating to his script for *All The President's Men*. Moreover, witness this comment to Richard Andersen: "I don't have a lot of friends in the picture business because I have a lot of ego, and I'll say, 'No, you're wrong. That's a good scene. Leave it.'" Asked by the current author why he would care so much if he was indifferent to the medium of the screenplay, he comes out with an unconvincing and waffling response: "Well, when you're writing a screenplay, if you're past the first draft and you're dealing with producers and directors who are involved with it and the fucking thing's going to get made, it's different. Because then all of a sudden you want it to have as much quality as you can and sometimes the people you work with are very smart, but sometimes they also have needs which are different from ours because they're in the world of business."

Listening to that, one wonders why Goldman doesn't just have done with it and admit that he enjoys writing scripts. He certainly came close to it in *Which Lie Did I Tell?,* where he said of the screenwriter's lot, "Not a bad occupation, truth to tell."

3

April 5, 1967, saw Goldman return to novels with *The Thing of It Is...*

Composer Amos McCracken is almost thirty-one and currently in London with his wife Lila on a trip designed to bolster a marriage being undermined by endless quarreling. Although the narrative that unfolds is third-person, it is all from Amos's point of view, apart from an irritatingly pointless omniscient passage that sees the author tell us details of London architecture of which Amos is not cognizant. Much of the narrative is colloquial, which necessarily involves occasional poor grammar, but this

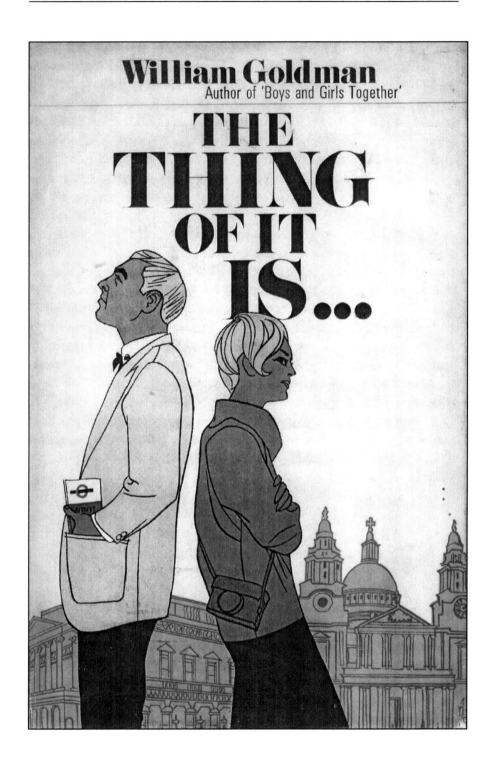

works reasonably well ("…he knew she was kidding, until he reached out and touched her").

The pair are accompanied by their four-year-old daughter Jessica, who possesses a face like that of Edward G. Robinson. Although Amos adores her, he can't bear to say her name because it is the same as that of his hated mother-in-law. Having both come from broken homes, Amos and Lila are anxious to save their own child from that fate.

When Amos had proposed six years before, it had been with the words, "…the thing of it is, I love you." At the time, Lila was under the impression that he was poor, a Protestant and from Princeton. In fact, he was from Illinois and already making good money from TV commercial jingles and stage musicals. He is also half-Jewish. "Amos never intended making a secret of his heritage," we are told. "Things just worked out that way." With only one living relative—aside from his mother, who has not been seen since she abandoned him when he was "quite young"—his secret is safe. Amos is now financially comfortable courtesy of 'Francie,' a song from the musical of the same name, which has been a number one hit and which blares out of radios, bandstands and cab drivers' mouths wherever in the world he goes. Although ambivalent about its qualities, he is not averse to exploiting in small ways the fact that he wrote it.

Amos has a bad back, something which will be a recurring theme in the work of Goldman, who himself has a weak disc. Understandably, he writes about it with verisimilitude. Another Goldman staple resounding with obvious personal knowledge is, of course, love of professional sports. One has to take one's hat off to Goldman at the reverse logic he employs to make the protagonist of this book a big baseball fan—it is partly the compensatory legacy of a childhood in which Amos was denied physical activity in case his gifted hands got injured. The text is accordingly littered with names of baseball players, some legendary some obscure (although, of course, pretty much all obscure to non-Americans). Less predictable in their authenticity are the occasions when Amos muses on songwriting technique and his works' permeation of the public consciousness.

Amos's frustrating exchange with a counter assistant at a lost property office in London is an example of something else destined to be a Goldman motif: humiliation at the hands of a petty and unsympathetic figure of minor officialdom.

Despite their good intentions, the couple argue relentlessly on their marriage-saving trip. Jessica is aware that there is something wrong in her parents' relationship and pulls stunts such as losing her beloved doll to distract them from their bickering. This is reasonably convincing, but her dialogue is not—Goldman is, as ever, clueless when it comes to children's speech ("I read it with my very own eyes"; "I'm not so much hungry as tired"). However, the adults' dialogue is sometimes not much better: both Amos and Lila are preternaturally—that is, unconvincingly—witty. Conversely, Goldman conveys well the broken English of Romans, in whose city Amos and Lila end up—alone—when they flee England after it does nothing but make them more irritated with each other.

The Rome section occasions the first piece of sustained good writing when Amos is suddenly fearful that a mystery tour provided by a friendly taxi driver has a sinister purpose. Somewhat less successful is a scene in a shop in which Lila is accused of stealing a gold watch: although it picks up, this set-piece remains boring for a dismayingly long time.

Part three is set in Venice. Amos has decided that, here, he and Lila will talk properly, "…so that the dove of peace might fly triumphant." His wife has other ideas, suggesting that they try a separation. As his heart shatters, Amos pretends that he too had decided this. Lila is dismayed when her mother turns up: having sensed the marriage of which she had always disapproved is moving toward a denouement, she has hurriedly made her way over, Jessica in tow. To pay her back, Lila arranges a mystery tour of the city's ghetto, the world's inaugural one. Unbeknownst to her, of course, the first locale in which Jews were hidden from view has a greater resonance for her husband than her mother. The dramatic revelation ("Kiss my Jewish ass," snaps Amos) is manufactured and underwhelming, not least because it is provoked not by an anti-Semitic diatribe by the mother-in-law but an anti-songwriter sermon (she had always frowned on his showbusiness profession).

The book has a surprise happy ending when Amos—deserted by the two women after his explosion—makes his way back to his hotel resigned to divorced life and part-time fatherhood only to find Lila reaching out to him by confessing that, despite her previous denials, she had in fact tried to steal the watch.

The book was only 163 pages in its first hardcover printing, but its insubstantiality comes more from its technique than its slimline constitution. The two main plot underpinnings are inadequate. The first—the dissolving marriage—too often strays toward the comic to manage to communicate the stakes involved. Amos and Lila's dialogue is really movie dialogue and, whereas we would more readily accept it as part of that medium's vocabulary, on the page it serves to move the narrative a step away from pathos.

The second, the shameful secret of Jewry, is strangely unconvincing for a man named Goldman. To have dramatic impact, some sort of conflicted state would have had to be conveyed, perhaps one based around previous forbearance in the face of provocation. The fact that Amos once had to endure the anti-Jew jokes of a college friend doesn't cut it on this score—not least because he had genuinely found the college friend's gags funny.

There is one laugh-out-loud line, prompted by Lila using the word "bloody" in a London taxi cab: "…in just seventy-two bloody hours my bloody wife speaks bloody English like a bloody native" snaps Amos. Mostly, though, the dialogue is neutral in quality and—due to the fact that a bickering couple is never exactly an attractive sight—mildly distressing.

Another aspect with a part to play in the fact that the narrative rarely grips is the not-exactly-charming nature of the lead characters, which Amos helpfully summarizes for us. "A happy coward" and a woman "prone to bitchy things" are not the first people one would invite to a dinner party.

All of these things mean that, although it's not a chore to read it, we never look forward to picking up *The Thing of It Is…*

Although the proposed movie version of *Boys and Girls Together* never happened, in 1968 the second movie adaptation of a Goldman novel hit the screens in the form of *No Way to Treat a Lady*.

In his screenplay, John Gay depicts Christopher Gill as the only killer in town. The sole remnant of the original double-murderer device is the fact that when the NYPD try to trick him into revealing his true description by claiming in the press that a suicide is one of his victims, it has the by-product of leading Gill to fleetingly assume that there is a rival killer on the streets. Although it was much to Goldman's chagrin that the movie jettisoned his book's device—or even unique selling point—it did have the consequence of enabling a *tour de force* acting performance from Rod Steiger.

Among other guises, Steiger kills as an Irish priest, a blue collar German and an effeminate wig-fitter—each time employing a wildly different accent and manner and each time communicating a barely-suppressed evil beneath the adopted avuncular exterior. He makes phone calls to Detective Morris Brummel (George Segal) in further guises. Only the traditional embarrassingly cartoonish American notion of cockney ("Cheerybye!") fails to impress.

The impressively slick and quite enjoyable film is less grim than the book. Moe Brummell does not suffer from ugliness. His girlfriend (Sarah Stone in the book but here renamed Kate Palmer) is not murdered. There

is a conventional showdown of a climax rather than the sadism of the book-ending.

Note: the phrase "The thing of it is" is employed several times in the dialogue.

No Way to Treat a Lady was the final time Goldman allowed a hand other than his own to turn one of his works into a film. (A screenplay by Barry Kemp of his 1986 novel *Brothers* was not produced.)

June 1, 1969, saw the publication of Goldman's first piece of journalism in the shape of a review of *The Goodbye Look*, the latest Lew Archer novel by Ross Macdonald. It appeared on the front of the *New York Times Book Review*.

"...it is evident that this is another stunning addition to the Archer books, the finest series of detective novels ever written by an American," opined Goldman. "Though the first half dozen or so were enormously influenced by Dashiell Hammett and Raymond Chandler ... Macdonald's novels of the last decade have been of a texture never done by anyone before ... Macdonald's work in the last decade has nothing remotely to do with hard-boiled detective novels. He is writing novels of character about people with ghosts." Taking a side-swipe at that year's critical literary sensation *Portnoy's Complaint*, which he felt "a repetitious bore," Goldman compared Macdonald to Alfred Hitchcock, stating that, like the film director, he was an "unpretentious artist." He summed up, "Classify him how you will, he is one of the best American novelists now operating, and all he does is keep on getting better."

Goldman later claimed that his 1,600-word review had made Macdonald a "cult figure," not so much because of him but the influence of the *New York Times*—an influence he publicly lamented had never been employed to grant him a similar seal of critical approval.

4

"I hated working for the theatre," Goldman baldly states of his experience on Broadway. A hefty book about the Great White Way, then, is not necessarily the most logical project for him at the other end of the decade in which his theatre experiences occurred.

His writing *The Season*, however, becomes more understandable when listening to Goldman's almost misty-eyed recollections of his experiences of live drama as a consumer. "My parents took me to the theatre in Chicago," he says. "I started going when I was eight or nine years old. The theatre was magical for me." He visited theatre's Mecca, Broadway, with his father when he was ten years old. "After my father's death, my mother brought my brother and myself to New York and we saw sixteen plays in two weeks. We went all day, every day, because that's what New York was."

Of the genesis of *The Season*, published on September 10, 1969, he explains, "I had wanted to try a piece of non-fiction. I was getting involved with movie writing and book writing and I'd never tried a piece of non-fiction. I was going to write an article called 'The Hatches' about the various places where if you had an insane child, a disturbed child, you would send them. The notion for the piece was not a great notion, but the notion was that the famous places where you would go if you were in trouble would be like colleges and they would send out 'Our food is this and our that is that' and all the rest of it. The most famous place in America at that time was Menninger's and I realized if they wouldn't help me I was screwed. Since the theatre has so many people who will talk to you and I'd been involved with the theatre and I'd gotten my Masters paper on the Comedy of Manners at Columbia, I thought I would try and write something non-fiction. *The Season* came out of it."

Asked how he found the process of writing non-fiction for the first time, Goldman almost seems to be going so far as to say he relished it before stopping himself: "Well I've done a lot of non-fiction over the last twenty years, haven't I? So I must have found it fairly... None of it's pleasurable. I don't like my writing, what can I tell you, I never have, but, non-fiction is, yeah I like doing some of it, I do." Queried on whether he finds non-fiction's attendant hunting down of statistics and dates tedious, he shrugs, "No, I don't think so." This is not a surprise in the context of Richard Seff's recollection: "Billy's always been one—a little like me—that likes statistics. He and I would sit and discuss Broadway grosses all over the place. We'd know what a show grossed in Cleveland. 'Cause it was interesting to us. We'd read *Variety* every week. He knew about things like what a show breaks even at and when does it make a profit and how are the royalties paid. Most writers don't know a thing about that. They rely totally on their agents or their managers or their accountants. Not Bill. He liked that aspect of *The Season*. It's full of facts."

In *The Season*, Goldman discusses all of the plays and musicals that appeared on New York's main theatre district in its 1967-68 season,

THE SEASON

A Candid Look At BROADWAY

WILLIAM GOLDMAN

With A New Introduction By Frank Rich

roughly in chronological order. Along the way, he takes the opportunity to explore the issues pertinent not just to individual shows but to Broadway and live theatre in general.

Goldman acknowledges in the text that Broadway is "statistically trivial," the 12,000 souls that its venues then cumulatively accommodated on an average Monday utterly dwarfed by the world's cinema audiences. Of course, that's not the point about the Great White Way (a phrase he never employs). Its cultural significance is as a theatre of dreams that serves as a microcosm of the American Dream itself and as an arena perceived (rightly or wrongly) to have intrinsically more class than the motion pictures and television programs that succeeded it, and which many then felt were superseding it. (Movies, incidentally, are put in their place in this book: their titles are in mere quote marks, with Broadway shows awarded the accolade of italics.)

The biggest revelation about this book is just how knowledgeable Goldman is about theatre in general and Broadway in particular. It shows him able to hold his own with any professional Broadway expert and put up convincing, detailed ripostes to received wisdom about productions, personnel, practice, and custom. The fact of his own Broadway shows aside, only in the theatre sections of *Boys and Girls Together* and *Father's Day* is there even a hint in his other work of this vast theatrical hinterland, a marked contrast to the way his knowledge about sports and movies glimmers, and sometime veritably glares, in many places in his oeuvre.

Billing pages from theatre magazine *Playbill* precede each chapter. Said chapters explore a huge span of subjects. How a show inevitably starts changing when the director leaves it ("It is always wisest to try and see a show as soon as possible after it opens"). What a Broadway season constitutes ("The season ends the last day in May, according to most theatrical records. No one quite knows why"). Snob hits ("There is nothing, *nothing*, you *should* like because some intellectual tells you to"). Changing times ("All those wild plot moments don't play well any more; television has educated us, and we're too smart now"). Critics ("…the critics are so execrable: they are the opposite of accurate. They do not report what's there …" He states that the *New York Times'* Clive Barnes—whose opinions could make or break a production—"is the most dangerous, the most crippling critic in modern Broadway history," although has good words to say about TV theatre critic Edwin Newman, with whom he tags along as he takes in, and files his copy on, the latest Tennessee Williams effort). Producer corruption (Goldman exposes the way producers keep turkeys going because their kick-backs and scams—"takes"—mean they can make money even if business is terrible). Box office corruption ("The box-office man ... *hates* selling tickets to people who come to the window. If it is even a halfway decent seat, selling it for the box-office price costs him money. No ice ... I have friends who have called up shows that were doing less than 10% of their capacity and were told by the box-office people that there were no seats available for six months"). Alternatives to Broadway (at a juncture marking a disillusion with Broadway amongst major theatrical figures, not only was the off-Broadway scene becoming more important but there was even a burgeoning, even more unconventional, off-off-Broadway). Critics' thespian darlings (who "all share this in common: extravagance of gesture. They gesticulate; they overdo. They are, in all ways, enormous. And they are all women"). Casting (Goldman's claim that "There are simply no words to describe the barbarity inherent in the audition system" is supported by a tragi-comic episode where an interview he has arranged with a casting agent is interrupted by an actor who "just thought I'd say 'hello'" and who gets down on his knees to beg the agent for a job in a gesture that does not come across as 100% humorous). Homosexuality in the theatre (Goldman declines to let his conviction that gays are "a persecuted minority group" prevent him from protesting that gay playwrights disguising homosexual relationships as heterosexual ones leads to a dramatic falseness). Theatre-party ladies (acting as liaisons between producers and fund-raising organizations, they possess such an inordinate influence on a show's success that they are able to turn the mediocre *How Now, Dow Jones* into a minor hit because they calculated that the husbands of the wives who hired them would not complain about being dragged along to a play if it was about the stock market. Their influence was felt by some to make producers inclined to gear plays to an overly conservative market). Broadway myths ("A smash helps the whole theatre" and "Don't admit to low attendance days" are a couple Goldman challenges with cogent reasoning and number-crunching). Internal strife ("Productions—all productions—are literally struggles for power ... every member of the group sees something in his head, and he wants that 'something' translated to stage"). The shallow gold dust of the annual Neil Simon comedy ("Simon has become perhaps the highest-paid writer in the world ... with all his skill he is trivial..."). The season's biggest controversy (*Leda Had a Little Swan*, a play by Bamber Gascoigne about bestiality, which literally engendered violence; Goldman's hilarious recounting of the spluttering outrage and lobby scuffles would make the basis of a good play in itself).

Its sub-title *A Candid Look at Broadway* might suggest a purely subjective book. While Goldman certainly isn't shy about proffering personal opinion, the book is also a fearsome exercise in research. Across eighteen months, Goldman took in every single one of the shows discussed, some of them five times. By the point he started watching, he had already read the scripts of many of them so that he could contrast and compare ambition with achievement. He conducted nearly a thousand interviews, and travelled to London, Boston, New Haven and Washington for additional insight. He also did something he claims no Broadway interests had ever done in commissioning a poll amongst theatregoers and potential theatregoers to find out who they were and why they attended or, indeed, didn't attend.

Goldman never explicitly refers to his own previous Broadway involvement. The closest he comes is a passage in which he unexpectedly starts using the first-person plural ("These people *paid*. Those of us standing in the back watching them come in are usually pretty talented people"). However, it is obvious that Goldman's judgments and revelations are suffused with knowledge no research can confer: "...this strange thing happens: with the substitution of the new number, some of what preceded it—at the very least the song lead-in—is different, and everything that follows it is in some way affected. So another number or scene that was working perfectly may suddenly, crankily, stop working. Or something following the old (bad) number, which seemed adequate, may, in the light of the new (good) number, turn rotten. So we've got to change that. And when you change *that*, everything else changes. Out of town, it's a constant wild race: changing, trying like hell to fix and patch, and forget what you said the show was about back before rehearsal; under the gun you go with what works. And slowly, without anyone knowing it at first, the whole giant structure begins to change direction." He also does something no mere theatre scholar would do: writes play scenes to illustrate points.

Although the book constitutes a weighty exploration of an important subject (one perhaps best summed up by a line from an old Paul Simon song: "Is the theatre really dead?"), Goldman is frequently conversational and playful. For example: "At this point, I would like to talk briefly about the nature of Spanish and Portuguese comedy. (Ignore this paragraph; look at the one above.) Spanish comedy differs from Portuguese comedy in that ... (Reread that paragraph above; do you see it?) ... and, of course, one cannot estimate the effect of Franco and his consequent censorship ... (You've got to have it by this time: the adapters were writing a play about a man who believes in Providence, while the director was directing a play about a man who has an occupation for when Providence fails him.)" Sometimes, Goldman is just plain hilarious: "Look: I am a reasonably intelligent man, with a reasonable amount of interest in the world around me and a reasonable curiosity about the past, but why should anyone expect me to give a shit about Victoria and Palmerston?"

In a chapter designed as a demolition of Harold Pinter, he presents us with a finale to one of Pinter's plays along with extracts of reviews theorizing on the meaning of its enigmatic dialogue—before revealing that he has made it all up as a means of exposing the emperor as unclothed. While Goldman's corpus, both fiction and non-fiction, is littered with the technique of reversal, this has to go down as the most audacious example of all.

He also not only employs another soon-to-be familiar Goldman device, but signposts it: "And one final difference, one that is so numbing I want to set it off by itself in a separate paragraph…" Another present-and-correct Goldman trait is shoehorning in of sports references. This time they take the form of metaphors. They are in no way helpful, and one of them about Willie Mays sprawls over three pages. That he has no need (or excuse) for the sports metaphors is proven by the fact that Goldman also employs more generalized metaphors to good effect. Referring to a song that doesn't really fit into a musical but is enjoyable nonetheless, he says, "Like a bar in the back of an automobile: it doesn't make the motor go, but it helps make the trip enjoyable." (It's an amusing fact, incidentally, that when Goldman did get around to writing the non-fiction sports tome he had clearly long been itching to, he could have legitimately titled that *The Season* too.)

Although Goldman's interviews with behind-the-scenes unknowns are no less insightful and enlightening than those of celebrities, it is impressive the way he drops in lines like, "I talked to Pinter about it," "I arranged … to visit Mr. [Tennessee] Williams…" and "I went to see Kazan about casting." Some of his quotes are anonymous, something particularly necessary in the chapter on ticket corruption. However, he often manages to elicit bridge-burning frankness, such as George C. Scott's comment on Burl Ives, whom Scott was directing in Ira Levin's *Dr. Cook's Garden*: "What's working against him is this incredible lack of acting ability."

One part of the book is such a thought-provoking piece of writing, it bears reprinting at length without commentary:

Before You Go *told the story of a lost, homely girl who finds a lost, homely guy and perhaps happiness after the curtain comes down. To repeat: love will find a way. And Marian Seldes was so touching, so sad, so vulnerable as the homely girl that she made the whole thing true.*

But she's homely.

She is a tall, gawky, graceless thing and she is playing a tall, gawky, graceless thing, which would seem to be terrific casting; and it would be, but not in the Popular Theatre. If you want to do a comedy about a homely girl in the Popular Theatre, you've got to cast Lauren Bacall as the homely girl, which is what they did in Cactus Flower *and one of the reasons why it ran for more than 1,000 performances. When they say that Bacall is a dog in* Cactus Flower, *we know that they're wrong. My God, how can she be a dog? She was a movie star when she was barely out of her teens. Gorgeous? No. But never unattractive. And the fact that she was really glamorous Lauren Bacall frees us to enjoy the laughter in* Cactus Flower, *whereas the laughter in* Before You Go, *much of it caused by Miss Seldes' brilliant performance, never came easily or wholeheartedly because it was too true, and because it was true, too painful. Conclusion: if you're going to do a piece of Popular Theatre, there are certain requirements that must be met. Since Popular Theatre must never be unsettling, the minute you unsettle us you're dead."*

Sometimes Goldman's judgment seems awry. He waxes enthusiastic about a play called *Johnny No-Trump* by Mary Mercier and reproduces a chunk of it with the comment, "Is there any doubt the lady is a writer?" To which the answer is yes: the sample of dialogue he presents is false and flowery. He ridicules Clive Barnes for dismissing Tennessee Williams as unimportant but then prints with a lack of comment that implies agreement a quote from Edwin Newman: "You know what Williams has done, and you're terribly cast down by the knowledge of how long it has been since he has done it and how much greater the odds are against his doing it again." (Admittedly Barnes may have meant Williams had always been unimportant rather than had become unimportant by virtue of decline, but this isn't made clear.) Goldman's claim regarding critics, "…we are dealing with failures who have suddenly been given POWER. (But not enough. That's what kills them)," may or may not be correct but, in the interests of openness, should Goldman not have mentioned that, with two short-lived, sometimes lambasted Broadway ventures of his own behind him, he could be posited both as a failure and a man with a vested interest in dismissing critics? This becomes particularly apposite when he ridicules a producer of a failed show for saying, "The lack of attendance is a devastating commentary on the New York theatre-going public." Goldman presumably himself feels that when the public voted with their feet in regards to *Blood, Sweat and Stanley Poole* and *A Family Affair*, their judgment was wrong.

A couple of times, Goldman states as fact stuff that you wonder how he can possibly know to be anything other than assertion ("She was out of control, and no one could stop her," he states with no provenance of Sandy Dennis, already damned by him as a critics' darling). However, while he does not pretend to be impartial, he attempts to be fair, questioning his own judgments and seeking out those with opinions opposing his. Additionally, although he allows himself to be over-charmed by *Trial of Lee Harvey Oswald* actor Peter Masterson (the three pages he devotes to a précis of his acting career are boring and indulgent), he does no favors to friends. He acknowledges the talent of Kander and Ebb—one half of which songwriting team worked with Goldman on *A Family Affair*—but also bluntly opines, "…their work simply does not stack up to Bock and Harnick … and … Rodgers and Hammerstein…"

In the final chapter, Goldman number-crunches—primarily using the data from the survey he commissioned—to try to work out what it is about Broadway that is currently failing to enchant the public. His breezy, informed pronouncements are persuasive, even overwhelming—until we bump up against a statement that does not seem supported by the facts he lays out, such as his assertion that it is the cost of visiting theatres that is a barrier for the public rather than the entire cost of the evening out, which seems a misinterpretation of the reported answers. He also demolishes his own suggestion that Broadway is a decaying part of the entertainment industry slowly being obliterated by motion pictures: "With *Dolly!* and *Fiddler* running forever, and Neil Simon making millions for three short plays, it is simply not an industry that can vanish. It's a high-risk enterprise—it always has been—but when you hit, you are almost set for life. Any business that can hold out that promise is going to be around awhile."

Goldman occasionally shows the sloppiness of an author who doesn't believe much in reading back what he's written (he treats us to a definition of the *auteur* theory twice), but overall the book is astoundingly sure-footed, stylistically and structurally.

Goldman had the luck of the devil in choosing to cover the season he did. It was a non-calendar year in which several revolutionary things occurred on Broadway and its environs: sexual frankness (that sex comedies had traditionally lacked sex was a state of affairs clearly coming to an end in the new permissive climate, a smattering of the season's plays containing "the admission of intercourse without shame"); homosexuality (his stated hope that that year's off-Broadway success of unashamedly gay play *The Boys in the Band* would lead to a sexual freedom on stage has come true: no longer does Goldman or anyone else have to question the authenticity of bedroom scenes written by playwrights everybody knows have never shared a boudoir with a woman); alternative and younger outlooks (*Hair* finally brought the concerns of insurrectionary youth to the comfortable, middle-aged theatre district); and credit card bookings (possibly more revolutionary in the long term than the first three put together).

However, Goldman triumphantly capitalizes on his luck. *The Season* is a thumpingly substantial (432 pages in its first hardcover edition) and solid piece of journalism. It is reportage of the best kind: it achieves the feat of being a page-turner even for those readers whose interest in the subject is negligible.

As with any journalism, part of its value comes from its depicting the way things are, but is it still relevant now that Now is Then? The fact that there is much detail on plays that were short-lived and are long-forgotten is in the nature of the beast, but some parts of the book inevitably feel redundant. The box office corruption Goldman explores was, over the following years, made largely a thing of history by the advent of the age of the credit card and the computer, which made it more difficult. (Declining shame on the part of theatres in selling discount tickets also played a part in this process.) He also gets some stuff wrong; his guess that activity would shift from Broadway to off-Broadway is just about the opposite of what actually transpired, with *Hair* being only the first of many shows to travel in the opposite direction and become a mainstream smash, the most famous example of which being *A Chorus Line* in 1975.

Yet in very few places do we get a feeling of an era with whose concerns we cannot identify, and when we do it is mostly a matter of sentences referring to once newsworthy topics that have been made incomprehensible by the passage of time ("...if Grayson Kirk had only been more loving, Columbia University wouldn't have gone"). Overall, the book retains a consequence not as a snapshot of Broadway in a bygone age but because it encapsulates the perennial issues of what happens at the point where art meets commerce in the contexts of an immediate, paying audience and financiers worried about their stake who are able to steer artistic direction. "That was a bible," summarizes Richard Seff. "It's fascinating. He tackled every subject that we all think about. He just took one season as an example, but it's very cogent. It's still valid today."

A Goldman comment on Snob Hits—"...no one really knows what's worthy"—will cause a bell to ring with those who have encountered a later, more famous Goldman line about a different industry—"Nobody knows anything." It's not the only precursor to his 1983 book *Adventures in the Screen Trade*, another, to use Seff's word, "bible." Goldman's observation, "...the thing that characterizes Popular Theatre is this: it wants to tell us either a truth that we already know or a falsehood we want to believe in" is identical to Goldman's definition of a Hollywood as opposed to art film as purveyed in his 2000 book *The Big Picture*, one of his works on cinema made possible by *Screen Trade*. For those wondering why reference to those similarities has not been saved for the section on that book herein, it is to underline the fact that, although *The Season* is by far the less well-known work, it is easily the equal of *Adventures in the Screen Trade*.

To write the definitive book on one industry is impressive. To write another on a completely different industry is nigh miraculous.

5

In November 1967, Goldman found himself famous, as American woke up to the news that a writer had been paid the jaw-dropping sum of $400,000 for a screenplay. The script was for a prospective film then still titled *The Sundance Kid and Butch Cassidy*.

"I worked on *Butch Cassidy* for years," recalls Goldman. "I read whatever there was on Cassidy and Longbaugh." Butch Cassidy and Harry 'Sundance Kid' Longbaugh had been famous in the days of the Wild West but were not well-known to the contemporary public. "There were no books about," says Goldman. "If anybody has heard of Butch Cassidy in the industry now [it's] because of the screenplay was so huge and all of a sudden people started writing books about them." Goldman was intrigued by the pair because they were popular outlaws who did not kill. Becoming too notorious for comfort in America, they fled to Bolivia, where they resumed their old robbing ways before coming to a bloody end: "The whole reason I wrote the fucking thing, there is a famous line that Scott Fitzgerald wrote, who was one of my heroes: 'There are no second acts in American lives.' When I read about Cassidy and Longbaugh and the super-posse coming after them—that's phenomenal material. They ran to South America and lived there for eight years and that was what thrilled me: they had a second act. They were more legendary in South America than they had been in the Old West … It's a great story. These two guys and that pretty girl going down to South America and all that stuff. It just seems to me it's a wonderful piece of material."

Although for many years he would consider himself a novelist who happened to also write screenplays, the Christmas vacation of 1965-66, when Goldman was teaching creative writing at Princeton University, found him with no novel itching for release. He therefore turned his hand to something he had never written before: an original screenplay, one employing all that research he had done on the two outlaws over the course of several years. "In those years people did not really write much original screenplays," he says.

He states that there was never a possibility that he could have turned this material into a novel: "I didn't want to do that research. I don't like riding horses. And I didn't want to do all the research that you would have had to do to have an authentic thing about the two guys on the run and did they build a fire and how did they build it and what did they eat and all that shit. I didn't want to write that."

Of the screenplay, he says, "Every studio but one rejected it … The studio head said, 'Well, I'll buy it if they don't go to South America.' I said, 'But they went there!' He said, 'I don't give a shit. All I know is John

Wayne don't run away.' That's one of the great lines that was ever said to me. Anyway I re-wrote, didn't change it more than a few pages, and for reasons passing understanding every studio wanted it. There was a great agent in California and there was this insane auction and it went for four hundred thousand dollars, which is a lot of money today but when you're talking forty years ago was really a lot of money, and it made headlines— small headlines—all across the country in the entertainment sections of newspapers. I think maybe one screenplay before had gone for two hundred thousand dollars, but that had been when there had been a star attached and this was just a plain unadorned screenplay."

Butch Cassidy and the Sundance Kid—as it was renamed because a famous actor was playing Butch and an unknown Sundance—was released on October 24, 1969. It gets off to an uncertain start. What is actually scene two should have been its preamble: the Sundance Kid (Robert Redford) in the company of a nervous Butch Cassidy (Paul Newman) spins to shoot a gun out of the hand of a man who falsely accuses him of cheating at gambling. However, outside of James Bond, pre-title sequences barely existed in 1969, and the movie starts with a boring, flickering title sequence of mock-contemporaneous photography followed by an unremarkable interlude involving Butch casing a bank for robbery. Things proceed to get a lot better in a film that helped ensure that Westerns would never again adhere to the formula to which they broadly had since their inception.

The opening two scenes are shot in sepia, the film emerging into glorious color when the start of scene three finds the title characters clip-clopping through a beautiful landscape to meet their comrades in the Hole in the Wall outlaw gang. Butch is the brains of the outfit, Sundance the brawn insofar as legends of his gunplay are enough to make hardened men tremble at his name. However, they don't kill people. Threats, charm and dynamite are their preferred methods for stripping bank vaults and train carriage safes of their contents.

What has been cited as the picture's overarching post-modernism begins when Butch has a fight with a rebellious member of his crew. The sneaky kick in the crotch that Butch executes—and Sundance's "1-2-3-go!" collusion—is not within the gentlemanly code of previous cinema cowboys. That this isn't *High Noon* or *Gunfight at the OK Corral* is underlined when Sundance forces a woman—a schoolteacher named Etta (Katharine Ross)—to strip at gunpoint before it is revealed that this is the bedroom role-play of two long-term lovers. Adding to the air of the unusual is Butch and Etta frolicking on a bicycle to an infectious (and debatably anachronistic) pop backdrop. (The snagging of a new tune by Bacharach & David—the premier middle-of-the-road chart merchants of the age—was probably as much of a coup as securing the acting services of Newman.) Also unusual is the fact that the bicycle frolicking does not involve a pair of lovers, even if their conversation states that, if Etta hadn't met Sundance first, they might have ended up together.

Whereas the first part of the narrative triptych covers the fun and games of being a train and bank robber, the middle section focuses on the soured mood engendered by Butch and Sundance being hunted and hounded. A railroad owner hires a super-posse led by a preternaturally skilled Indian tracker, spending more money on this objective than anything Butch and Sundance ever stole from him. "That's bad business!" Butch says in outrage (a wonderful piece of acting by Newman). The pair have no option but to flee, choosing Bolivia as their destination. Etta tags along. The transition to their expatriate status is a passage of time represented by a peculiar montage of still photographs whose backing is one of the film's few pieces of music outside of the bicycle frolic song.

The final part concentrates on the duo's exile. The half-hour in Bolivia sees the pair become the Banditos Yanquis. (Their own temporary pseudonym of Smith and Jones was co-opted by the makers of the seventies television series *Alias Smith and Jones*, a take-off that gives an indication of the industry this beloved movie spawned.) They kill for the first time as a result of a temporary detour into respectable employment, which involves them protecting a payroll. Etta –who had always said she wouldn't hang around to watch Sundance die—returns to the States.

The only conventional mass Western gunfight of the picture occurs when the pair are finally cornered towards the end. Their death has a real pathos, partly because they had been discussing their plans for a new life in Australia, partly because they do not know that an entire army division lies in wait for them and partly because of the sheer unfairness of them being so outnumbered.

Butch Cassidy and the Sundance Kid came out in the same year as *Easy Rider* and, in its own way, is of a piece with that hippie road journey movie, which demonstrated to Hollywood that the era of Doris Day pictures and other clean-cut vehicles designed to tell America what it wanted to believe about itself—or indeed human beings in general—was over. It also followed only two years after *Bonnie and Clyde*, whose non-judgmentalness about a pair of real-life outlaws far nastier than Butch and Sundance was shocking to generations steeped in the upright values of the Hays Code.

The Western genre's hitherto square-jawed, morally unambiguous paradigm made *Butch Cassidy and the Sundance Kid* seem very fresh and new at the time, as did the main characters' stage comedian-like double-act repartee. However, this is not really the post-modern Western some cite it as. (Nor even a modern Western, if such a thing is to be defined by bloodspill, nudity or profanity, all of which are absent with the exception of a never completed "Shiiiiiit!" during the famous jump into the river.) Instead, it is simply the style familiar to devotees of Goldman's books—a glib tone, wiseacre call-and-response dialogue, multiple reversals, laconic undermining of dramatic convention—superimposed onto the Wild West.

Recalls Goldman, "When the movie came out, it got terrible reviews in the east because all the critics in the east were pissed, and they'd say so in the reviews sometimes: 'This screenplay went for so much money, why would anybody...'" Scorn for the trade of screenwriter and bad reviews on the East Coast, however, turned out to be utterly irrelevant. As Goldman recalls, "I was walking with the director, George Roy Hill, and we were in despair 'cause we both liked *Butch Cassidy* and it had gotten just crucified in the media. We were walking along the streets of New York at night and George said, 'Let's go into that theatre and talk to the manager.' The manager came up to us and George said, 'Why are you smiling?' and the manager said, 'Because we're selling out every performance and the audience loves us.' George and I walked off [and], as we separated to go to our apartments, he said, 'Maybe it's not a disaster after all,' which was what we thought we had at that moment. It turned out to be an Oscar winner and a freak commercial success ... I never thought of myself as successful until the *Butch Cassidy* sale ... It became the most successful anything I've ever been involved with and that was a huge, huge plus for me."

It was also a huge plus for screenwriters everywhere. "In those years nobody thought we were anything," Goldman avers. "They thought the stars made up all the lines and the directors had all the visual concepts ... That was a famous movie sale ... It was for years and years the biggest screenplay sold. Now it's nothing particularly—thank God writers are getting more than that."

Top Hollywood screenwriter Ernest Lehman (*North By Northwest, West Side Story, The King And I*) claimed that the film also had the effect of opening up Hollywood to screenwriters who wanted to create a narrative that was something other than an adaptation. "…originals were not smiled upon in those days, believe it or not," he told John Brady in his book *The Craft of the Screenwriter*. "There was *very* little interest in originals in those days. That all came later. Studios, distributors wanted the assurance of someone else having thought a property worth publishing, or it had been on the best-seller list, or a hit Broadway play … It started changing, I think, with Bill Goldman's sale of *Butch Cassidy and the Sundance Kid* … It served notice to writers that if they wrote a screenplay that someone wanted to do very badly, it would sell."

His first original screenplay ultimately earned Goldman a lot more than that record-breaking fee: fame, acclaim, and an Oscar. Goldman didn't attend the ceremony to pick up his Academy Award for Best Original Screenplay both because he thought he wouldn't win and he was more interested in attending a New York Knicks match crucial to that year's National Basketball Association championship. (The film also won in Cinematography, Music and Song categories.)

Bantam seemed to have confidence that *Butch Cassidy and the Sundance Kid* would do well. Perhaps it was due to the knowledge of how much the script had sold for, but, in lieu of a novelization, they issued a mass market paperback version of the screenplay to accompany the film's release. This highly unusual move introduced many to the format of the movie script, then not very widely known. Goldman readily admitted in an introductory author's note that "any film is a community effort in which the screenplay is the blue-print" and that what followed had benefited from the input of "many people," including Paul Newman, Robert Redford, and George Roy Hill. However, he did take the measure of reinstating his original sub-title: "Not that it matters, but most of what follows is true." Hill had deleted the first four words when he noticed in previews that the caption was generating laughs.

Other parts of an industry spawned by the film are the 1979 'prequel' picture *Butch & Sundance: The Early Days*, with which Goldman's main connection was a coproducer credit ("role" probably being an exaggeration). This project itself spun off a novelization by D. R. Bensen. In the same opportunistic/parasitical spirit as *Alias Smith and Jones* was "*Whadda we do now, Butch?*," a 1978 novel by Shel Talmy, which, though it didn't technically breach intellectual property laws, was patently based on the characters of Butch Cassidy and the Sundance Kid as established by Goldman in his film and not confirmed by historical evidence. Meanwhile, the paucity of research material Goldman found when preparing his script turned into a deluge as historians and documentary makers began investigating these now-household names.

The movie proceeded to lodge itself in the popular consciousness as few do. What is startling about watching *Butch Cassidy and the Sundance Kid* now is the fact that it is its own 'Greatest Hits.' Such is the fame and affection achieved by so many of its events or sections of its dialogue that there is barely an unfamiliar moment. Iconic scene follows iconic scene: the opening legend "Most of what follows is true"; the wince-making kick in the balls following the puzzled "Rules? In a knife fight? No *rules*"; the sweet 'Raindrops Keep Falling On My Head' interlude; Butch's high-pitched imitation of a woman in distress in order to trick a train employee into opening a carriage door; the complaint "All of 'em? What's the matter with *those* guys?" when the posse only follow Butch and Sundance after the pursued gang splits up; the repeated cry "Who *are* those guys?" as a tracker sticks doggedly, almost eerily, to the pair's trail; Butch's "Why, you crazy! The fall'll probably kill ya!" prior to the duo evading their pursuers by making a stomach-churning jump off a cliff into a foaming river; Sundance's comment when told of the low cost of living in sleepy Bolivia, "What could they have here that you could possibly want to buy?"; the "Is that what you call cover?"/ "Is that what you call running?" bitching as the pair fight for their very lives; and the final freeze-frame of Butch and Sundance charging their opponents darkening to sepia as the army's volleys resound… In fact, a précis could almost be written in shorthand: everybody knows what you mean when you say of *Butch Cassidy and the Sundance Kid*, "The knife fight" or "The jump off the cliff …"

Is *Butch Cassidy and the Sundance Kid* even, anymore, a movie, rather than a cultural reference point? While it's certainly never boring, can it nowadays be enjoyed unselfconsciously as a piece of art? Perhaps not, but most of its scenes are overly familiar for a reason: the picture's immense and enduring popularity brought about by its high-quality, twinkle-eyed craftsmanship.

That the publication of *The Season*, incontestably his most heavyweight offering in any genre, came in the same year as the release of *Butch Cassidy and the Sundance Kid*, his most populist and popular piece of work, demonstrates that 1969 was Goldman's *annus mirabilis*.

6

Considering how slight and unengaging was *The Thing of It Is...* a sequel to that Goldman novel sounds like a very unwise course of action. However, *Father's Day*, published in January 1971 is, although flawed, unexpectedly good.

That this is a sequel, incidentally, is nowhere made overt within its pages: despite the use of the same characters and even one inclusion of the phrase "The thing of it is...," *Father's Day* can be a standalone reading experience. Another way it feels unrelated to its predecessor is how engaging it frequently is: it is a much more eventful and fast-moving story, even if some of that lively and vibrant narrative, slightly contradictorily, consists of flashbacks.

Jessica McCracken is six years old and now more resembles Bert Lahr than Edward G. Robinson in her homeliness. (Amos McCracken can now bear to enunciate her name. Presumably Goldman has forgotten about this aspect of the predecessor, just as he appears to have forgotten Amos's resentment of his wife's meager bottom, him aggrieved now only by her flat chest.) *Francine* is about to enter its third year on Broadway. However, Amos's latest musical, *Annie's Day*, has opened to "as ruthless a set of notices as any within memory." Although his marriage has staggered on this far, it is deteriorating again as proceedings open.

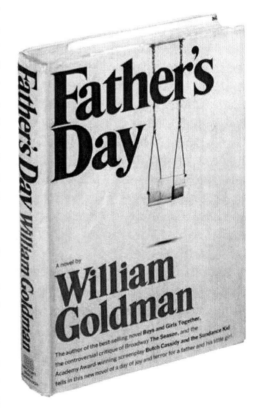

There is then a trick jump-cut wherein Goldman fools us into thinking Amos is making love to Lila when it is her short-term successor Betsy with whom he is enjoying congress. Lila, in fact, infuriatingly provides the *interruptus* to their *coitus* by ringing Amos to remind him that he is looking after their daughter that day. The scene, like several, is genuinely funny. Also like several scenes, the dialogue is crackling but movie-style false. In other scenes, while the dialogue is completely convincing, such as the spluttering of a cab driver whom Amos suggests doesn't know New York well, the motivation is movie-style false: Amos had decided to wind up the cabbie simply so as to be battle-hardened for an audience with a fractious Lila.

Amos is presented as sometimes irrational (drifting off into fantasies that aren't even always ones that idealize life) and dislikeable (lines such as "Amos liked the little man about as much as he liked anybody" hint at a sociopathic nature). This deterioration from the fairly straightforward character represented in *The Thing of It Is...* is transparently a device to engender drama. As before, the narrative is third person but the point of view entirely Amos's.

In a powerful scene, we are taken back to the agonies Amos was enduring when he ran dry during the out of town tryouts of *Annie's Day*. When he can't come up with the required songs, he is informed by producer 'Angel' Harding that he is being replaced by one Merle Lewis for the New York opening. The show's librettist, Donny Klein, is horrified when Amos tells him of Harding's behavior and insists he will not be party to it, passionately reassuring him and persuading him to plot with him to stymie the producer's treacherous plans. However, Amos is then visited by Betsy, who has a small part in the show and has been effectively delegated to express concern over the rumors that he has been canned, which disturb the cast because they imply trouble with the production. She brings news that Merle Lewis watched a matinée performance in the company of Donny Klein. "Donny's devious, but he's not that devious," Amos insists. But when Amos confronts Klein on the phone when the latter makes a supportive call, it transpires that indeed he is. This sort of thing is what will become quintessential Goldman: Long fond of reversals, he is now making them more and more elaborate, adopting a policy of a succession of switcheroosthat leave the reader almost as sucker-punch-drunk as his protagonist. This one is deftly and ingeniously done, even if, as always, there is something slightly implausible about the intricacy: human beings simply aren't as Machiavellian as this.

In an illustration of Goldman's ambiguity toward his protagonist, Amos is depicted as consciously batting away thoughts that Klein is justified in his actions.

Seeing as the crux of the book is a day that the now single Amos spends with his daughter, it is more than a little unfortunate that the scenes with Jessica are by far the weakest. The author's reasonable skill in rendering colloquial speech once again deserts him when it comes to a child. As a man who by now had two daughters, Goldman must have known that no six-year-old would come out with stuff like, "There's just no question it was a spell and I think we would be making the most horrible kind of mistake if we didn't even take a peek at the Astor, Daddy." Compounding Jessica's sophisticated syntax is Pierre, a zany French chef prone to malapropisms who has been invented by Amos to amuse his daughter out of her mild anorexia. The substantial sections in which Amos conspires with Jessica to pretend Pierre is not her father in a false moustache jar via their non-naturalism.

Amos accidentally injures Jessica when they play on swings in a park, him losing concentration as he tries to find a way out of his on-going composer's block. As she is being treated in hospital, Amos makes a call to Lila. His confrontation with an obstreperous old woman in the queue for telephones is another laugh-out-loud scene, although what follows blackens the mood: Lila tells him down the line she will ensure he can no longer gain access to his daughter.

Amos elects to go on the run with his bandaged child, reasoning that if he lays low long enough, Lila will come round. He seeks financial help from people Lila either doesn't know or won't expect him to. A visit to an unsympathetic Donny elicits one of Goldman's new trademark verbal exchanges that are slightly too pat but glitter anyway:

> "I didn't even know you were queer, Donny."
> "Your naiveté cannot be blamed on me."
> "I thought we were friends."
> "Your naiveté cannot be blamed on me."

Amos then visits Betsy, who had walked out on him that very morning and is more than a little alarmed by his manic state and his daughter's semi-comatose one. Needing untraceable finance quickly, he asks her to give back him a gift of a gold bracelet. When she hesitates, the pitiless way he reveals to her that it had been intended for Lila before their split ("It was never yours…") crowns a compellingly ugly scene.

When a cop hears Amos enunciating his name in a pawn shop (Amos has temporarily left Jessica with Betsy), he recognizes it from an All-Points Bulletin. The chase is on. A diversion caused by two fruitcakes in a darkened cinema in which Amos takes refuge provides a comedic tinge to the thrills. So do, in some instances, the protagonist's continued imagining of alternate realities, which sometimes make it difficult for the reader to keep track of 'real' events. This is more of Goldman's playful reversal tactics, but a fantasy in which Amos imagines his daughter dead at the airport to which he has taken her isn't exactly filled with levity. Finally, his daughter's imploring words to Pierre, whom she insists Amos makes appear, cause Amos to apprehend the insanity of his plans: "I don't want to be with my daddy … he's gone all scary…"

It's all a curious mixture of comedy, drama, tragi-comedy, and suspense but, for the most part, it works. The prose is stylishly informal ("He had gone, for the first inconceivable time in his life, dry"). It is also often breathless, Goldman conveying action and momentum with extremely elongated sentences. A fight scene between Amos and his estranged wife's new lover runs three pages without a full-stop, as does a fantasy sequence in which Amos imagines he is being attacked by a wild dog and his daughter has been made to look beautiful by a surgeon.

There is some more bad-back stuff whose verisimilitude is plainly wrenched from personal experience. The author also deploys well theatre knowledge he has clearly picked up from his own sojourns there—particularly the intrigues and agony involved in being doctored or replaced. More impressively, as Amos's brain strains for an elusive melodic progression, Goldman convinces us he fully understands a composer's psyche.

The New York Post's review declared, "Goldman is very much the NOW writer." Four decades on, his zeitgeist-riding is of course not so immediately apparent but it becomes obvious when one thinks about it. In addition to that then-new informality of language, there are other signs of the freshly irreverent times, such as explicitness about the mechanics and messiness of sex and an allusion to rumors of J. Edgar Hoover's homosexuality. (Such candor didn't yet feature in Goldman's screenplays: Hollywood dragged behind literature in terms of liberalization.) In some ways, *Father's Day* is even ahead of the times. Although the book features the sort of dismissive comments about "fags" and "queers" commonplace to the era, it is surprisingly proto-PC, with Amos in various parts fretting over being seen as anti-Semitic, anti-Irish, and anti-black.

In addition to its aesthetic merits, the very fact of following up a very worthy piece of journalism like *The Season* and a spectacularly mainstream piece of filmmaking like *Butch Cassidy and the Sundance Kid* with a small-scale literary novel such as *Father's Day* served to reinforce the position Goldman was lately carving out for himself of Renaissance Man.

Goldman once talked of making the Amos McCracken saga a trilogy by writing a book called *The Settle for Less Club*. However, even as he told Richard Andersen of the idea in the mid-seventies, he was unsure if it was still a viable project: changing cinema fashions had made passé his plot idea of Amos's musical being adapted for film. Goldman seems no more enthusiastic about the third part now. "I don't know if I'll do that, but who knows," he shrugs.

7

Surprisingly, considering the success of *Butch Cassidy and the Sundance Kid*, there were no further original screenplays from Goldman until *The Year of the Comet* nearly a quarter of a century later, although the caveat should be added that *The Great Waldo Pepper* (1975) could be posited as an original screenplay and *The Year of the Comet* was written far in advance of its production.

Although now one of the hottest movie writers in the world, Goldman opted to primarily continue the way he had started: adaptation. Does he have a preference? "Well they're all different," he shrugs. "You can do adaptations or originals or adaptations of your own originals—and I've done all three—and they're all hard. You don't know what you're doing, you don't know what's going to work. It's always a crapshoot—I can't stress that enough." When he is asked if it is not more fulfilling to do something that is entirely his own idea rather than an interpretation of another person's, it elicits that quote included earlier in this text: "I don't mean to piss on screenwriting, but I don't know that fulfilling is the word you would use."

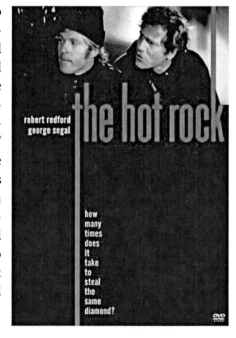

Goldman's follow-up to *Butch Cassidy and the Sundance Kid* was *The Hot Rock*, released in January 1972. "It was based on a wonderful, very funny book by Donald Westlake," he says. "He does all kinds of things but one of the things he wrote was wonderfully funny thrillers. I was a Westlake fan. I don't know if *Hot Rock* was my idea to do. I can't believe somebody came to me with it."

Dortmunder (Robert Redford) is a thief just released from another of his regular incarcerations. He is picked up straight out of prison by his brother-in-law Andrew (George Segal). Andrew has a proposition for him: an audacious raid on a museum to steal a huge, perfect diamond, the hot rock of the film's title. The person commissioning the crime is Dr. Amusa (Moses Gunn), an ostensibly respectable African diplomat but in fact a man burning up with the injustice of a foreign country having possession of the rock, which he believes is the property of his own people.

After initial misgivings—with his expert eye, Dortmunder observes that, because there is no alarm system attached to the locked glass case in which the diamond is on display, the guards will not get complacent—he agrees to the proposition. Andrew hires two aides and their plan is put into action.

Said plan is the sort only criminals in films would attempt. It involves a diversionary tactic, which sees one of the conspirators crash a car in spectacular fashion outside the museum and demand the guards—who rush out—call him an ambulance for the relief of his theatrical agonies. The glibness of this scene actually prohibits any tension attaching to the one simultaneously being played out inside as his colleagues—disguised in guard uniforms—pick the locks on the cabinet hosting the diamond. The team inside are discovered. One of them, Alan (Paul Sand), is captured, although not before surreptitiously swallowing the diamond.

Alan turns out to be the son of Abe Greenberg, a colossally corrupt and immensely overweight lawyer, played in typically delightful over-the-top style by Zero Mostel. Greenberg arranges for his son to be sprung from prison. After their plan is executed (if not without a hitch), Alan reveals that he doesn't have the rock, having secreted it in the police station in which he had been held after being arrested. The solution? Naturally, to break into the police station. A diversionary tactic involving smoke bombs is arranged, the reaction to which by the precinct house's police chief is pure comedy: he thinks it is the beginning of a revolution. It makes one think that, had the rest of the film been written this way, it would have made the general implausibility much more easy to swallow.

The diamond turns out not to be in the police station after all; Alan's father has double-crossed everyone and has it stashed in a safe deposit box. This information is gleaned after an utterly ludicrous scene in which Alan's colleagues pretend to throw Alan down a deep shaft in an abandoned building in order to terrify Greenberg.

Now the team have to find a way to get into the safety deposit box, which requires a signature: Greenberg won't cooperate with them and they can't bluff him twice. Enter yet more absurdity in the form of a criminally inclined female hypnotist whom Dortmunder suddenly recalls knowing. She readily agrees to make the man responsible for the safety deposit section susceptible to mind manipulation. Dortmunder gets his prize, even despite Greenberg betraying them yet again by negotiating directly with Amusa.

The Hot Rock is a real mixed bag, not only undecided as to whether to pursue comedy or drama, but also—for all its then modernistic trappings—a throwback to the stylized approach of old-time movies (something underlined by the absence of profanities). The fisticuffs and car crashes are comic book stuff. The failings of the movie are summed up by a scene in a park where Dortmunder is taken to meet Amusa. They speak at a bench's distance from each other. This is meant to convey the idea that they are being careful not to be seen together, but the attempt at *demi monde* verisimilitude has the opposite effect: any passer-by would overhear their felonious negotiations. Also nonsense is Robert Redford's casting. Even taking into account artistic license and box office business sense, it is still difficult to accept that someone who looks like him would be a jailbird rather than, say, a male model.

There are, however, some good scenes. The segment in which a nervous Redford prepares to utter the trigger word that will make the bank employee become acquiescent is genuinely tense. The film ends in an almost exhilarating and refreshingly non-climactic way via a fairly lengthy section in which a jubilant Dortmunder walks to meet his colleagues with the diamond safely in his possession and is barely able to refrain from demonstrating his joy to the world. Also impressive—and terrifying for those who don't like heights—are skyscraper-skimming scenes in a helicopter.

8

"The only book of mine that I like is *The Princess Bride*," says Goldman. He also says, "That's different from anything else I ever wrote."

He's certainly right on one point. *The Princess Bride* (published September 12, 1973) is an absolute *non sequitur* of a book. It goes against the grain of the contemporary, urban tone of Goldman's previous novels to explore the terrain of the fairytale. It is, though, a post-modern fairytale, juxtaposing contemporary irreverence with the formality of olden times while throwing in the odd humorous piece of subversion ("Not surprisingly, the Duchess's grumpiness became legendary as Voltaire has so ably chronicled. Except this was before Voltaire"). In the same knowing spirit is a mania for the sort of ranking lists associated with the pages of magazines, with heroine Buttercup starting the novel as just inside the top twenty of the world's most beautiful women and gradually climbing said table as the narrative proceeds, even though in a world before mass media she would not have come to sufficient attention, and there would not be adequate comparative mechanisms, for this to be tabulated.

Buttercup has a stable boy named Westley to whom she is initially haughty and demanding. He perennially responds to her instructions with the devoted mantra, "As you wish." Buttercup's beauty attracts the attention of royalty—hence the title—but she has become smitten by Westley, to whom she pledges her heart. Following their forced separation, Westley becomes a feared but mysterious masked swordsman. Their paths dovetail in the expected happy-ever-after fashion (albeit with a slight twist). Goldman peoples this narrative with fairytale staples like kings, queens, brutes, hunchbacks, blacksmiths and pirates in one of his longest novels so far (308 pages in its first hardcover edition).

Yet, the central literary conceit of *The Princess Bride* is that it is a vintage book written by S. Morgenstern, a one-time citizen of defunct European country Florin, and that this "good parts"

version is simply an edited highlights package that strips away Morgenstern's unwieldy and dated satire for the sake of the gripping adventure that so enthralled Goldman when his own father first read it to him when he was a boy. Explains Goldman, "I had all these stories but didn't know how to get there. I was walking around the city and the book was disappearing on me and then I got the notion that I didn't write it, that Morgenstern wrote it and I had just abridged it. Once that happened, the whole thing flew. It's so freaky. It was a great, great experience for me. I could read what I'd written and not be horrified and all the rest of it."

Goldman sets the scene with a long opening chapter detailing his supposed history with the book. Throughout the rest of the text, he drops in commentary and explanatory asides. Although he says the conceit was a matter of practicality, the knowing, ironic slant this gives the book is beneficial in another sense, for it was probably the only way of making such a work commercially viable as adult fiction. Whatever the reason, he certainly invests much energy into making the conceit seem real, dropping in references to *The Temple of Gold* and his work on *Butch Cassidy and the Sundance Kid* (he 'reveals' that its famous scene involving the titular heroes jumping off a cliff to have been inspired by *The Princess Bride*'s Cliffs of Insanity section). He also constructs childhood vignettes involving a beloved teacher named Miss Roginski. This all reaches a surreal crescendo when Goldman implores the reader to write to his real-life editor to request a free copy of a section he has reluctantly excised from *The Princess Bride*, providing the genuine address for that purpose. The giveaways are the pat, switcheroo quality of the supposedly autobiographical scenes and the machine gun prose, convoluted, spikey dialogue and modernistic clauses and sub-clauses in Morgenstern's prose: all are strangely reminiscent of Goldman's own techniques. That in itself would not be a problem, and potentially could be part of the fun. Unfortunately, this ingenious, intriguing and even innovative project doesn't work on any level.

Although Goldman drops in occasional slang like "slummy," the necessary general lack of colloquialism leads to stilted, florid dialogue that sits dead on the page ("I have lived my life with only the prayer that some sudden dawn you might glance in my direction"). He also throws in stuff that is embarrassingly neither colloquialism nor traditional cod-antediluvian fairytale speech ("I could kill my tongue"). There are also exchanges that seek to put one over on the square-jawed certainties of fairytales but which are themselves suffocatingly smug ("Catch up quickly." "Don't I always?"). Conversely, Goldman buys into the absolutism of fairytale superheroism ("Domingo slept only when he dropped from exhaustion. He ate only when Inigo would force him to") and implausible timeframes (a whole year to perfect a commissioned sword), to even more soporific effect. His prattling playfulness often kills momentum ("Inigo allowed Fezzick to open the door, not because he wished to hide behind the giant's strength but, rather, because the giant's strength was crucial to their entering: someone would have to force the thick door from its hinges, and that was right up Fezzick's alley"). He sometimes gives the impression of making it up as he goes along ("...milkmen still were in charge of bones, the logic being that since milk was so good for bones, who would know more about broken bones than a milkman?"). As is the nature of whimsy, this can induce contempt as easily as it can create indulgence.

The mention of Australia as a repository of convicts—transportation to that colony by the British did not start until 1787—rather plays havoc with the period, which, although vague and a mishmash, is overwhelmingly medieval.

The Princess Bride is not too dissimilar to *Butch Cassidy and the Sundance Kid* in the fact of its subversion of generic and historical expectation. Leaving aside the fact that that work was exhilarating where this one is tedious, the similarity rather exposes a one-dimensionality to Goldman's writing. Whereas, for example, his brother could adopt the traditions and vernacular of period, Goldman is here betraying the fact that he is unable to write with any mind-set except that of a contemporary American.

All of which makes it painfully ironic that in the 'autobiographical' sections, Goldman is frequently to be found claiming that he jettisoned parts of Morgenstern's original to spare the reader ("Dreary? Not to be believed"). Those 'autobiographical' sections themselves are often funny and possessed of vitality, especially Goldman's operatic tussles over long distance telephone lines with New York bookstores reluctant to help him locate Morgenstern's book. Expanded, the 'autobiographical' material might have led to a good novel but, as it is constituted, *The Princess Bride* is boring where it is not pleased with itself and is a real chore to get through.

Not for its author, though. "*The Princess Bride* is the best experience I've ever had as a writer," says Goldman. "I don't like my writing and all the rest of it. I just had such a wonderful time. Westley was lying dead by the machine and I remember thinking as I was walking in my office, how was I going to save him, how was I going to save him, and I got to my office and I read the papers and I sat down and all of a sudden I realized, 'Oh my God, you're not going to' and for the only time in my life I burst into hysterical tears and I went running to the bathroom to put water on my face. I can still remember the way I looked. My face was red and distorted and everything and I just was hysterical."

Goldman's fondness for this book probably lies partly in its real impetus: he came up with the idea after his two daughters told him they wanted their next bedtime stories to be about brides and princesses.

Incidentally, in the heyday of snail mail, those who wrote to the publisher to request *A Princess Bride*'s missing scene were sent a convoluted letter telling them a tall tale of why it was not legally possible. Goldman and the publisher were still playing along in the age of the internet, emailing a twice-revised apologia (copyrighted 1973, 1998 and 2003) to anyone who clicked on the link "Request the Missing Scene" on the book's webpage.

Goldman admits he has been surprised by the number of people who have requested the 'missing' chapter. Did he think back in the day that anybody at all would write in? "Never, come on. It didn't happen when the book came out and it didn't happen when the movie came out, and then suddenly over the last couple of years it's bigger now than ever in terms of getting stuff to me. It's very strange. It's wonderful. I'm thrilled about it, but it shocks me … It's the freak thing I've been connected with. It's republished and people love the book and they love the movie and that thrills me."

Family life was clearly important for Goldman at this juncture. "My daughters," he states as his motive for penning his next book. "The same reason I wrote *Princess Bride*. One of my kids had a security blanket that she called Wigger and so I wrote a book about it." Published on September 18, 1974, *Wigger* is Goldman's sole foray into children's writing.

The book tells the tale of Susanna, who, like many children, is emotionally attached to a security, or comfort, blanket. Her one is a pink rag she has named Wigger and invested with a personality and a vocabulary, both rather superior. The two frequently engage in banter.

That, at seven, Susanna is unusually old for such things is explained by the fact that she has lost her parents in an accident. Although she is a placid child, her grandmother and four aunts one by one find an excuse not to care for her and she ends up in a children's home run by a stern regime, albeit one boasting a kindly nurse. As she careens from rejection to rejection, Wigger becomes her only source of stability in an unreliable world.

Susanna gets caught up in a bank robbery executed by a man in a Santa Claus suit—much of the book takes place during the Christmas

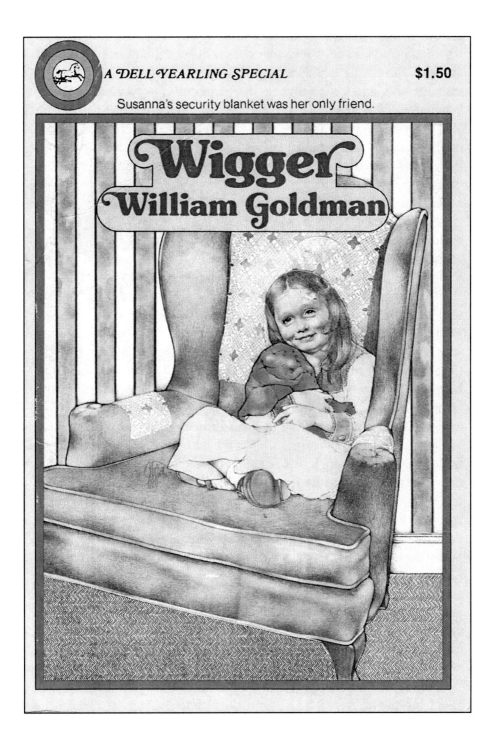

A DELL YEARLING SPECIAL $1.50

Susanna's security blanket was her only friend.

Wigger
William Goldman

season—during which the bank robber grabs at Wigger to hide his face when his beard falls off. The robber gets on a plane bound for Switzerland. With Susanna initially oblivious of the theft of her companion, Wigger embarks on a series of adventures as it is passed from person to person. When the robber dispenses with the pink rag on the plane, it is appropriated by a rich duchess as a receptacle for her jewelry, which she is worried might be stolen if it is made conspicuous by being in a jewel case. Once the rag has served its purpose for the duchess, she dispenses with it in a garbage pail at her Zurich hotel. It is retrieved from said pail by a hotel maid, who finds it a good implement for cleaning. The maid disposes of the now well-used rag in a street garbage basket. From there, it ends up in the possession of a bohemian and somewhat under-talented artist and composer, who takes it up to the top of a mountain and uses it as a flag as a symbol of the fact that the ugly can be beautiful, just like his art.

Meanwhile, back over in the States, Susanna has discovered the loss of Wigger and is rapidly wilting. So acute is her condition that she is admitted to hospital, where she proceeds to baffle the doctors. An egotistical specialist performs all manner of tests on her before coming to the startling conclusion that she is drowning. However, the miracle concoction he whips up to stop her internal weeping proves ineffective and the dread form of Katz—a coffin-maker for children—is called in. Katz, however, is somewhat more good-natured than his profession would suggest and is less interested in new custom than in saving the child. However, his realization that the problem is that Susanna is alone in the world at Christmas time doesn't mean that he is able to do anything to pull her out of her condition. He regretfully concludes that he will indeed have to construct her death casket.

At that point, over in Zurich, a great wind begins developing. It deposits the duchess into a fountain and spins the bank robber into a police station before whipping Wigger from its place on the pole atop the mountain. (That the wind is portrayed whistling through the stars might perplex a schoolteacher trying to explain to her charges that space is a vacuum.) As Susanna is being placed in her coffin, two people working for Katz notice a pink rag in her hand. They try to wrench it out but her grip is too tight. They desist when Susanna slaps at their hands.

The reconciled Wigger and Susanna start up their bantering again. There is hope on Susanna's horizon now—Katz seems like the kind of person who might adopt her—but this is not so important as the fact that she has Wigger. That will always be enough.

It's difficult to work out how to assess *Wigger*. The seven-to-ten age group at whom it's aimed will quite possibly find the book as heart-lifting and charming as it's clearly intended to be. That demographic will presumably be too young to worry about the inconsistencies that the adult brain registers. In describing the car crash that killed the protagonist's parents, Goldman's language is both so opaque and so advanced—"the car slipped one snowy night … so the wreckers towed the car away while the undertaker shouldered the burden of the others"—that it seems unlikely any youngster below twelve or thirteen would grasp it without parental guidance. Lines like this betray Goldman's unfamiliarity with the children's market. Moreover, one would think that the experience of having children himself would have apprised him of the fact that he needed to narrow his linguistic parameters.

There is also a certain glibness and laziness about some of the dialogue, while the soothing mantras that Wigger attempts to teach Susanna—"A cheery face is worth diamonds," "A good first impression is worth ground sirloin"—are ungainly.

There is an absence of logic in the denouement. How is Wigger able to co-opt wind? If it has this power, why did it not use it at an earlier stage, thus saving Susanna from a close brush with death? It wouldn't have taken much for Goldman to seed a piece of internal logic to Wigger's return, such as a pledge from the rag that should Susanna ever be at death's door some force would reunite it with her.

That said, Goldman's breezy tone will probably go down well with kids, and some of his characters like Katz and the Nurse are endearing. Additionally, chapter eight—the bank robbery scene and its immediate aftermath—is a good piece of writing.

Whatever qualities *Wigger* does have, however, the *Booklist* review that spoke of "blunt, sometimes stunning writing" and the fact that it was voted a Book of the Year by the Child Study Association strike one as the desperation of parents who want to get down with the kids.

Asked if it was harder or easier than he thought it would be to produce a children's book, Goldman says, "Those are not words that I ever would connect to writing. You never know what's going to happen and you hope you can get finished and you hope someone will like it, but you don't know." What about the fact that with a children's book, an author is aiming his writing at an age group that doesn't know as much as he does about the world? Goldman: "You're asking me stuff that I wish you wouldn't because you're looking for coherent, intelligent answers. I wish you would understand that I don't know what I'm doing, that I'm totally instinctive. Do you think I'm sitting here smirking, thinking, 'I'm going to fuck this kid around?' I really know exactly what I'm doing? I have thousands of pages of notes? I know what my next eight books are going to be? No."

While Goldman says it is "lovely" that *Wigger* was adjudged one of the best children's books of its year, asked if he has ever thought of writing another 'juvenile', he says, "I haven't really, no."

■

PART III

The Peak Years

1

In December 1973, Goldman's long-term editor Hiram Haydn died of a heart attack at his home on Martha's Vineyard. The sudden absence in his life of the man who had never quite understood the populist instincts behind, and audience for, ideas like *No Way To Treat a Lady* led to Goldman reinventing himself as a novelist.

One measure Goldman took was to sign with Delacorte Press. "He switched publishers at that point," says Ross Claiborne, then editor at Delacorte. "He left Harcourt and came to us. I was thrilled … I started to publish Bill with *Marathon Man* and *Tinsel* and *Magic*, so I published some of Bill's good books … I published ten of William Goldman's books." A second change was financial arrangements: for the first time, Goldman did not write a book on spec but signed a contract and took an advance. A third measure was a switch in direction.

Recalls Goldman, "I had a whole bunch of ideas for what I guess you could call popular fiction. When I wrote *No Way to Treat a Lady*, Hiram never saw it 'til it was done. He never wanted me to write that and we published it under a pseudonym. When he died, I began to write, for good or ill, a different kind of novel … I was a huge fan of Graham Greene and I thought, 'God, wouldn't it be wonderful to write a spy thriller or something?' *Marathon Man* was a commercial piece. I don't know why I wrote *Marathon Man* then, but Hiram was dead and it rocked me. I was sure if Hiram had lived I would never have written *Marathon Man* then. The instinct for the book was I was walking in the diamond district in

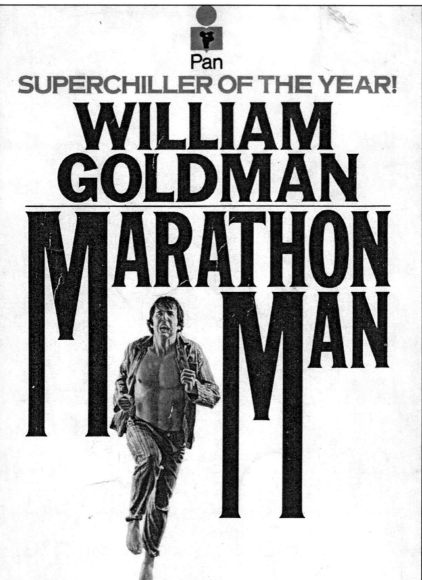

Pan

SUPERCHILLER OF THE YEAR!

WILLIAM GOLDMAN

MARATHON MAN

'Keeps you
on the edge of your
seat with that
combination of
terror and pleasure
only the superb
thriller can achieve'*

New York once. It was filled with all these Jews with scars from the Nazis in their little shops and I felt, 'Oh my God, how great would it be if a Nazi was walking in this street.' How many years before I finally wrote it I don't know, but that was where that came from."

A gritty, contemporary, urban, pacey, profane and blood-splattered thriller, *Marathon Man*—published on October 1, 1974—is a book whose tone could not be more of a contrast to that of *A Princess Bride*. The chapters are rarely more than half a dozen pages but it is not solely this that is responsible for the sometimes dizzying feel: the narrative switches rapidly between disparate characters and situations with, initially, no obvious connection. A case in point is 'Before the Beginning,' a prologue dedicated to the death of a grumpy old man in a car accident. Although it is a crackling and sometimes funny curtain-raiser that sums up the bad-tempered bustle of New York, its significance as the catalyst for all that will follow—the dead man is the father of a fugitive Nazi named Christian Szell, who must now come out of hiding to retrieve his diamonds from the safe deposit box his father had supervised for him—will not be revealed until well into the book. Beyond the relaying of the fact of the death, it's also unnecessary.

The marathon man of the title is T. Babington Levy, a twenty-five-year-old majoring in history at Columbia University courtesy of an athletic scholarship. He is known as "Babe" to his beloved elder brother by ten years, Hank, who is "Doc" to Babe. They are the sons of a professor driven to suicide by the McCarthyite anti-communist witch hunts. Babe's vague ideas for revenge, which his handgun skills were acquired to assist, are really fantasy: he is a lanky, comical, gentle naïf.

Other chapters are devoted to the point of view of Scylla, who works for "The Division," identified as an organization existing between the crevices of the different, bickering arms of state. He is one of, if not the, best in his business of assassination. When we first meet him at an airport bar, he has run into one of his counterparts, a short, toupéed man named Ape currently working for "the Arabs." Ape knows there is a contract on his life—people aren't allowed to retire in this line of work—and this has unleashed a melancholy: "I was thinking that there has never been a woman I didn't pay for, or a child who knew my name, or a wig that enhanced me," he mutters into his drink. This has some pathos, as does the fact that Scylla is subsequently outraged when Ape is denied dignity in his inevitable death when he is taken out on the toilet by a killing crew. The dense detail about assassin craft in Scylla's chapters is robbed of its semi-authenticity, however, by other elements that are sheer comic-book: Scylla is paradoxically so much a celebrity of a hitman that fellow assassins apprehend his identity just from his slick modus operandi.

Scylla has his stomach ripped open by a bull-shouldered man who is the focus of other chapters and whose significance will, like so many things, take time to become clear. When Doc bursts through Babe's front door and dies in his arms, we apprehend that he is Scylla, although that's not as big a surprise as a crew-cutted government type named Janeway who arrives at the scene telling Babe his friends call him "Janey": it's only then that we realize that in the passages in which Scylla had been depicted thinking about the person we assumed was his girlfriend, Goldman had never used a female pronoun. Babe is captured and subjected to dental torture by the bull-shouldered man who keeps asking him, "Is it safe?" Babe is bewildered. The reader is also bewildered when it later transpires that the bull-shouldered man desires to know if he will be robbed of his diamonds if he empties the safe deposit box. Why didn't he just explain that to Babe in the first place? To Babe's heart-stopping relief, Janeway rescues him and explains all about Szell—for the bull-shouldered man is he—in the getaway car. Doc had worked as a courier for Szell in exchange for the latter turning in other Nazis (although was no angel, having skimmed off the top). When Janeway's probings about why Doc should have dragged himself across town to die in Babe's arms draw a blank, Janeway brings the car to an infuriated halt and Babe realizes he is back at the scene of his torture and that Janeway is one of the bad guys. It's another in a brilliant series of switchbacks. Following this ploy by Doc's faithless ex-lover, more nerve-shredding dental torture is practiced before Szell comes to the conclusion that Babe doesn't know anything, which just leaves Szell's cohorts with the task of disposing of him.

Outside, Babe takes advantage of being left unguarded for a moment to slip away. Naturally, the villains give chase, but even though he is in his pajamas, barefoot and suffering mightily from his tortured teeth, Babe knows that if he hangs in there he can evade them: a sprinter is no match for a marathon man over distance. In a scene with impressive swells of emotion, Babe imagines his Olympic heroes urging him past the pain barrier. It is the height of the sporting references that abound herein, with characters frequently using baseball, basketball and track events and participants as metaphors.

There is one more kick in the teeth awaiting Babe. His girlfriend Elsa, to whom he turns for assistance, transpires to also be working for the Nazi's crew. This is not as much of a jolt for the reader: Goldman all but revealed this on her first appearance, a somewhat surprising narrative choice considering there was no reason to let us in on it and considering the author's skillful toying with reader expectation everywhere else.

The book's relative shortness (309 pages in its first hardcover edition, a couple of hundred in paperback) makes its structure of lightning shifts between contrasting scenes even more unusual. The power conferred by this, though, is undermined by sometimes atrocious prose. Goldman piles on metaphor to the point where his text loses plausibility and drama: "...if you didn't have someone to cling to, the currents were too strong; the swirling rumors were enough to knock you down, steal your air, drag you out to sea." It is littered with awkwardly glib phrases like "logic was his" and clunkily show-offy and utterly unidiomatic passages such as, "Summing up, he was uncomfortable, completely captive, undoubtedly the helpless victim of relentless sadistic destroyers."

The dialogue itself rarely rings true. The banter between the two brothers is haunted by the ghost of cheesy sitcom repartee ("What do you do for fun if there isn't a vampire picture playing in town?"; "It's Elsa, *Elsa* you got that, Not Ilse or Ella or Eva, not Hilda or Leila or Lida, not Lily, not Lola"). Meanwhile, the way a Latin street kid mocks Babe ("I just absolutely *adore* your chateau") is simply absurd.

The unglamorous realism of the espionage scenes (in how many spy books or movies is a toupéedassassin who is dejected about his ugliness and loneliness murdered while defecating?) is undermined by superheroics, such as Scylla being able to move unmolested about a small darkened room in which is located a man he has told he is going to kill, taunting his quarry as he goes, and incredible elements such as the fact of freelance assassins hiring themselves out to governments.

A final weakness is that although its adroitly revealed twists, as well as the usual under-punctuated Goldman breathlessness, keep the reader turning pages, upon a second reading *Marathon Man* begins to fall apart a little as the third eye begins to ask questions previously unposed, such as why would Elsa play so hard to get when she is a honey trap, and how could the baddies coming for a basking Babe be taking the hinges off his bathroom door when hinges are on the inside?

Yet right at the death, a fairly flimsy book acquires gravitas courtesy of a sequence of four highly impressive chapters. Babe confronts Szell's henchpeople, but just when he is beginning to feel predictable disappointment with himself over not having the guts to use his handgun on them, he wipes them all out. Then Szell visits New York's diamond district to get an idea of what his fortune is worth, only to be identified in this Jew-heavy area by two of the people on whom he performed grotesque experiments on behalf of the Third Reich. The chapter—one of the book's longer ones—is a sweaty, claustrophobic exploration of the mind of a monster at bay. The next one sees Szell sniveling for his life when Babe catches up with him. Hardened by his experiences, Babe avoids the fearsome retractable knife hidden up Szell's sleeve, which had done for Doc, and tells the newly bullet-riddled Nazi that the Jews are waiting for him on the Other Side. The final chapter is a wisp in which a young cop, attracted by the gunshots, finds a calm Babe methodically skimming what seem to be pebbles across Central Park's reservoir: they are in fact Szell's priceless diamond haul.

Although a massively flawed book, its structural idiosyncrasies, taut pace and powerful flourish of a finale generated enough good reviews and word-of-mouth to send *Marathon Man* up the bestseller lists. Goldman had had million-selling American paperbacks as far back as the mid-sixties, but, by early 1976, *Marathon Man* had been sold to a dozen countries outside the US, something that not even his biggest-selling books hitherto had managed.

The book also reinvented Goldman in a highly lucrative way. Because the seventies was a juncture in history where rising living standards had created a greater demand for entertainment product but was just before video recorders became affordable to the bulk of the populace, it was a boom era for paperback sales, and many of those sales came from men, who favored action-oriented, frankly spoken fare like this.

2

'The Simple Pleasures of the Rich,' published in *Transatlantic Review* No. 50 (Autumn-Winter 1974), was William Goldman's farewell to short stories.

His agent's campaign to place this effort resulted in an ego-deflating 60 to 75 rejection slips, ultimately forcing Goldman to effectively call upon the charity of friends: he was reduced to offering it to the *Transatlantic Review*, whose staff had always clearly been less concerned with the quality of his stories than the sentiment of personal association. As Gold-man told Richard Andersen, "...the intense rejection from everybody of what was the best I could do made me stop writing short stories ... I went on to doing movies between novels. Screenplays haven't been like the short stories. I haven't been beating my head against the wall trying to get a screenplay accepted. It's nice to be wanted."

"The best I could do" turns out to be a seven-page effort that lurches between nondescript to mediocre to incompetent.

'The Simple Pleasures of the Rich' ventures into territory even more effete than *A Family Affair*, depicting the whim-drenched activities and rivalries of a clutch of elderly people with too much time on their hands and more money than sense. The point of view is that of Peckham, a man-servant to a Mr. Churchill. The latter summons him to inform him of his intention to build a road on his estate. ("It wouldn't necessarily have to lead anywhere.") The two men attempt for no directly stated reason to keep the project secret from Agatha, Churchill's wheelchair-bound, peremptory sister. When the men's clandestine activities are discovered, it leads to an awkward atmosphere in the house, with Agatha mocking them in front of her half-dotty, equally contemptuous bridge companion 'the Duchess.'

An emotional shift occurs when the news comes that the Duchess has—like many of the group's friends over recent years—'gone to Europe.' This transpires to be a euphemism for death. Agatha retreats to her room, only emerging a month later to inspect the road. She submits that she can assist by smoothing its edges. The two men acquiesce, but when she suggests a servant be quick in fetching a roller from the guest garage, the group come to an agreement that in fact he should not be quick. "We have time," says Agatha. The road is eventually completed "long long after" this incident.

This wisp of a story strives for the claustrophobia that comes from detailing the minutiae of a hermetically sealed part of human existence and tilts for a sense of aching misery behind trimmed hedges and fine manners. It does so primarily via subtly communicating the meaning be-hind inflections of dialogue and exchanged glances. Goldman is clearly attempting to emulate the understatement and elegance of masters like Irwin Shaw and F. Scott Fitzgerald. The text proves that he just doesn't have the requisite talent.

The story's problems start with the opening sentences: "When his buzzer rang out—at half past four in the morning—even Peckham was sur-prised. Being Mr. Churchill's man for fifty-one years now, going on fifty-two, had prepared him for many things; but not for having his buzzer ring out, piercing sharp above his head, at half past four in the morning." That passage should really read, "When his buzzer rang out, even Peckham was surprised. Being Mr. Churchill's man for fifty-one years now, going on fifty-two, had prepared him for many things; but not for having his buzzer ring out at half past four in the morning." As it stands, it's simply self-conscious, convoluted and overly colloquial for a story of this timbre. The choice of the name Churchill doesn't help: it takes a few paragraphs to get past the initial assumption that this is a story about Britain's iconic World War II leader.

Ungainly choices of words and phraseology mount up quickly. "So he buzzed back quickly, one-two, fast presses of his thumb, and then sat up, rubbing his eyes gently, whisking sleep away. Later he stood, draped his robe about him, left his room…" The "later" makes it sound as though the author is talking of a passage of at least several minutes when the context soon makes it clear that he means straightaway. When the summoned Peckham is standing in front of Churchill, Goldman writes, "So the minutes ticked by, as they usually do, with not a word thrown out to alter their progress." Yet it becomes quite clear that Goldman cannot possibly mean minutes but moments.

Several other things cause the reader to crinkle his brow or snort. Why does Peckham—a man so lowly in his employer's eyes as to have his sleep disturbed by him quite arbitrarily—have the presumption to sit beside Churchill at the dinner table? Goldman includes the line, "And don't spare the horses," without any suggestion of humor on the part of the speaker, which of course renders it a parody of upper-class speech. Agatha's wheelchair is pushed by her own manservant Bergen, but both employee and means of transportation are spectral presences, neither ever described.

Columbia's William Goldman Papers purport to contain nearly fifty separate short stories by Goldman, testament to the fact that the man whose life was changed by Irwin Shaw's *Mixed Company* desperately wanted to succeed in this medium. "I'm going to guess they weren't any fucking good," Goldman responds when asked why he didn't, adding, "I don't know why." Goldman is always disinclined to analyze his writing, but seems to have wondered enough about his failure in this direction to be bewildered by it.

Some will assume that anyone who can string together a sufficient number of sentences to produce a more-than-competent novel, as Goldman has so many times, will axiomatically be able to do it on a smaller scale. Goldman would appear to be one such person. However, the short story is not simply a miniature novel but a completely different beast, a form in which it is particularly difficult to strike the right balance. Character and motivation have to be explored in a restricted space, description and incident have to be pared right back to essentials lest a reader make unintended inferences, emotional resonance must be generated despite the reader barely having time to care for the characters or apprehend the milieu, and the ending must feel like a resolution regardless of the fact that set-up has barely occurred. Even good short stories face a problem that is a function of their success: the fact that no sooner has a reader come to be interested in a character than that character is departing the stage.

Many writers excel across multiples of tens of thousands of words in populating a structure that boasts a beginning, middle and end with characters about whom the reader cares. A smaller number can also do it across a mere few thousand words. That Goldman falls into the former category but not the latter cannot be because of the fact of him, by his own admission, not being a stylist: many celebrated short story writers have relied on propulsion of plot and vividness of character rather than elegance of prose. Moreover, it is not down to the fact that Goldman's writing needs to be able to breathe and stretch its muscles: as touched on in this text, there are plenty of sections of his novels that, isolated, would serve as fine pieces of short fiction. Rather it would seem a matter of self-consciousness. Goldman always seemed to feel the baleful stares of Shaw and others on the back of his head as he constructed short stories. Accordingly, he put in them not what he wanted to or felt comfortable with but what he felt he should: archetypes abound in this quadrant of his oeuvre, as do character types beyond his obvious comfort zone.

As stated previously, it is often difficult to establish the degree of a screenwriter's importance to the success or otherwise of a motion picture. Nowhere is that more the case than with *The Stepford Wives*, released on February 12, 1975.

Goldman did a lot of work on this project. Instead of just relying on Ira Levin's 1972 novel, he investigated the Women's Liberation movement that is central to its plot: a box in Columbia's William Goldman Papers contains various feminist books, magazines and cuttings he read. Much of this work transpired to be futile. Although the screenplay of the movie is credited to him alone, Goldman claims that director Bryan Forbes rewrote his script so comprehensively that he felt compelled to try to dissociate himself from it. ("I wanted my name off it, and they didn't take it off," he told author John Brady.)

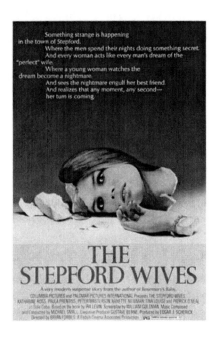

Caught in the middle of a to-and-fro between Forbes and Goldman was the movie's male lead Peter Masterson. A friend of Goldman's (Goldman shone a spotlight on his career in *The Season*), Masterson claims that Goldman told him he had delivered a final draft to Forbes, whereas the director told Masterson no final draft had arrived and set about work on a new pass. Masterson says he was making telephone calls to Goldman during filming, which resulted in him surreptitiously re-inserting the writer's original intentions.

One of Goldman's most famous movie anecdotes revolved around this project. He wrote in *Adventures in the Screen Trade* that he considered the project to be "more than likely doomed" when Forbes suggested his actress wife Nanette Newman for one of the roles. That Newman did not meet the description of the women in Ira Levin's source material, whose universal youth and shapeliness is a mystery with sinister roots, was not something he felt able to point out to her husband. "She's a hell of an actress but whatever I wrote, I wrote," says Goldman. "You can't say that to somebody about their wife. I certainly couldn't." So what was it like continuing to work on the project with the conviction in the back of his mind that it was now undermined? "I don't want to answer that. When you're contracted to write a movie, you have the original to get in and usually they have a re-write and then another re-write that you get paid for and that's your contract and you don't want to break contract." However, he says that he did not think the work was futile at any point: "You're assuming that somebody fucking knows that the movie's going to work. That movie could have been the biggest hit of all time because of Nanette Newman and you don't know that. Nobody has the least idea what's going to work. Talk to any director or star or producer about their hits and flops and say, 'Why did this happen?' They don't know."

The Eberharts—Walter ((Masterson) and Joanna (Katharine Ross, Sundance's love interest in *Butch Cassidy*)—escape the seediness of New York by relocating to the well-tended, picturesque village of Stepford. That their new neighbor Carol Van Sant (Nanette Newman) is eerily docile and stiff is the first sign of something not quite right about their new locale. Further clues are provided by the fact that the village women pay inordinate attention to their appearances and are so house-proud that they spurn maids. Moreover, the area's husbands spend much of their time in the antiquated environs of the Stepford Men's Association.

Joanna makes friends with the resentful Bobbie Markowe (Paula Prentiss), who has also recently relocated from the city with her spouse. Their decision to bring "Women's Lib" to Stepford runs up against a brick wall of ladies too busy to participate because of children and baking. They set about trying to get to the bottom of this mystery of female servitude.

Whoever is responsible for the *Stepford Wives* script, it has to be said that the finished film contains much stilted dialogue and is so slow and lacking dramatic and scenic layering that most of it resembles a seventies American made-for-TV movie. It's interesting that Goldman claimed to John Brady, "Bryan [Forbes] rewrote all of *Stepford*, until the last twenty minutes of the film, which is mine," because things only really pick up in three powerful passages toward the end. When Joanna visits a psychiatrist on the insistence of her husband, the way she unburdens herself to the female doctor has more vitality and tension (and, come to that, good acting) than everything that has preceded it. A scene where Joanna finds that Bobbie has been 'turned'—her spiky friend is suddenly as subservient, overly groomed and intellectually vacuous as all the other women in the village—is fairly eerie: Bobbie's only reaction when a desperate Joanna stabs her in the stomach is to go about doing domestic tasks with the mindless repetition of a stuck record. Joanna then goes searching for her missing children at the Men's Association building, where she is told the awful solution of the mystery of Stepford by the sinister Diz Coba. The scene ratchets up the tension to the levels of a horror or chase movie and culminates in her encountering her robotic replacement, who currently resembles her in every way except for black, blank eye sockets. Her double advances on her with a stocking held menacingly in her hands. The final scene shows 'Joanna' with the rest of the Stepford Wives meekly but happily shopping for the family at the local supermarket.

Even that well-executed shock ending starts falling apart once the in-the-moment enjoyment fades and the mind starts asking questions. For instance, whatever the fantasies of dominance that may reside in the subconscious of the average male, why would any of these men agree to be part of a conspiracy that ends with the murder of the mother of their children? Walter should have been given a hinterland of misogyny, chauvinism or even psychosis to make his behavior plausible. The perfunctory early scene in which he drunkenly expresses to Joanna feelings of inadequacy simply does not suffice in this regard. Additionally, why would the men of the superior abilities of those in Stepford need to engage in this conspiracy at all? People so gifted as to be capable of constructing utterly life-like robots from sketches, voice recordings and contacts in the local fecund computer industry would constitute a super-race who could command the submissiveness they desire by simple dint of the vast influence and wealth that would accrue from their talents.

Although parts of it may seem banal and anodyne today, the fact that *The Stepford Wives* was dropped directly into the still raging waters of the Women's Liberation movement made it a controversial movie upon its release. Yet despite the male triumvirate of Levin, Goldman and Forbes behind it, there is no denying the unusually distaff timbre of the picture. Moreover, that the intention of the film was the polar opposite of what was assumed by those feminists who demonstrated against it is proven by the fact that "Stepford Wife" has now entered the popular lexicon as a pejorative to describe docile or conventional housewifery.

Asked if he has requested that his name be removed from a movie's credits at any other time, Goldman says, "No. You don't know what's going to happen with a movie. Remember, it's years before the movie hits the screens. God knows how many studio heads are going to get fired before the movie hits the screens, what directors are going to do…"

3

On March 13, 1975, just a month after the appearance of *The Stepford Wives*, came the release of *The Great Waldo Pepper*. It was a project that augured well, reuniting as it did Goldman with the director and one of the stars of *Butch Cassidy and the Sundance Kid*.

The writing credits for this picture read, "Screenplay by William Goldman, Story by George Roy Hill." "Waldo was basically an original screenplay of mine," explains Goldman. "I say 'basically' because the pulse of the movie came from George Hill, the director, and we worked for ten days on a story. So *Waldo* wasn't as original as *Butch*, but it was a hell of a lot more mine than any adaptation I've ever done." Of Hill, he says, "It was his great passion. George had been a pilot in two wars … George really wanted to do a movie about old airplanes … George was the great director for me that I ever worked with but I didn't realize quite how brilliant he was then. We did the two movies. It was something I did in a sense [because] we had a great experience on *Butch*."

At one point in *The Great Waldo Pepper*, the titular protagonist (Robert Redford) laments that in the year of 1926 the public simply isn't as impressed as it once was by airplanes, hence the reduced circumstances in which he is living as he uses the skills he learned as a pilot in the Great War to earn a buck taking people for sky-rides. Yet part of this film's *raison d'etre* is the assumption of the continued appeal to the modern, movie-going public of seeing daredevils looping the loop and wingwalking. It provokes the question whether, by the film's end, that continued appeal has been confirmed. The answer is a qualified yes.

Ironically, one of the reasons for that continued appeal is something that wasn't available to daredevils of Pepper's generation: the patina of age. The trappings of the 1920s that we see in *The Great Waldo Pepper*—fashions, customs and equipment—can't help but seem somehow exotic. The combination of this, awesome cinematography from Robert Surtees and great direction from Hill make the film very easy on the eye. Also impressive is the fact that airplane jargon and custom is clearly well-researched. The faithfulness to the period is spoilt only by Redford's luxuriant and non-brillianteened hair—but then nobody had the power to tell the biggest star in the world to get his famous blond thatch cut. In mild mitigation, a sex symbol attractive by contemporary standards is another thing that makes the film appetizing to contemporary folk.

Pepper is putting most of his meager earnings towards having a new plane built. To his reluctance, his engineer Ezra Stiles (Edward Herrmann) is constructing a monoplane: Ezra Informs him that biplanes are on their way to becoming museum pieces. When Pepper sees the work in progress, he realizes it is so sturdy that it will enable him to perform an outside loop—an almost mythical stunt, which not even the great Ernst Kessler has managed. Pepper knows he is good but that he is only second-

best in the world to Kessler, a German Great War fighter pilot similar to the Red Baron, only, unlike the Red Baron, he survived the hostilities and is now resident and performing feats of aerial derring-do for a living in the United States. Pepper—who has never met Kessler—idolizes the German to the extent of telling tall tales to impressionable women of dogfights with him.

One of said women is Mary Beth (Susan Sarandon), whom Pepper and his one-time rival, now colleague, Axel Olsson (Bo Svenson) recruit as a piece of eye candy in their never-ending quest to satisfy the requirements of a jaded public. Mary Beth is game when it is suggested she appear partially clothed on the wing of an airplane in flight. However, the publicity stunt goes wrong when Mary Beth suddenly freezes in fear. There follows a superb, white-knuckle sequence wherein Pepper jumps from one plane to another, climbs over the pilot and attempts to escort Mary Beth back toward the seats. Pepper has almost succeeded in his task when Mary Beth misses his outstretched hand. Up until now, the film has not been particularly gritty, with one early scene involving the implausible discovery of sabotage just on the point of take-off not far above the level of a comic strip. When Mary Beth falls to her death, it becomes jarringly apparent that this is not *Those Magnificent Men in Their Flying Machines*.

Pepper, somewhat unjustly, is suspended for his part in the death by the Civil Aviation Authority, which newly formed regulatory body is the closest thing to a villain in the film, even though its agent Newt (Geoffrey Lewis) is a wartime buddy of Pepper's and not completely unsympathetic to the daredevils. Pepper being grounded (yes, that's where that expression comes from) leads Ezra to decide to try the outside loop in the now completed monoplane at the aviation circus of which Pepper is now in the employ. However, Ezra doesn't have the technical dexterity of Pepper and crashes. Another decidedly non-comic strip scene follows in which Pepper desperately tries to pull a wounded and trapped Ezra from the wreckage. A cigarette being smoked by a bystander ignites the spilt fuel around the plane. A desperate and terrified Pepper—realizing the inevitability of Ezra being burnt alive—knocks his friend out with a metal bar so as to relieve the agony of his final moments. Pepper then climbs in a plane and furiously flies it at the gawking bystanders to scatter them. As a consequence, he is grounded permanently.

When Pepper hears of aerial stunt work in Hollywood, he can't resist signing up under an assumed name. He is amazed and thrilled to then discover that the movie in which he will be performing is a biopic of Kessler. He is even more thrilled when he discovers that Kessler is the film's technical adviser. (A photogenic young man is playing Kessler, about which the German remains philosophical.) When Pepper and Kessler meet, there is an instant rapport. Kessler—played by Bo Brundin—insists to the producers that the stunt pilot with whom he will work in the dog-fight scenes is not the man scheduled for the task but Pepper.

The film's finale is somewhat misjudged. The Civil Aviation Authority is hot on Pepper's trail, Newt watching from the ground as Pepper performs with Kessler for the cameras. He intends to arrest Pepper on landing but the movie dogfight is unexpectedly played for real by the two rivals. Although not firing guns, their playing chicken and clipping of each other's vehicles does such damage that both know they will be unable to land. Kessler peels away from Pepper, saluting him in respect before he does—just like Pepper had falsely told Mary Beth he had done when spinning a tall tale. A closing caption then reveals that Pepper died in 1931. It's an ending that is simply too subtle: it's easy to miss the fact that the climactic dogfight leads to the hero's death.

An old-fashioned yarn, *The Great Waldo Pepper* is bland and quasi-soporific in places, inspired and thrilling in others.

4

Nineteen-seventy-six was quite a year for Goldman.

As if the two movies credited to him in 1975 weren't enough, the following year saw the release of the Goldman-scripted movies *All The President's Men* (which eventually garnered him an Oscar) and *Marathon Man*, plus his novel *Magic*. He would continue to be prolific through to the end of the decade. An eye condition caused by a type of pneumonia was the main impetus for Goldman's jaw-dropping productivity: alerted for the first time to his own mortality, he began to worry for the financial security of his family in the event of anything happening to him. That, however, doesn't explain the high quality of the work he was veritably ladling out. In the late seventies, Goldman was, creatively, a man on fire.

Having said that, some motion pictures are so sociologically important that their aesthetic quality is almost incidental. *All The President's Men* is an example of such.

On June 17, 1972, five men were arrested at the Democratic Party's National Committee headquarters in the Watergate building in Washington D.C. Peculiarly, they were dressed in formal attire. Even more peculiarly—as *Washington Post* reporter Bob Woodward discovered when he attended their arraignment hearing in a routine assignment—one of them was a former CIA employee. When Woodward then found out that the name of E. Howard Hunt, an aide of a White House official, had been found in the address books of two of those men, he and his *Post* colleague Carl Bernstein set off on a trail that would uncover one of the

most sensational stories in the history of journalism: a secret campaign conducted from the White House, almost certainly authorized by President Richard Nixon, designed to destabilize the opposition to the ruling Republican Party via dirty tricks, which included criminal activity.

Robert Redford decided he wanted to make a movie out of the David-versus-Goliath scenario of two humble young reporters exposing wrongdoing in the highest office in the land (and, unbeknownst to anyone then, ultimately bringing down the president). He helped shape the direction of *All The President's Men*, the book the two reporters wrote about the events stemming from the Watergate burglary, by suggesting that they provide not merely a recitation of facts but a human narrative in which their sleuthing methods featured. It was natural for him to contact Goldman, with whom he'd had great success previously, for the screenwriting job.

Despite the incremental uncovering of facts involved in a newspaper investigation being inherently undramatic, Goldman says he had no qualms about accepting the job offer: "Because it was one of those things you had to do it. It was just such a big story in America. It wanted to be a movie, if it got made, that would have some quote-quote importance to it. They didn't want to make it then. No studio would make something like that now, unless they had a big, big star who would do it. We had a huge problem, which was the President's men were so powerful. The book had come out and no one had sued the book. A lawsuit is killing to a movie company—it means they can't release the movie until after the lawsuit is settled—so anything that was in the book was fair game for the movie, and we could change Woodward and Bernstein's lives because they didn't mind that, but for the most part it had to be just as accurate as could be. So we stayed very close. My memory is it's very close to the book. We didn't know if the movie was going to get made."

The combination of it being a true story with a mundane newspaper office backdrop and the fact of some cast members' love of improvisation makes *All The President's Men* possibly the most naturalistic movie ever shot. Its mock-documentary approach includes characters mishearing each other and stumbling over words and correcting themselves, as well as 'real' sound (it's hard to make out the dialogue in one scene as planes fly overhead). It has none of the standard smooth Hollywood rhythm explained by Goldman at length in his book *Which Lie Did I Tell?* and exemplified by such things as movie characters always finding a parking space outside a building to which they need urgent access, possessing the right change for a cabbie, etc. etc. As the two men piece together a story of whose substance and direction they are not sure by stumbling on names and ferreting out fragments of information, the action is as bitty, staccato, stuttering, repetitive, error-strewn and unglamorous as life.

During the movie's elongated gestation period, momentous events occurred in the United States. In November 1972, Nixon secured a second presidential term after the dirty tracks campaign of which the Watergate burglary was one part ensured he had lame election opposition in the shape of George McGovern. In August 1974, Nixon became the first president in history to resign as his personal complicity in at least covering up the dirty tricks campaign became apparent. The producers resisted the urge to change the nature of the project to one which fully addressed these events: the plot remains focused on the uncovering of the story, with the shattering consequences of that uncovering restricted to bulletins hammered out by a teletype machine right at the un-climactic end.

The main casting of *All the President's Men*, released on April 9, 1976, is about the only non-naturalistic part of the whole enterprise. That Redford would costar as Woodward was the condition of Warner Bros., the studio that bought the movie rights. What with Dustin Hoffman being cast as Bernstein, the unfortunate, absurd notion was planted in the audience's subconscious that the news floor of the *Washington Post* was a repository of smoldering sex bombs. However, Redford and Hoffman are professional enough that we soon forget about the unlikely physical beauty of their characters and start to believe in them as hustling hacks. Jane Alexander is very good as the petrified but dignified bookkeeper informant Judy Hoback. Jason Robards is perfect as the barnacle-encrusted, battle-scarred *Washington Post* executive editor Ben Bradlee. Hal Holbrook is suitably mysterious and grim as Deep Throat, the ribald nickname given to the anonymous 'deep background' source.

The feeling of the movie being right in its time is heightened by the presence in a Goldman-scripted movie for the first time of cuss words, although with "rat-fucking" the term of choice for their activities by the dirty tricks brigade it could hardly be any other way.

All The President's Men is in many ways a non-film: talky, repetitive, largely static and with no proper second act. Added to this is its, for the time, extraordinary length of two-and-a-third hours. If the events it relates were not true, it would be unwatchable. However, that it is highly watchable is not just because those unbelievable events actually happened but because of great craftsmanship.

On this project, Goldman felt badly treated by Carl Bernstein (for trying to supplant his script with one of his own), Redford (for being prepared to contemplate using Bernstein's script) and director Alan Pakula (for replacing him with an anonymous doctor towards the project's end and not bothering to tell him, even if, Goldman later wrote, what appeared on screen "seemed very much to resemble what I'd done"; a claim by Redford in a 2011 authorized biography that only ten per cent of Goldman's script remained after he and Pakula worked on it was refuted by journalist Richard Stayton via an analysis of different drafts of the screenplay and the finished film). He went so far as to write in *Adventures In The Screen Trade* that if he were to be asked what he would change if he had his movie life over again, his reply would be that he wouldn't have gone near *All The President's Men*. "The movie's fine and Alan Pakula did a swell job, etc," he says now. However, he also observes, "It was a terrible experience. Most of the time you don't give a shit, but that was a very unpleasant experience." In this context, his Academy Award (Best Screenplay Adaptation from Another Medium) is the irony of ironies. As with his *Butch Cassidy* nomination, Goldman didn't attend the award ceremony. "I didn't want to go out there," he says. "I was there once because I was helping to write the show that time. When I won the Oscars, God bless, the Academy Awards were not as important as they are now. They're really a big deal now."

Not so easy to formally quantify as awards but indubitable is the fact that with *All The President's Men*—along with *Butch Cassidy and the Sundance Kid* and *The Stepford Wives*—Goldman had for the third time in seven years succeeded in getting his name in the credits of something destined to be less a movie and more a cultural landmark.

5

The publication on September 1 of his latest novel, *Magic*, confirmed Goldman's new direction as a writer of thrillers.

"*Magic* is an odd book," says Goldman. "*Magic* was an idea I'd [had] for years about a ventriloquist."

The book's epigram is a distillation of the philosophy of the magician's craft of Merlin, Jr. Said performer's division of the craft into three stages –"effect," "preparation," and "the work is done"—gives the book its triptych structure. The phrase/philosophy is somewhat clumsy—surely "the work is done" should have been something pithier like "execution"?—and the very fact that Merlin, Jr. is in fact fictitious (he's a character in this novel) feels like cheating. Interestingly, though, Christopher Priest's similarly-themed 1995 novel *The Prestige* seems to be nodding to *Magic* in its insistence on an intrinsic three-pronged nature to the art of stage illusion (in this case, "setup," "performance," and "prestige").

An italicized tendril of an opening sees an old hunter drawn nervously to screams in a resort cabin. Similarly darkly portentous is *The Wisdom According to Fats*, extracts of a diary stated to now be a police exhibit. Fats, we understand, is being verbally abused by his friend Corky. Events will show us that this is not, in fact, possible.

A couple of chapters follow in which Goldman seems to be suggesting that his protagonist Corky Withers is a serial killer. The way the book develops, though, betrays this as mere groping around for direction or tone by the author: no blood is spilled by Corky until much later. Similarly sloppy is Goldman's dialogue: as in too many places throughout, it is too glib to be realistic ("You're still frightened?" I'm down to edgy").

We meet Ben Greene, an ancient showbusiness agent nicknamed "The Postman" because, money-wise, he always comes through. Corky arrives for a restaurant meeting with Greene, who adores his shtick, which is magic-related. Corky (just turned thirty and Greene's client for over two years) disappoints the agent by jeopardizing a CBS pilot Greene has secured him: he doesn't want to take the contractual medical examination. "Just principle," he vaguely says. The Postman is relaxed about it, saying he'll see about getting it waived. In the following chapter, Fats's diary reveals that he himself is far from relaxed and that a screaming match had taken place about it between he and Corky. The 'Effect' part ends with Corky leaving town when the Postman tells him over the phone that he couldn't get CBS to budge about the medical and that he wants to see him.

'Preparation'—a flashback to Corky's formative years—is the best part of the novel. A native of Normandy, a dreary town 90 miles from New York, Corky is insecure both because of his inability to physically take on bullies and the fact that he, his father and his jock brother Willie were abandoned by his mother when he was aged eight. The passage in which we are shown his mom bidding him a tearful farewell is well-written and moving. Also possessing a verisimilitude—if a more amusing one—are Corky's experiences with seeking to take up a course from the Charles Atlas company, whose promises to make musclemen out of ninety-pound weaklings appeared in American comic books of the era of Corky's childhood and beyond with suffocating regularity. Corky's trepidation at a suggested visit by an Atlas field representative of awesome imagined dimensions, and his terror that he might be jailed over his failure to check the box on their coupon to indicate he was under fourteen, make for a delightful and funny evocation of children's inexact grip on reality.

On finding out about the Charles Atlas stuff, Corky's snarling father Mutt—who believes that the gods have pissed on him all his life—tells him, "God gave you the brains. The muscles leave to Willie." However, when Willie is killed in a car crash, Mutt tries to remold a skeptical Corky as a footballer. Cue huge wodges of the sports folklore Goldman loves. (The section on a miraculous, temporary comeback by football legend Nagurski is based on Goldman's own eyewitness experience as a child.) If the suspicion is that it is with something approaching brute force that Goldman is working this material into a story about a very non-athletic protagonist, the good writing and the fine colloquialism makes us not mind. In any case, the fact that after much build-up Corky gets both legs broken on the football field, ending his dad's ambitions for him at a stroke, is an enjoyably familiar type of Goldman reversal. It also swings us smoothly back into the book's central narrative thread, for it is while recovering in hospital that Corky discovers magic via a copy of *Classy Classics Volume I* by Merlin, Jr. The same sensitive hands that make Corky adept at whittling mean he is a natural at card decks.

Corky has to leave behind his unrequited high school crush Peggy Ann Snow when Mutt gets a "big break" in Chicago. When we meet Corky again, aged just under nineteen, it appears that his father has been pissed on by the gods once more, for Corky engages the tutelage of Merlin, Jr. for three thousand dollars gained from Mutt's life insurance. Merlin, Jr. is a sick old widower down on his luck. Corky moves in with him as Merlin takes him on as stage assistant. The process of Corky's refining of his card tricks and coin palms is depicted at fair length, but just when we seem set for a novel based around abracadabra stuff (it is titled *Magic*, after all), Goldman pulls the rug again.

At the age of twenty-six, shortly after Merlin's death, Corky finally musters the courage to perform on his own for the first time by entering a club's open night. He is shocked to his core when his intricate and uncommonly skillful card tricks, built up over years of intensive training, fail to impress or hold the attention of a buzzing, inebriated venue. Although Goldman depicts well Corky's gut-churning tension before he takes the stage and his sweat-drenched embarrassment when performing, his attempts to convince us that Corky's humiliation could immediately engender a severe personality disorder—specifically schizophrenia—are completely unconvincing. Goldman had set up Corky's loserdom with the depiction of that loveless, upheaval-punctuated childhood, but Corky's intellectual brightness and the fact that he is "astonishingly good at picking up girls in bars" because, the women told him, he "seemed to be nice," don't strike one as severe dysfunction territory. When Corky later turns on the gas in his apartment and lies down to die, a voice in his head calls him back, talking him out of his attitude of, "I just don't want to fail any more, I'm tired."

Cut to more than a year later, when the Postman first encountered Corky and his new stage act. Corky still does magic tricks but the crucial aspect of the act is that he does them to a chorus of abuse from the world's first X-rated ventriloquist's dummy (implicitly whittled by Corky). The presence of the dummy also provides a heightened version of that element essential for a magician—misdirection. When we learn that the dummy is named Fats, the pieces of the jigsaw thus far presented by Goldman begin to fall into place.

The way Fats keeps up the snide repartee even when Corky is off-stage is as much a part of Fats's charm as the formal entertainment. Yet the caliber of Fats's wisecracks—"You'll strain your pacemaker," "Is it true you've never missed a show of Captain Kangaroo?"—is so feeble as to make the idea of a weather-beaten character like the Postman being one of his devotees mystifying. As is the fact that, in contrast to the years of intensive training necessary to acquire his magic skills, Corky has become adept at ventriloquism in a mere year. Ditto for who taught him those ventriloquism skills.

The 'Work Is Done' section (more than half of the book) brings us back to the present. In fleeing the suspicious Postman, Corky ends up taking a taxi to his childhood stamping ground. Here, he rents a cabin in a resort deserted at this time of year. It just so happens that it is run by Peggy Ann Snow and her husband the Duke, another ex-high schoolmate of Corky's. In Duke's temporary absence, Corky and Peggy start a romance. Like Peggy, Corky feels trapped in an unhappy marriage. His marriage, however, is very different to that of Peggy: when he is alone in his cabin, a muffled voice demands from his suitcase, "Open up, open up..."

Peggy is enchanted by Fats, and here Goldman convincingly conveys the fact that Corky is only socially functional with the dummy on his arm. His dialogue between Corky and Peggy is less convincing. The line, "Years ago, Ronnie told me, 'Whenever possible, Birdseye'"—a way of her indicating her family's preference for junk food—is false enough without Peggy then following it up an exchange or two later with, "You didn't pick up on Ronnie," a reference to her alluding to the fact that she is taken. Real people don't talk in such pseudo-sage and elliptical ways. Bizarrely, the barbed exchanges behind closed doors between Corky and his increasingly obstreperous dummy have a greater authenticity.

Peggy is also enchanted by Corky's facility with cards and coins. However, despite his previous references to misdirection having long conceded the point that magic tricks are mere illusion, Goldman proceeds to confuse illusion with reality: Corky might be able to make coins looks as though they're strolling on his palm, but he couldn't, as he does, make them appear beneath a seated Peggy's bottom.

Goldman then seems to get similarly confused by the issue of Fats's sentience. In his cabin, Corky has a snarling argument with Fats, who is anxious to get back to New York City. The operatic dispute is brought to an abrupt end by the fact that Corky/Fats realizes that the Postman is watching from the doorway—yet it's Fats who is stated as screaming in shock at a sight Corky can't see. This is not the last instance of this muddle.

When the calm but sad Postman asks, "How long you been like this, kid?" and "Is this why you wouldn't take the medical exam?" Corky tries to bluff his way out of it. The Postman says he won't contact the medical authorities if Corky can make the dummy shut up for five minutes. The countdown that follows, and which culminates in Corky closing his eyes and admitting, "I can't make it," has a tension, but the revelation of Corky's dependence on Fats is also inconsistent with previous scenes showing Corky interacting perfectly normally with Peggy while on his own, which themselves were inconsistent with previous suggestions of Corky only being able to charm Peggy with Fats on his arm.

In a blind panic, Corky uses Fats to bludgeon the departing Postman to death. It is Fats—at least in Corky's bifurcated mind—who tells Corky to drop Greene in the middle of the resort's lake. Meanwhile, the Duke— the man whose partner Corky is hoping to steal—has arrived back. He is extremely suspicious when he discovers the Postman's expensive Rolls Royce in the woods. An increasingly aggressive Duke—who unnerves Corky with the vague preternatural intuition common to secondary characters in thrillers—goes nosing around in his guest's cabin and is rewarded for his pains by being stabbed to death.

Corky decides to break the tie with the increasingly controlling Fats ("I'm doing a single from now on"). In another virulent man-and-puppet argument, Fats threatens to expose Corky. He does, but not in the expected way. When Peggy comes knocking, Fats reveals to her that an incident in which Corky had apparently successfully willed Peggy to mentally transmit the thought of a card—touching her deeply because it seemed to suggest a real connection between them—was a well-worn sleight of hand. When Peggy storms out, Fats tells Corky that she too must be permanently disposed of ("Where was she when the gas was on?"), making Corky crawl around the floor to demonstrate his control over him.

Corky goes to see Peggy on the pretext of giving her a heart he has whittled. He explains through her locked bedroom door that he executed the mind-reading trick because he didn't think anyone as perfect as her would be interested in him otherwise. Opening the door, Peggy is surprised by the knives in his hands.

Back in the cabin, Corky drops the bloody knives on a chair and then sobs. Fats says, "I don't know how to say this since I haven't got a stomach but my stomach hurts." Corky explains that after he had come away from Peggy's door, he had turned the knives on himself.

The final chapter is a mere paragraph long and is the final reversal in a book chockfull of them. Peggy is so touched by Corky's whittled heart that she decides to go down to the cabin to tell him. It is joyful to realize that the blood on the knives was not hers. However, we now realize that the screams the old hunter had heard at the beginning were Peggy's upon her discovery of the corpse of Corky, who—baulking at harming her—had freed himself from the madness.

Weird piece of writing: "There was a tiny hole in the door, a protective device through which you could see who was standing there without opening." Considering all the knowledge Goldman assumes on the part of the reader about the sometimes obscure pop culture figures he references—characters frequently use them as historical or achievement yardsticks—it's bizarre that he thinks the reader won't know what a spyhole is. A bad or at least inappropriate piece of writing is: "In the next room, in the overstuffed chair, eyes wide, sat Fats, his head slightly turned, as if listening." This is a movie script stage direction that has no place in a novel. A similar losing of sight dictates Goldman making the Duke think he is being stabbed by Fats. There's no logical, as opposed to stylistic, reason why Corky would take on the already difficult task of stabbing someone while both holding the dummy and hiding behind a curtain.

As with almost all Goldman fiction, *Magic* impresses less on a re-reading. Firstly, because its currency of plot twists and switcheroos is by definition debased when expected. Secondly, because the mild sloppiness that we have by now long learnt is part of Goldman's work, leads to unconvincing psychology and inconsistent quality of dialogue, verbal, and interior. Overall, however, *Magic* is a good, unusual, intriguing, and easy-rolling piece of work and was further confirmation that Goldman was now a guaranteed entertaining diversion for anybody facing a train journey, plane ride or night shift.

The month after the publication of *Magic*, came the opening of *Marathon Man*, whose credits state, "Screenplay by William Goldman from his novel." It was Goldman's first such accreditation. There would be three more like it over the following decade or so, and Goldman's insistence on not allowing other screenwriters to, as he saw it, traduce his work paid dividends: with the one exception of *Heat*, all were high-quality films that did justice to their source.

The *Marathon Man* movie, released on October 8, 1976, was actually set in motion before the parent book was published, the producers having been impressed by galleys. Snagging two-time Oscar nominee Dustin Hoffman for the lead role in this (as the movie posters put it) "thriller" was a coup but at the same time skirting risible: he was pushing forty. Although he is assisted by his diminutive stature and perennial youthfulness, Hoffman is amazingly convincing as a college-age naïf. Roy Scheider, with whom the entire world had just become familiar via *Jaws* (already on its way to creating a new blockbuster movie paradigm that Goldman would come to loathe), is well-cast as Scylla. William Devane—whose boyish, toothy, befringed visage was prevalent in the seventies—is good as Janey. Most impressive is Laurence Olivier. Who would have thought that a refined knight of the stage could inhabit so exquisitely grimly the character of an old Nazi brute?

The film makes changes to the story for a variety of reasons: stylization (when out running, Babe happens to see the automobile conflagration that takes the life of Szell) and simplification (some characters are changed or merged). A new ending—written by an uncredited Robert Towne—was devised at the insistence of Hoffman, who felt discomforted by Babe's sudden ruthlessness: Szell impales himself on his retractable knife after a tumble. (Elsa also avoids death at the hands of Babe.) Goldman's assessment of said ending as "Hollywood horseshit" (*Marathon Man* DVD bonus feature) is half-right. The rewriting means the sacrifice

of the pathos of Babe knowing that Szell killed his bother and the tension of him not knowing that he has a hidden weapon. However, the section (also not written by Goldman) where Babe says to Szell of the diamonds, "You can keep as many as you can swallow" is bleakly powerful stuff.

Other alterations seem to have been made because when faced with the unfamiliar (in a sense, unprecedented) task of revisiting his material, Goldman noticed flaws: he doesn't give away Elsa's secret early here; Scylla's preternatural talents, like being able to hide from an enemy in a small, darkened room while taunting him, are jettisoned; when Szell is wandering the diamond district, he, unlike in the book, is uncomfortably aware of security cameras. One change was made not by Goldman or Hoffman but by the producers nervous about preview audience repulsion: Scylla's demolition of the crew who murder the wretched Ape in the men's room was cut in an era when such screen violence might have been increasingly fashionable but was a fashion that alienated many.

The ending sees Babe, rather than being resigned to capture, walking free as a bird back through the park that has been shown as the site of his running practice.

The transition to film sometimes improves things as a matter of course. We can believe the all-reaching power of the Division because Goldman gets no chance in this medium to waffle about it. The threat of Szell's dentistry tools is all the more menacing because they can be seen whirring in our faces. In the set-piece chase scene, adroit incidental music by Michael Small adds to the atmosphere and tension.

Despite the toning down of the original violence, the *Marathon Man* movie continued Goldman's reinvention as a gritty, contemporary writer. The bloodshed, the bare backside of Hoffman, the bare breasts of Marthe Keller (Elsa) and the profanities ensured it was a certificate 'R' ('X' in the UK).

Did Goldman find it hard being objective adapting his own material? "It's all hard. Because you don't know what's going to work. I don't know. I can't answer the question. It's all tricky." Goldman did say to John Brady, "It's very hard, because one is not *ruthless* enough doing screenplays of your own novels." Considering that the original book is so dialogue-heavy as to almost resemble a film script, some might be surprised that Goldman made as many changes as he did for the movie version, but as he explained to Brady, "...there's only one scene in the novel that translates well to film and that's Szell in the diamond district. That's an exterior scene. All the rest of the book is interior and was extremely difficult to try and make play in terms of a movie."

In the process of adapting one of his own books, has Goldman ever concluded that it would have been more suited to the medium of film in the first place? "No," he says. "The forms are so different. One of them you can sprawl and go on forever and the other one has got time constraints."

Goldman says that this was one of the few of his movies whose filming he attended. "I don't go to the filming of much of anything. I don't like being around. I was around for a little bit of *Marathon Man* 'cause it's shot in New York, but if something doesn't shoot in New York, I don't really want to. If you've written the screenplay, all the drafts of the screenplay and all the meetings on the screenplay, you're so fucking sick of it. And it's boring being around a movie that's shooting."

7

A Bridge Too Far—released on June 15, 1977—is a movie based on the non-fiction book of the same name by Cornelius Ryan. This work told of the attempt in September 1944 to fulfill the audacious plan of British Field Marshall Montgomery to hasten the end of World War II by seizing a series of bridges in Holland, thus providing a clear route for an advance into Germany. Operation Market Garden would involve the biggest airborne operation in history, and it was to be prepared and executed within the space of seven days. The plan was abandoned with the loss of eight thousand men, which means that—highly unusually for Hollywood in the era—the war film based on the book is one that traced the arc of a defeat, and a spectacular one at that.

The ambitions of the film adaptation of *A Bridge Too Far* were almost as lofty as Montgomery's. It was the most expensive motion picture ever made up to that point. As such, it was probably inevitable that Goldman— by now unquestionably the major screenwriter of the seventies—would be offered the gig of adaptation by producer Joseph E. Levine. Nonetheless, his retention for this project was as peculiar as the deployment of the inexperienced Richard Attenborough as director. The film's orientation around logistics and explosions makes it utterly unlike anything else scripted by Goldman.

Despite the bang-bang stuff, *A Bridge Too Far* could be postulated as an anti-war movie, one of the first motion pictures to try to take the

glamour out of war. "Probably because Attenborough felt that and it was his baby," says Goldman. "Well, you can't be pro-war really. This was such a terrible experience for all those young men who got killed. It's a wonderful piece of material for a movie."

The film's introduction is awful. Compounding the laziness of an explanatory voiceover is the strange decision to make the voice female, foreign-accented and stilted. We're already being made irritated and bored. Things don't pick up much for a long time after that. Some wags dubbed the film *An Hour Too Long.* That putdown may sound too conveniently slick to be truthful, but much of the first sixty minutes certainly drags. Lengthy scenes in which plans are explained to officers via maps and aerial photographs might be novel and brave but are also as boring as a school lesson in a chilly lecture hall. Portraying Germans as human beings as valid as the Allies is also relatively new territory, but having to read sub-titles because the enemy are filmed in their native language only adds to the depressing feeling of being stuck in a classroom.

The work of Richard Attenborough—directing his third film—is rarely remarkable, and is sometimes positively clumsy. A scene where Staff Sergeant Eddie Dohun (James Caan) is driving a wounded comrade through woods mystifies the viewer when he parks his jeep in close proximity to Germans facing his way who incomprehensibly take an age to spot him. When Major General Roy Urquhart (Sean Connery) shoots a German through the window of a house, the enemy soldier takes forever—and multiple bullets—before he starts falling. One impressive sight Attenborough does conjure is the Allies filling the skies like aerial jellyfish upon their mass parachute drop.

Goldman's script is pedestrian verging on poor. When Dohun holds a gun to a doctor/superior officer's head until he agrees to examine his wounded friend and the doctor refuses to court martial him upon discovery that Dohun was right about his friend being alive—ostentatiously telling an MP to arrest him and then release him after ten seconds—it is an example of the way Goldman consistently manages herein to give real-life stories the flavor of all-American corn. He seems to imagine that he is consistently spurning Hollywood cliché, but what else are we to call the scene where General Frost gasps out an explanation for his mysterious trademark umbrella and then immediately dies? Whenever he strains for poignancy, Goldman comes up short. A scene where soldiers engage in negotiations with a reluctant Dutch woman about using her home for the treatment of the wounded can do nothing but provoke a "So what?" because another family's house had been matter-of-factly depicted being commandeered by the Allies for billeting purposes earlier. When the operation's officers decide to order a retreat without their mission accomplished, their conversation after all the bloodshed and sacrifice is ridiculously perfunctory.

Admittedly, these flaws could conceivably be the director's fault, but Goldman would seem to be responsible for one particular major flaw at least. In *Adventures in the Screen Trade,* he tells of how he decided that the best way to adapt Ryan's book was to remove the stories depicting the feats that led to the award of five Victoria Crosses, Britain's highest military honor for valor: they didn't fit in with his Calvary-Doesn't-Come-To-The-Rescue structure. There is no doubting that the script of *A Bridge Too Far* is a feat of engineering as incredible as the titular Arnhem Bridge itself, Goldman marshaling and intertwining facts for optimum pacing and contrast effect. An engineering feat, however, is all it is. One can't help but feel that spurning the human interest content inherent in such material as the VC stories is the primary reason that the finished film has no heart.

One of the movie's rare instances of either pathos or impressive photography comes right at the end when Arnhem residents who had provided shelter to the Allied soldiers and lost everything in the process are seen against a pink sun taking away their few possessions on a cart.

In *The Big Picture*, Goldman launched into an attack on *Saving Private Ryan*. Goldman's assessment of the 1998 Steven Spielberg war epic as being overrated and clumsily executed is interesting in light of the deep similarities between that picture and *A Bridge Too Far*: both are nearly three hours long; both are explorations of the ideas War is Hell, and The Enemy Are People Too; both feature a crucial sequence involving a raid mounted from water; and both contain a battle for a bridge. Only one is a powerful, mesmerizing piece of cinema—and it's not *A Bridge Too Far*.

142 • *William Goldman: The Reluctant Storyteller*

A *Bridge Too Far* is as antiquated a movie as *Marathon Man* was contemporary, and that's not a reference to the time period in which the respective movies are set. Far from being the radical break with war films it was portrayed as, *A Bridge Too Far* firmly adhered to the square-jawed, clean-cut archetype of the genre. The acknowledgment of the fact of battlefield failure aside, it was creakingly old-fashioned even for the seventies, turning its face from a new morally ambiguous paradigm for war movies created a full decade previously by *The Dirty Dozen* and continued by the likes of *Kelly's Heroes* in 1970. Moreover, whereas in *Saving Private Ryan*, we are put directly into the heart of battle—we almost feel that our ears are ringing from artillery explosions and that bullets are thudding into the bodies of men beside us—in *A Bridge Too Far*, we are treated to a crisp, clean vista in which nowhere is sweat, gore, blood, pain, misery or cacophony ever properly conveyed.

Despite this, the film did very good box office, partly because it was one of those pictures whose release was a huge event by default, partly because its realism about conflict was still novel enough to make less important the deficiencies in execution, partly because of an astonishingly stellar cast, which numbered not just Caan and Connery but Dirk Bogarde, Michael Caine, Edward Fox, Elliott Gould, Gene Hackman, Anthony Hopkins, Ryan O'Neal, Robert Redford, Denholm Elliott, Maximilian Schell, Laurence Olivier, and Liv Ullmann. A film that included all those luminaries was virtually guaranteed to attract their individual fan sets, collectively a large body of people. Redford is quite good as Major Julian Cook, even if he does look preposterously like a seventies California playboy: he decided that he would get neither a period-correct haircut (just as in *The Great Waldo Pepper*) or a military-correct one. Most impressive in the cast is Sean Connery, who is unflashily authoritative and decent. Or perhaps that stand-out accolade really belongs to Gene Hackman. That his Maj. Gen. Stanisław Sosabowski is so unpleasant that the viewer feels disinclined to admire either the character or the actor portraying him is a paradoxical triumph of Hackman's craft.

Some viewers found the film surreal in the way that famous cinematic faces pop up in such number, but Goldman seems to feel criticism on this score betrays naïveté about the industry. "The movie doesn't get made," he says of the alternative. "Remember, this was a movie that was paid for by the producer. It was not a studio. It was Mr. Levine's money and the only way Mr. Levine was ever going to make his money back was if he had enough stars in it because stars, at this period at least, were very valuable around the world. The closest thing we have today are the *Oceans* movies. That's an all-star cast. They don't do many of them anymore because stars are so expensive, but that was the kind of filmmaking that was. Mr. Levine needed those people."

Although the film is not one of those Goldman projects that have become iconic, the title phrase has. "I think we may be going a bridge too far" was uttered by one of the commanders before operations commenced and is included in Goldman's script, albeit in slightly different form and circumstances. "A bridge too far" has now entered the language to mean a task doomed to failure by over-extension.

To coincide with the release of *A Bridge Too Far*, Dell put out on July 1, 1977, a small paperback titled *William Goldman's Story of A Bridge Too Far*.

It is an example of a type of book now pretty much obsolete. The home consumption of films made possible by video cassettes, later DVDs, made redundant artifacts that offered merely an experience of the film by proxy. Prior to the 1990s, however, just about every major or middling cinema release had a 'tie-in'. They usually took the form of fiction (novelizations), but that option was hardly open for the tie-in to Joseph E. Levine's movie: it would be treading on the toes of Cornelius Ryan's original book, which had a novel-like narrative. Levine instead opted for something more akin to a souvenir, essentially a collection of photographs, albeit monochrome ones reproduced rather small because of the A-format. (The screenplay of *The Great Waldo Pepper* published by Dell in March 1975 had a similar heavily illustrated, B&W, A-format.) Goldman's contribution is actually relatively minimal—there is barely enough text to constitute a clutch of essays—but this inauspicious little volume transpired to be quite important in Goldman's career.

The book is divided into three parts. In part two, "A BRIDGE TOO FAR: The Story in Pictures," the captions that Goldman supplies to more than 150 sequential photographs from the film actually serve to clarify some of the sometimes confusing or overpowering details of the movie's plot (and, most valuably, without putting the reader through the ordeal of watching it again). Part three, "STARS AND HEROES," finds some of the movie's actors and some of the men they played telling Goldman their thoughts on the project and war in general. Their opinions and observations are interesting, and judiciously edited to flow smoothly in a way verbatim transcripts don't.

It is part one, though, which will be of most interest to the Goldman aficionado. In "Reflections on Filmmaking in General and A BRIDGE

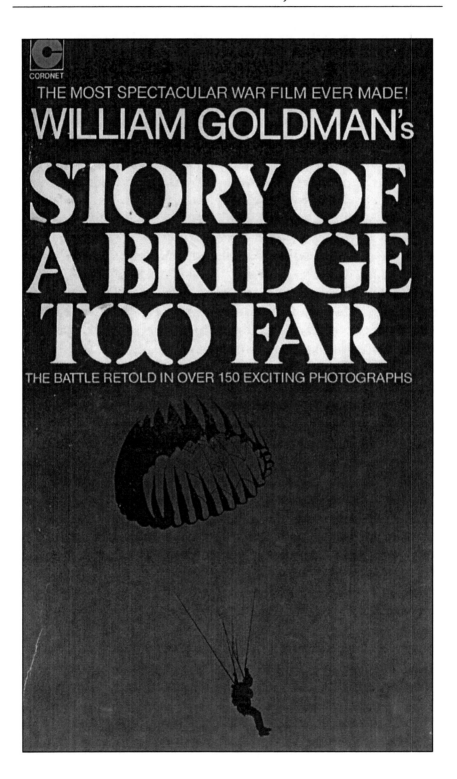

TOO FAR Very Particularly," he regales us with his opinions on filmmaking, screenwriting, directors (particularly Richard Attenborough) and Joseph E. Levine. He also provides behind-the-scenes revelations about the making of the film ranging from the technicalities of shooting a crucial passage that would have sent the movie millions of dollars over budget if not completed within a single day to Steve McQueen's mind-boggling conditions to appear that included Levine buying a house the actor owned, an escalating madness only brought to an end by Redford's signing-up, which meant there was no star part left for McQueen to play. Goldman's "Filmmaking in General" observations include status debunking ("…the director, more often than any of the [other creative staff], is first among equals. But no more than that") and technical insight ("Dialogue may be among the least of a screenwriter's contributions; it's certainly far less important than structure"). This is all delivered in a chatty, irreverent style full of sentences italicized for emphasis, narrative reversals and digressions. Several pages are spent on analysis of a scene from *Rocky*. One section is even laid out in movie script format. In other words, it all reads remarkably like a miniature precursor to his celebrated *Adventures in the Screen Trade*—in which, it should be noted, parts of this book are reproduced verbatim.

Its author no doubt considered *William Goldman's Story of a Bridge Too Far* a minor project. Explains Goldman, "Joseph E. Levine was very kind to me and I had a great experience on *A Bridge Too Far*. It was my first movie with Richard Attenborough and he's a marvelous human being. A lot of movies are shit, the experience is just terrible, and *Bridge* was wonderful and Mr. Levine wanted something to publicize the movie so I wrote that for him. It was just something like I've never done, but it was as a favor for Mr. Levine." Moreover, the book had a built-in limited shelf-life, probably going out of print quicker than anything else Goldman ever wrote.

However, the favor rendered Levine could be posited as a pivotal act in Goldman's career, for it seems unlikely that this book didn't later serve, at least partly, as a spur to him writing *Adventures in the Screen Trade*. The latter is not merely one of the key works in Goldman's canon, but important on other levels. It span off several other books. It also kept Goldman's reputation alive when his screenwriting career was in the doldrums.

8

That *Magic*—released on November 8, 1978—was Goldman's second movie adaptation of one of his books in the space of two years begs the question of whether, when he was writing the novel, he wasn't already thinking of how it might translate to the screen.

"Oh, never," he veritably splutters. "Good God, no. Never, ever, ever. No. It's, like, basically, 'Why did they buy this?' and 'Why didn't they buy that?' You never know what the hell they're thinking, so no, absolutely not. I never dreamt it was going to be a movie. I was thrilled that it was bought and I was thrilled we had those two performers."

That *Magic,* the movie, is significantly different to *Magic,* the novel, is evident right from the opening, which shows us Corky trying to fool his landlord Merlin, Jr. into believing that his open night performance was successful. This scene is not in the book: Merlin was dead by then. We then jump-cut to the point where the Postman is proudly showing a television executive his new client, a magician with an X-rated dummy. Apart from a brief, silent flashback, all of Corky's childhood scenes—the moving stuff about his fractured home life, the hilarious Charles Atlas course passage, the powerful sequence wherein Corky is forcibly immersed in gridiron lore—have been dispensed with. Also gone are the extracts from Fats's diaries and the unresolved teases that Corky might be a serial killer. None of these cuts are unwise. Some worked in the book, some didn't, but all would be inappropriate for, or unwieldy in, the taut motion picture aimed for here. Moreover, in a visual medium it would not have been possible to maintain the surprise of the fact that the diary was 'written' by a ventriloquist's dummy.

As with *Marathon Man*, revisiting his mate-rial seems to lead Goldman to spot and rectify faults in his original story. Unlike the book, he has Corky impress Peggy with tricks that are actually humanly possible. Most of the other improvements revolve around the incongrui-ties of the way Fats was previously portrayed. For instance, the apparent stabbing of Duke by Fats—Corky behind the curtain—may still be manufactured and exploitative of the audience but the fact of optics confers a logic to it being purveyed that never existed on the page. None-

theless, a moment remains where the writer forgets that Corky's belief in the sentient life of his dummy is illusory: it is still Fats, not Corky, who screamingly 'sees' the Postman when the latter turns up at the resort cabin. (Another scene in which Fats's eyes move after Corky has walked away was a mistake left in for reasons of whimsy.) In the interests of deepening the suspense, the Postman's body gets washed up on the shore of the lake into which Corky dumped him.

With the exigencies of celluloid causing the story to be stripped back to the issue of Corky's mental illness and his determination to not allow it to be exposed, *Magic* becomes Hitchcockian—a twist-laden depiction of a man becoming ever more paranoid and panic-stricken as he tries to outrun the consequences of his actions.

The chosen actors elevate the quality. The line "I think his old man was a limey" is inserted in a feeble attempt to explain away Anthony Hopkins's bad American accent, but otherwise he is good casting as Corky, both acting well and—in a skill somewhat less called-upon from thespians—throwing his voice ably. Most importantly, he looks the part: there is an edginess glinting behind his good looks. Ann-Margret is not the most obvious casting for a classic American high school dreamgirl like Peggy Ann Snow but this ceases to matter when the viewer registers her excellent acting chops and, in one scene, the beauty of her semi-naked body. Ed Lauter impresses as Duke, both visually—a balding man with an over-compensatory bushy beard is a perfect metaphor for an over-the-hill high school jock and equally past-it Lothario—and performance-wise, simmering with suspicion (except when Fats charms him). Also a commanding screen presence is, ahem, Fats. An oversize doll modeled on Hopkins but with bulbous features, it often looks menacing even in a doll's equivalent of repose. Best of all is Burgess Meredith as Ben Greene. His cigar-chewing, old-as-Methuselah, rich-as-Croesus Postman is exactly how you pictured the book's character.

Richard Attenborough's direction is as good as it was mediocre in *A Bridge Too Far*, him using every opportunity to employ atmospherically exaggerated shadows and making full use of the scenic Catskills landscapes. How peculiar it is that he couldn't make violence in a war movie believable but does so effortlessly here: Corky's assault on the Postman is genuinely distressing.

Magic garnered Goldman his second Best Motion Picture Edgar Award. It may or may not have been consolation to him for the fact that, with this movie, his screenwriting hot streak came to an end and he would never be quite the same force again.

He didn't lose his abilities, but more the opportunity to ply his trade. He signed an exclusive deal with Joseph E. Levine (who produced *Magic*, as well as *A Bridge Too Far*). Goldman wrote two scripts for Levine, but the producer declined to make them because of the escalating costs of shooting movies. Following the end of his deal with Levine, a further three movie scripts went unproduced. This had the effect of a decreased profile for Goldman, which in itself gave him a whiff of failure in success- and visibility-orientated Hollywood. His being resident in New York and unable (and unwilling) to network exacerbated that process. The upshot was that there was not a movie in the theatres credited as written by Goldman for nine years following the release of *Magic*. "The movies business is a total crapshoot," says Goldman again. "In the seventies, everything I wrote got made and then suddenly it stopped being made and I have no idea why. Maybe the screenplays were terrible, but the movie world is such a strange world and there's no logic to it."

It was a sad close to the 1970s for a man whose track record over the decade had been extraordinary. *Butch Cassidy and the Sundance Kid* may have come out in 1969 but achieved much of its success in the following decade, one with whose tone it perfectly chimed in its glibness and informality. From there came a sequence of seven movies, a remarkable four of which became part of the public consciousness. *The Hot Rock, The Great Waldo Pepper* and *Magic* were prosaic for being merely competent-to-good pieces of cinema. Everything else—good cinema or bad—was either possessed of water-cooler moments (the dentist drill sequence in *Marathon Man*) or was epoch-marking in its entirety (the controversial contribution to the feminist zeitgeist of *The Stepford Wives*; the clarification for the public of the dizzying facts and allegations over grave constitutional impropriety provided by *All the President's Men*; and the old-timey celebrity extravaganza and pride-stirring of *A Bridge Too Far*).

Goldman would be back as a screenwriter and, as a consequence of the success of his book *Adventures in the Screen Trade*, to some extent the public perception of him as a top practitioner in that field would even increase. However, upon his return he was transformed from a man possessed of the aura of go-to guy for any director or producer who wanted guaranteed script quality to a jobbing dramatist. That 'reduction' is of course relative: he was operating in one of the most highly paid and fulfilling professions in the world, was getting his work into both multiplexes and the public's collective mind and continued to command great respect amongst both the cineastes (widely recognized as an expert and canvassed for quotes) and the ordinary public (not many dinner parties are unimpressed when someone at the table reveals his profession to be Hollywood screenwriter). Yet, while there have been plenty of Goldman-scripted movies since 1978, and some of them are very good, not a single one has been classic, zeitgeist-encapsulating or arguably even possessed of water-cooler moments.

When it is put to him that the second half of his screenwriting career is not as impressive as the first, Goldman simply says, "I'm not going to argue with you. The whole success that I've had in the movie world is still surprising to me 'cause it's not where I was headed."

Magic marked the preamble to the point where Goldman skipped a beat as a screenwriter and went through that universal process of career deflation defined, perhaps vulgarly, as, "Every dog has its day."

PART IV

The Wilderness Years

1

November 12, 1978, saw the publication of Goldman's second piece of journalism. As with his first, it appeared in the *New York Times*, was a book review and was an opportunity for him to extol one of his literary heroes, in this case Irwin Shaw.

The clunky opening line of his appraisal of *Irwin Shaw Short Stories: Five Decades* was unpromising: "If a writer deserves to be judged by his best work—and he does—then 'Five Decades' is far and away the major book of Irwin Shaw's remarkable career." One would be hard-pressed to find any critic—even the type of fiend who reviews Broadway shows—of the opinion that an artist should ultimately be judged on his worst work.

In fact, the review overall is of a somewhat bumptious tone, suggesting that Goldman has become a little full of himself in the near-decade since his previous one. However, he isn't so full of himself as to not give over nearly a quarter of his 1,100-word appraisal to quotes from Shaw's work. He also makes some good points: "There is narrative interest in everything the man puts down … Coupled with the narrative gift is the ability to write with an ease and a clarity that only Fitzgerald had. There is never a wrong word, a phrase that makes you stop, reread, make sure you've gotten the sense right … the vast majority of these pieces do work, and the dozen or so that work best … are as fine as any stories written by anybody since Shaw entered the arena …" As with his Ross Macdonald review, Goldman stakes a claim for his man being superior to some of the people anointed great by the critics: "…if he is not held in higher esteem by the literary establishment it is because, for all his skill, he was not skillful enough to surmount the ultimate obstacle: popularity," he asserts, before launching a broadside against Hemingway whose more macho themes have, he says, been dated by wide dissemination of Freudian thinking, which had exposed them as "sexual panic." In contrast, Goldman says, "Irwin Shaw stays."

These persuasive points are slightly undermined by him insisting that the Shaw story 'Girls in Their Summer Dresses' is a classic (it's both slight and confusing) and an awkwardly-phrased ending in which he summarizes Shaw as a writer who "wants only to get us safely through the terrors of the night. He asks only that we sit quietly in the cave, and build the fire high to frighten the wild animals outside. And just listen…"

His non-fiction works indicate that Goldman has a facility for what might be broadly termed criticism. It would certainly have been interesting to see more of his appraisals of writers. However, he says, "I don't know that I ever want to write another review." Yet when asked if that is due to insecurity about his own credentials, he gives a confused answer that suggests that he does indeed rather hanker for the role of critic: "It might be that, and it might be that no one's ever asked me. There are some writers who are review-happy and I guess they get lots of requests."

In early 1979, Goldman returned to the true-life Western genre with which he had done so well with *Butch Cassidy and the Sundance Kid*. His subject this time was Tom Horn, a figure as mythic as the two outlaws whose careers he had essayed previously, although better-known than Butch and Sundance had been when he wrote his film on them.

Asked when he got the idea to tackle Horn's life, Goldman says, "Oh, I guess when I was researching the Butch Cassidy material. Tom Horn

was a fabulous figure in the Old West and, in that era when I was growing up, Westerns were a big part of everybody's life. In the thirties and forties it was one of the things they used to make along with musicals, which they don't make any more, and I just thought Tom Horn was a fabulous story."

Mr. Horn was a mini-series broadcast on the American CBS television network on February 1 and 3, 1979. Each episode lasted two hours including commercials, which in those days amounted to a cumulative total of around two-and-a-half hours screen time. "I didn't write for television," says Goldman. "I wrote it as a movie and it happened to get made on television. I don't remember why it came out as a television thing." His memory was clearer in the eighties when he was speaking to John Brady, whom he told, "...it got to Lorimar and somebody timed it, which I had never done, and it came out to be three hours and twenty minutes—which is why I think someone said, 'Wait a minute—that's a four-hour television movie.'"

That Goldman had nothing to do with the novelization released to tie in with the broadcast—D. R. Bensen penned *William Goldman's Mr. Horn*, just as he would *Butch & Sundance: The Early Days* the following year—isn't much of a surprise. What will be to many is Goldman's statement on the *Mr. Horn* mini-series, "I don't think I've ever seen it." He explains, "It was an unpleasant experience. It was a wonderful piece of material and then it got all fucked up with television and all that stuff."

It's difficult to imagine the iconic success of *Butch Cassidy* not playing some part in the motivations of the producers in giving *Mr. Horn* the green light (or at least difficult for anybody except Goldman, who says, "No, I don't think so at all" to the suggestion). Unfortunately, once the project transmuted into a TVmini-series, it was never destined to be another *Butch Cassidy*. Not only was it hamstrung by limited budgets, which denied it the grandeur of motion pictures, and a family-viewing orientation that militated against grit and realism, but it was additionally constrained by the nature of the medium at that juncture in history. In the seventies, American TV drama was a byword for blandness. This nuance-free era of US television precluded the playfulness and moral ambivalence common in the form today.

Tom Horn is defined here as a "Talkin' boy" (meaning he is adept at languages) and a "White Indian" (meaning he can scout like a Native American) by Al Sieber (Richard Widmark), who procures his services as his "assistant" in 1885, in the hunt for legendary outlaw Indian Geronimo. Sieber's additional description of Horn as having "no close friends, lots of enemies" seeks to mythologize him in the traditional manner of Westerns. However, it has to be said that Horn's preternatural abilities on which the show is predicated are never clearly delineated, and are even called into question. For instance, when an injured Sieber has to pull out of the hunt, he is worried that a mere rookie like Horn might not be able to manage.

Snagging David Carradine to play the title role was a pretty big deal: he was still fondly remembered for a vastly successful TV Western series with a unique twist: *Kung Fu*. In the first half of *Mr. Horn*, the long-maned Carradine is young and heroic-looking, and the floppy hat furnished by the costume department makes him look refreshingly different to the run-of-the-mill, Stetson-topped screen cowboy. That his good looks don't resemble existing photographs of the man he plays is probably as irrelevant as the fact that the series is alleged to take liberties with history: it can only be judged as a piece of drama. Unfortunately, it's on that score that it falls down, and for reasons that seem to be over and above the medium's general level of mediocrity.

Problems with incomprehensible motive and sloppy writing start at the point where Horn and Sieber meet cavalry lieutenant Henry Lawton (an excellent depiction of self-regard by Clay Tanner), who is being taken by supposedly turncoat Apaches to capture Geronimo. An appalled Sieber points out that the men concerned are two of Geronimo's closest friends—but then he and Horn join the cavalrymen in walking into this obvious ambush. Meanwhile, the story attached to Mickey Free—to whom Horn is intriguingly told to stick close because "he can't get killed"—is never explained.

Everything feels generic, particularly the battle scenes, which, despite plenty of noise from the ricochets of rifle shots, are bloodless and uninvolving. The sound of crickets chirping in a scene involving a post-coital mellow moment with love interest Ernestina Crawford (Karen Black) is suffocatingly predictable. Moreover, the pace is sometimes soporifically plodding. Yet throughout, the dialogue, direction and, especially, music seek to claim a sense of majesty.

After having being dismissed by the glory-seeking Lawton, Sieber and Horn are reinstated by him in the search for Geronimo. Sieber seems to be getting ready to apologize for his denouncement of the lieutenant when he embarrassedly says he has something to tell him. This turns out to be, "I meant every damned word I said," a reversal that might have worked in a Goldman novel but here just seems another ornery Western cliché.

Horn manages to persuade Geronimo—whose supporters are now reduced to a rump—to give himself up on the promise that he will be allowed to stay in Arizona. Angered enough by Lawton aiding General Nelson Miles in taking the glory for capturing Geronimo, Horn and Sieber are absolutely appalled when it is revealed that the cavalry is exiling the Apache and his supporters to Florida, alien swamp land to these desert-raised people.

The second half of the mini-series takes place in 1901 and is essentially a courtroom procedural. Horn comes to Cheyenne, Wyoming where, by coincidence, he books into a rooming house run by Ernestina. Horn is hired as a cattle detective by a local syndicate. They have misgivings about his dilettantism and alcoholism but are persuaded by a display of gun prowess (which is curious, because it leaves the viewer yawning).

Despite his intact weaponry abilities, the mustachioed and booted-and-suited Horn is a very different figure to the hirsute, casually-dressed kid of the first episode. The make-up department impressively make Carradine look balding. The actor does the rest with a well-travelled air.

With local judicial corruption putting rustlers beyond the law, Horn's employers are obliged to upgrade his role to bounty hunter. The syndicate pay him $700 per rustler, provisional on the absolute deniability of their involvement. Horn starts executing the baddies, although gives each a get-outta-town warning first. He leaves a rock beneath the head of each corpse as a trademark to guarantee his payment.

One Joe LeFlors rides into town. Handily for those not quick on the uptake, he sports a black hat. When Horn is accused of the murder of a young boy whose bullet-riddled corpse has been left with a rock under its head, LeFlors claims that Horn confessed the dirty deed to him. An aged Sieber makes a return appearance to assert on the witness stand that LeFlors is a professional prosecution witness in rambling and often irrelevant testimony that surely would not have been allowed even in an Old West that permitted the type of prosecution ambush tactics also depicted. This courtroom narrative is pretty much without tension for the considerable part of the audience who already know the fate of Horn, although adroit use of a courtroom artist's work-in-progress helps leaven the tedium.

Horn tries to escape but his plan founders on his inability to kill an innocent man barring his way. His execution scene has mild historical interest for its depiction of the water-draining 'Julian Gallows' technique and a small amount of pathos for the way it cuts between Horn, the distressed Ernestina and Horn's smug ex-employers.

Mr. Horn has been little seen since its inaugural transmission. Although it received a VHS release, it has subsequently disappeared into a media black hole courtesy of the absence of a DVD edition. In addition, it was rather eclipsed by the theatrical release *Tom Horn* only a year later, which tackled much the same subject but with the added benefit of superstar Steve McQueen playing the title role and, of course, a much larger budget. (This was a curious semi-echo of the fact that *Butch Cassidy* had been filmed at the same time as another movie dealing with the Hole in the Wall Gang. Pekinpah's *The Wild Bunch*—another of the names applied to the gang—appeared four months before *Butch Cassidy*, although in this case both projects were successful and acclaimed.)

However, it has to be said that the world has not been denied much. Whoever's fault it is, *Mr. Horn* is rather reminiscent of *Centennial*, another self-consciously epic but flat seventies TV Western drama, which finished its first run in the very month that *Mr. Horn* was aired.

Columbia's William Goldman Papers list the following Goldman teleplays, all apparently unproduced: *Cash and Carry* (written with Bruce Geller), *Hog in a Hot Sump Pump*, *Madonna and Child* (with James Goldman), *Something in Fur* (with David Shaber) and *The Green Cunt* (David Shaber). (Note that the last Shaber cowrite has a title that no broadcaster would contemplate even today.)

All the titles merely inspire bafflement in Goldman, who says, "None of these have any memory for me. They were not an important part of my life. If you have information that these things were television it's because we failed in getting them anyplace else … David was a friend of mine who was a lovely fellow and a wonderful writer but was having a tough time. I think I probably just gave him my name … Writing for television was never a lure for me. I never wanted to write for television." Any particular reason? "It came late, relatively speaking."

However, this man whose vintage means he was weaned on cinema and the stage is cognizant of the fact that television today seems to be assuming cinema's mantle of the location of the worthiest filmed drama. Goldman: "I don't watch much television but I know right now that movies have gotten really pretty sucky compared to their golden periods and that television's really gotten better and the long TV shows people I know just adore." So if he'd been born at a different point in history, he might have ended up writing for *Mad Men* or *Boardwalk Empire*? "Absolutely, if I'd been lucky."

2

At the time he started writing *Tinsel*—and a long time after he finished it—Goldman could have had no idea either that his golden days in Hollywood had ended or that he was about to experience a decade in the screenwriting wilderness. It is simply massive coincidence, then, that *Tinsel*—published on August 11, 1979—feels like his revenge on Hollywood. "I wanted

to write a Hollywood novel," says Goldman. "It's such a bizarre place and it's a nutty place. I don't like California and I don't go there very often."

Tinsel follows a group of characters whose objective is variously to star in, produce, direct or score the titular movie. *Tinsel* will be, in producer Julian Garvey's words, "the first great sex film ever made." Not, he insists, a picture where a cut to fireworks exploding is made at the crucial moment but where sex and sexual fantasy "are an integral decent crucial weave of the fabric of the film." He encapsulates its plot thus: "The movie shows the last hours of a sex symbol but that's not what it's about: it's about us, out here, and what this town does to women, how it raises them up and dashes them down, skins them and discards them because the truth is and we know it out here—there's always a new pair of tits on the horizon."

Although the screenplay is the product of his son-in-law Robert Schwab, Julian genuinely believes in its merits. The reader is less convinced. The problem is the innovations of which Goldman's characters speak as making the crucial difference between tawdriness and art: a flash-cut device will bring sexual fantasy into the day-to-day lives of the characters; a separate theme for each of the rooms in the lead character's house will turn the accompanying music into one of the film's characters. We are asked to accept these as not only credible ideas but neat ones, when both we and Goldman know the contemptuous response he would have received from a producer or director if he had inserted them in one of his screenplays.

Indeed, at times, it becomes hard to credit that Goldman is a very successful screenwriter steeped in the practices and methods of 'Tinseltown.' He certainly never convinces us that the characters would be prepared to disrupt their lives and risk wrecking their marriages to come aboard *Tinsel*.

The action opens with the daily activities of Dixie Kern, who we only realize is not the archetypal Hollywood housewife when a grocery delivery man asks for her autograph and it transpires she is relatively well-known under her maiden name of Crowder: she played the character Daisy Mae in a now cancelled TV show called *Dogpatch*. She has dispensed with her ambitions to revive her faltering acting career at the request of new husband Mel, a rich dentist beneath whose blunt personality resides a genuine love. The son of a failed, tragic starlet, Mel has a lifelong antipathy toward the movie industry.

Dixie and Mel have a game of tennis with a friend who, to Mel's displeasure, has invited Julian Garvey along. It turns out that Dixie has her own reason to be discomforted by Garvey's presence: they have slept together. Yet before this revelation we had seen her become outraged by her husband's suspicion that they might be old lovers. If Dixie could act that well, her acting career would never have gotten into the doldrums. This is symptomatic of the over-elaboration now afflicting Goldman's reversals. Another example occurs when Julian tells an aspiring actress to leave his office after she has sneaked in on a pretext of being a reporter of whose appointment his secretary had neglected to inform him. When she comes back and they have sex, the revelation that Julian can only get aroused by such role-playing is momentarily delightful in its upending of expectation, but the third eye quickly sours that delight: Julian's previous fury over the woman's subterfuge and his scathing comments about her thespian delusions were just too involved and intense. Julian's sex life is peculiar on another level. Involved in a marriage of convenience, he keeps records of his many conquests on three-by-five index cards.

Julian would like his son Noel to be *Tinsel*'s producer. That Noel has no movie experience is less important to him than the fact that he is, according to Julian, "Fragile … one of the permanent victims of the 1960s." He feels that getting Noel interested in movie work will give him the sense of purpose that a book he is preparing, which centers on the symbolism in the songs of The Beatles and Bob Dylan, will not. Goldman is not of the vintage to be a rock fan but he has done his research well enough to convince us of Noel's ardor in that direction. Even the peculiar fact that Noel is puzzled by why Bob Dylan characterizes the morning "as jingle jangle" in 'Mr. Tambourine Man' (surely it's because that's the sound a tambourine makes?) is hardly a fatal flaw when so many knowledgeable rock fans can't agree on the meaning of Dylan's lyrics. Meanwhile, while Goldman's subtext that all drug users are doomed is questionable, his flashbacks to the sixties exploits of Noel and his friends in Haight-Ashbury has a stoned verisimilitude. Only a soliloquy on the origins of the term "psychedelic" gives rise to a picture of the author earnestly consulting the authoritative works on a subject with which he is not comfortable.

Julian manages to convince Noel to come on board for a one-month trial by explaining he has testicular cancer. He fights back tears as he tells Noel of his illness, but we later learn that he has a secret negotiating ploy: weak lachrymal glands, which enable welling up at opportune moments in life. Whether Julian manipulated his son is something that is not really cleared up, not least because Goldman later reveals the cancer scare was real but a false alarm.

When the scare hit, Julian had taken stock of his life and realized he had under-achieved as a husband, lover, father and, worst, producer. "What he had given the world for three decades was shit … Over forty features, over twenty-five hits, and not one would tax the mentality of a ten-year-old." *Tinsel* is so important to him because he thinks it might be the project that will prevent a *Los Angeles Times* headline on his death amounting to, "JULIAN GARVEY, 58, FAILURE."

Julian gives his son a crash course in the job of producer, a transparent device by Goldman to convey to the reader the singular workings of Hollywood, and a reasonable one, even if he does seem to take inordinate pleasure in explaining the Machiavellian aspects: how to create mystique via prevarication, how to play one potential investor off against another, how to pretend to be withholding a project from a studio in order to make it desperate to invest. Some of it is plausible (if never palatable), but when, for instance, Julian says to Noel, "What just happened?" after a fleeting and apparently innocuous encounter with a studio head that transpires to have contained a welter of psychology and manipulation, it feels like we are in trash bestseller territory. The same applies to a successful prediction by Garvey of the exact time of day that a studio head will confront him about being apparently cut out of his hot project.

We are then introduced to Pig, real name Patsy Higgins. A drifter in life, she is a former Playmate of the Month, sometime jobbing small-time stage actress and currently "maybe the world's oldest groupie" on account of being shacked up with fading rock star Johnny Small. Goldman's non-rock background begins to betray him here. He has Small's second album as going platinum just months after his first album's release. He also has Johnny incorrectly term the Mamas and the Papas a "super-group."

In his most contrived shoehorning in of sports content yet, Goldman makes it so that Pig, before she became a passive and large-breasted blonde, was a complete tomboy, which is why she relaxes by flicking through *Who's Who in Baseball* and how, when she lost her virginity (shown in detail in flashback), she prevented her partner's early ejaculation with chitchat about the game's major players. An additional flashback story thread about her male, baseball-adept childhood friends is enjoyable enough but absolutely irrelevant to *Tinsel's* plot.

Schwab—set to be director as well as writer—is dispatched to persuade Johnny to write the music for *Tinsel*. Pig reads the script and finds she is desperate to play the lead (never actually named except as "the Monroe part" on account of it being loosely based on Marilyn). She is crushed and embarrassed when Schwab informs her that Raquel Welch has been cast.

Except Welch pulls out of the picture. The withdrawal of Welch means that Julian loses his financier, so at his wife's advice he opts to independently produce with his own money. The movie will cost an astronomical $3 million, but, as he has $20 million in the bank, this will not be a huge problem other than the fact that an unknown will have to be picked to play the lead. Which means every beautiful and well-endowed woman past a certain age wants to audition.

In a chapter written whimsically in screenplay format, Julian, Schwab and Noel discuss lead possibilities. Noel suggests Dixie Crowder, whose *Dogpatch* role had been a formative influence on his sexuality. Dixie is skeptical about the project. Noel gives her a pep talk about her being able to handle emotional stuff now that she has experienced a bit more of life since the *Dogpatch* days. As with a previous scene that showed he has quickly become adept at bullshitting studio heads, one wonders whether he would know all this sort of stuff less than a month into the producer's role. For her part, Dixie doubts that she will still be such a valuable trinket to Mel when her looks fade; success in the project is something that might make her valuable to him in a different way. Which doesn't stop her starting an affair with Noel.

Ginger Abraham is a raven-haired, violet-eyed beauty with a troubled past. Parts of her backstory are not only tedious but interchangeable with those of other characters. Nonetheless, a journey into her childhood anorexia nervosa is a twisting, turning, absorbing, and powerful thing, even if—like many other story threads in *Tinsel*—just a little too manipulative of the reader's emotions and just a little too eager to provide a ringside seat to heightened human malice, such as the campaign Ginger wages to make her mother fat. Her unwanted hothouse education at least provides Ginger a preternatural composure, which leads to a movie contract with a smitten (but rebuffed) Julian Garvey. Julian confiding in her his worries about Noel leads to a deft piece of dovetailing as Ginger tries to help via an explanation, so far withheld by Goldman, of how she got over her own illness.

Ginger's movie career was short and bitter, her becoming tabloid fodder on account of childhood anorexia photographs and a scandalous affair with a married actor who died in a car crash. The start of concluding section "Final Casting" finds her happily retired from acting and living in a lesbian relationship in the boondocks. When Julian turns up with the

Tinsel script, she provides a piece of distaff verisimilitude: "...fucking a man is not such a terrific thing in and of itself. Most men couldn't pass Intercourse One. They weigh a ton, they've got next to no control..." When Ginger reads the script Julian has left with her, she contacts her former agent about reviving her career.

Meanwhile, Pig is trying to contact Rickie Metzenbaum, a director who had first spotted the hidden depths of her acting abilities, to put in a good word for her with Julian. Her telephone tussles with Rickie's cold, vigilant secretary, and her stomach-churning anxiety as she waits for a return call that doesn't come while simultaneously trying to get some sun on the breasts she knows are her chief assets, are overdone but nonetheless suspenseful. She is humiliated when she catches up with Rickie in person ("...all your talent's in your tits, Pig").

Meanwhile, Dixie's marriage has been wrecked by Mel's discovery of her double betrayal with Noel and Hollywood. Their break-up is a compelling scene, a stoned Mel playing some early-hours tennis shots before leaving the matrimonial home, coldly indifferent to her pleadings. He says, "I realized, 'My God, she really thinks she's gonna be a star, it's not going away.'" Dixie thinks, "Goddam civilians, they never understood." Mel later hunts down Noel and beats him to a pulp, crying as he does.

Meanwhile, Rickie Metzenbaum has had an attack of conscience and put in a word for Pig. Unaware of this, Pig—ever insecure about the continued perkiness of her breasts—has decided to have them 'done.' An amusing scene follows in which she consults a plastic surgeon and is embarrassed to find her nipples hardening as he dispassionately, if slightly eccentrically, inspects them.

Meanwhile, Ginger has met Julian in a hotel room. Somewhere during their intercourse, the deal to award Ginger the lead role in *Tinsel* is wordlessly completed. Julian has decided to leave his wife for Ginger, although doesn't inform Ginger of this. It's a confusing and badly-written chapter. Not only does Ginger still seem unsure whether to take the part, making her cold decision to dispense with her female lover unconvincing, but there has been no reason established for Julian to imagine Ginger would want to be with him on a permanent romantic basis. Somewhat better-crafted is Julian's showdown with wife Estelle, who coldly knits (*Click-click. Stitch*) as she informs him that she has no intention of being humiliated by Hollywood gossip and that, should he feel inclined to argue the point of her refusing to grant a divorce, she has in her safe Xeroxes of all his three-by-five conquest cards, many of which detail encounters with women who went on to become wives of studio executives, studio heads, and network vice presidents: "Think how popular you'd be ... Oh, they'd love making deals with you ... how old will you be when they let you back inside... say good-bye to Miss Abraham for me ... I'm afraid, my sweet, that the rest of your days will be spent with none other than plain old dreary titless me." To the sound of more *Click-click. Stitch*, Julian spins and flees.

Pig wakes up in the middle of the night to find one of her treated breasts ballooning grotesquely, courtesy of a blood vessel having come untied. When she is lying recovering in hospital, she is gently dumped by Johnny, who says he is off to work with a female lyricist to ensure he gets the *Tinsel* gig, although Pig suspects that more than work is involved. She rings her agent and finds she can't even get summer stock work.

The downfall of the third *Tinsel* lead hopeful is only shown in pre-amble form. Ginger is sitting in her agent Harry's house asking him how much she should demand for appearing. Harry excuses himself to go to the kitchen where he says to his wife, "She doesn't know. It's all over town, the barbers in the Beverly Hills Hotel know, the hookers in Hollywood know ... I can't tell her. I won't be the one."

The news Harry can't bear to break is that, during his day-and-a-half disappearance, Julian Garvey conducted marathon negotiations, which resulted in Barbra Streisand signing on to play the lead in *Tinsel*. This of course has led to a major change of emphasis: "There will be no nudity anymore," Julian light-headedly explains to Estelle and Noel upon his re-appearance. "She will not be a fading sex star, she will be a fading singing star..." It's a great deal for him, Streisand being successful in so many fields and the music-as-star concept creating the possibility of vast sub-sidiary profits. When Noel brings up all the people his father has screwed by signing Streisand, Julian says, "Myself among others..." Although he has locked himself back into the gilded cage of a career that is only su-perficially fulfilling—there will now be nothing innovative about the pic-ture—there is one solace for Julian in the form of his son's salvation. As he says to Noel, "You've loved this month and you know it and you're good and you'll get better..."

The book ends with a quintessential Goldman switcheroo. Having been led to believe that a previous encounter between Mel and Dixie was the precursor to a reconciliation, the reader is presented with a sad little half-pager of a final chapter wherein the grocery delivery man who had asked for Mel's autograph at the beginning of the book is told by the maid in the Kerns' house that they will no longer be requiring his services: "Divorcing, get me. It was bad here and it's gonna get real bad."

Tinsel has writing that is sometimes possessed of contrived portentousness ("*Dogpatch* got cancelled," is given a line to itself like it's a world-shattering event) and sloppy phraseology ("Roger … hit a Porsche on the Pacific Coast Highway and died of fire"). However, the writing is generally adequate-to-good, as is the plot. Other aspects are more open to fault. For instance, the universally smart-alecky thought processes of most characters. It's hard to believe that such frequently philistine or dim people are possessed of interior dialogue as laconic and witty as, "Dixie thought that was pretty funny but she was the only one in the vicinity who did."

Much of the dialogue suffers from a similar problem. Sexually betrayed Ginger expels, "Upset? *Upset?* I just left hysteria far far behind…" Ginger's doctor says to her, "I've known you since womb time…" Despite this phony eloquence, we are also asked to believe that a studio head has never heard the word "encapsulate." Some of the dialogue is not just arch, it doesn't even make sense: "Use my own money. They'll probably drum me out of the producer's union. Strip me of my epaulettes and illiteracy card." As the fact of Julian using his own money to fund *Tinsel* is what is supposed to render him stupid, the illiteracy card part of his ostracization contradicts this: how would an illiterate have gotten rich? When a realistic piece of dialogue does come along, it makes one wish everything else were as unshowy: "I hate Rickie Metzenbaum. He doesn't speak to me hardly anymore." With crushing predictability for a Goldman work, the worst dialogue is that of children, in this case the main characters depicted in flashback. A thirteen-year-old says of an underwater masturbatory experiment: "It stayeth in a flabby state. Pud-pull as I would, I could not make the cursed thing obey me."

Inevitably names of celebrities—many of whom Goldman would have worked or socialized with—pepper the text. They are worked in reasonably well. The Hollywood anecdotes and legends deployed by characters to illustrate points strike one as being slightly less natural—but then again Goldman would know better than we whether this is simply what takes place in conversations in that self-absorbed town. Indisputably unrealistic, though, is Goldman's obsession with making so many characters remarkably similar in appearance to movie stars: Julian has the looks of Leslie Howard, Ginger is a ringer for Elizabeth Taylor, Mel uncannily resembles Robert Duvall…

Goldman slips in movie jargon without feeling the need for explanation (e.g., "double coverage") and the reader instantly picks up the meaning from the context. This makes all the more puzzling sections wherein he feels the need to take a more strenuous approach to clarifying aspects of the industry. Some of Goldman's revelations have inevitably become banal: the did-you-know unveiling of the fact that actresses use body doubles for nude scenes had a resonance in the late seventies, which it no longer possesses for a better-informed public.

Telling several people's stories requires length. At nearly 350 pages in its first edition, this is a substantial tome. Thankfully, Goldman has learnt some discipline since *Boys and Girls Together*, which a decade-and-a-half previously took twice as long to explore a cast of character's ambitions to participate in a dramatic production. Nonetheless, the text is denser for longer periods than we have seen in a Goldman book since *Boys and Girls Together*.

It is not, however, substantial in content. This is no *The Day of the Locust*, *What Makes Sammy Run* or *The Last Tycoon*. While ostensibly in their tradition of an insider's work that illuminates how the mainstream American movie industry operates and why those who are involved in it behave in the unusual ways they do, its methods mean that it has none of those novels' gravitas. The title of *Tinsel* is apt because Goldman has stepped down a grade with this book to produce something flashily exploitative of human foible. This is not the terrain of Nathaniel West, Budd Schulberg or F. Scott Fitzgerald but that of Peter Benchley or even Harold Robbins, although admittedly with a little more wit, depth, humanity, and writing finesse.

Despite all this and the fact that it's always a little too glib, manufactured and pleased with itself, *Tinsel* is an entertaining and fast-moving read. It's also, in its own quasi-spiteful way, a morality tale.

Hollywood, of course, is a wide target. "*Tinsel* is not the first novel that's ever been written about that material," Goldman semi-agrees. He adds, "It's a weird fucking place and it's crazier now. In other words if I was to write a Hollywood novel now, it would not be anything remotely like *Tinsel*. It's a different world out there now and not, I don't think, a very good one."

After *Tinsel*, there was a three-year gap before any further work of Goldman's reached the public, even though he was busy with ultimately stymied screenplays of *Grand Hotel* and *The Right Stuff*. However, it was at this juncture that he began to receive some serious critical attention.

Nineteen-seventy-nine saw Goldman achieve the accolade of being the subject of a book on his work. An entry in the long-running Twayne's United States Authors Series (no. 326, no less), found academic and author Richard Andersen analyzing Goldman's output thus far, with an emphasis on the books. Some—particularly the type of people who enjoy Goldman's style—might bristle at Andersen's overwrought intellectualizing ("Generally, his protagonists are fleeing a society that encroaches on their desire to lead their own lives, but their flights also include an abandonment of innocence and former values for the discovery of adult realities and the rebirth of new identities"). However, Andersen deserves credit for doing something that heavyweight critics have been reluctant to in acknowledging his subject's worth as a writer ("Goldman's works produce an unassailable argument against the novel-is-dead critics"). Moreover, the quotes from the interview Goldman granted Andersen in February 1976, speckled throughout his text, are fascinating and, from this end of Goldman's career, often eyebrow-raising.

It was Goldman's movie work that was given the spotlight in John Brady's book *The Craft of the Screenwriter*, published in 1981. Brady interviewed half a dozen of the most acclaimed screenwriters of recent years. Goldman was chosen as a subject alongside Paddy Chayefsky, Ernest Lehman, Paul Schrader, Neil Simon and Robert Towne because he was one of the elite group of writers who could demand a six-figure sum for his work.

The chapter on him contains probably the best insight into Goldman's work for motion pictures ever published outside of his own books on the movie business. In some respects, it even bests the likes of *Adventures in the Screen Trade*, because the interrogatives of a third party force Goldman to focus on matters that otherwise would not have occurred to him. Brady has also done his homework, questioning Goldman over variations in different drafts of his scripts. At ninety-seven pages in the book's paperback edition, the chapter is only eleven pages shy of Andersen's entire book on Goldman, and much of the latter is, of course, taken up by the author's appraisals of Goldman's output. In Brady's book, the editorializing is restricted to a brief chapter introduction (in Goldman's case, two pages), with the remainder given over to Q&A.

As with the Andersen book, some of the quotes are eye-opening in retrospect, but the entire interview is fascinating and revelatory *per se.* Goldman is speaking close enough to the events to have lucid recollections. One can also assume that part of the reason for the quality of his answers is the fact that he still very much viewed himself as a working screenwriter. Because the issues addressed mattered to him in the here-and-now, rather than being a slowly misting overhang of his past, he felt them worth chewing over at length and in depth.

The Goldman photographs used on the front and back covers of this book were taken by Brady in Goldman's office in the summer of 1981.

3

"Many puzzling observations have turned up in medicine, psychology, and anthropology. In all these areas, effects have been reported that would seem possibly to be the result of some sort of psychic causation, although at this stage it is impossible, of course, to say what the explanation is." This epigraph from *Control*—published on March 29, 1982—is a quote from *New World of the Mind* by J.B. Rhine. It indicates that we are about to enter Goldman's first and (with the exception of parts of *Brothers*) only science fiction novel.

The book is divided into three sections: 'Victims,' 'Trackers,' and 'Confrontations.' The 'Victims' section is rather reminiscent of the early stages of *Marathon Man* in presenting multiple and not obviously connected narratives. Although these narratives do eventually dovetail, they do so with a twist.

Edith Mazursky is the subject of the first chapter. It, like many other sections in the book, is dense with detail that feels not so much necessary but a means of filling pages. Her related love of shopping at Bloomingdale's and her friendship with a lesbian named Sally Levinson are germane, but banal, colloquial waffling like this serves no plot development: "The major reason Edith never expected trouble around 59th and Lex was simply this: Edith *never* expected trouble, period. And with good reason. She rarely experienced any."

In a flashback to Edith's childhood, we are told of her father, "...the last of the ninth came and went for Sol not much more than a year later, and though he tried like hell to force it into extra innings, it was no go..." Goldman's squeezing in of a sporting metaphor is not so smooth this time: Edith is not presented as an aficionado, so the mention of baseball floats free of logic. Her father's early death and mother's grief makes Edith terrified of the idea of loss of control and leads her to deliberately underachieve academically. Only later as a contented housewife does she pursue her artistic muse, although the brilliance of her "Blues" series is not acknowledged by the male critical art establishment.

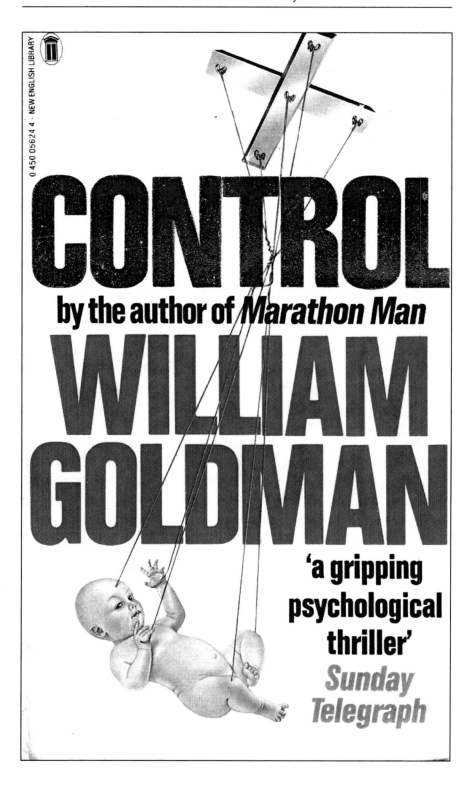

William "Billy Boy" Winslow—subject of the next chapter—is not most people's idea of a victim. We meet him as he is breaking out of prison. In addition to his colossal size and lack of conscience, he has an additional weapon in his nefarious activities, making "a fist of his right hand, a club of his arm..." This preamble to a huge punch is an awkward description by Goldman. Despite it being used repeatedly, one never quite fixes in one's mind the flow of the action it's meant to define. Also ungainly is the explanation of a yet further ability: "Billy Boy *sensed* things. He didn't know how, he didn't know why..." Yet while this supposedly prompts him to know when to, say, abandon a getaway car, we don't see any proof that this is the right decision. Billy Boy makes his way to New York City, where occur further examples of the tenuous grasp Goldman has on his character's psychic abilities.

For a reason that will eventually become evident, Goldman's usually sassy, contemporary tone is not in evidence in the chapters dealing with 'victims' Theo and Charlotte. Charlotte is the wife of businessman W. Nelson Stewart. Theodore Duncan is a stunted young man who is a tutor to the Stewarts' children. In his spare time, he is a Romantic poet and Charlotte's lover. Something else that will also become clear is that his and Charlotte's sex being rendered so explicitly would seem to be a double-bluff on the author's part.

"Haggerty's Kid" is a victim who is not seen. Instead we learn of the debt that the father of Frank Haggerty, Jr. owes to a psychiatrist named Ike Lorber for helping his troubled son back on the straight and narrow in a section that is not padding as such but not exactly necessary. When Lorber's son Eric shows a hankering to become a police officer, the psychiatrist asks Haggerty Sr. to return the debt and "show him the reality" and "scare the shit out of him." Nothing though—not the advice as sporting metaphor Haggerty gives him (it amounts to, sometimes you just have to let crimes go like sometimes you let basketball rebounds go) nor a savage beating meted out by some kids whose newsstand robbery he attempts to foil—can diminish Eric's law enforcement ambitions.

Eric's first section is reasonably realistic up to the point where he seeks out someone to help him in the art of night-fighting, lack of which skillset had led to his savage beating: "Randolph had been a fighter and in the merchant marine and he knew many things, how to hurt with your fingertips, how to banish, momentarily, pain, how to make an ally of darkness." Not only is this myth-making nonsense, but it's *Karate Kid*-level cartoonish.

When we return to Edith, it is with a strong chapter containing funny incident (she hails a cab and then decides to the cabbie's incredulous disgust that walking will do her good) and believable dialogue (she bumps into an ex-lover named Doyle who says, "Okay, fifteen years in thirty seconds, you wanna go first or me?")

Having reached the Big Apple, Billy Boy starts approaching fortune tellers to find out if he will be lucky in his criminal endeavors. Why he would need to do this when it has already been suggested he has abilities in that area himself seems a mystery, especially as we are informed that he also has the ability to spot if said fortune tellers are faking. The answer to the mystery is that it is a clumsy authorial device to bring Billy Boy to the attention of one Leo Trude, a man who works for a government agency researching psychic issues: a blind, black fortune teller called the Duchess tips off Trude about good candidates for his treatment in exchange for a fee. When the Duchess says to him, "You've been here before, don't deny it," and Billy Boy responds, "I don't like to talk about that," he reveals himself as the quintessentially good candidate.

Billy Boy mugs a woman near Bloomingdales. Goldman tries to make us believe that the passer-by who gets killed by him for screaming for help is Edith.

While Stewart plans a trip to Boston, Theo and Charlotte continue their affair. Theo presents her with three poems and demands she works out which, if any, he has written for her. Charlotte reads the poems, all reproduced. She enters into deep reasoning as she eliminates those she doesn't think are of Theo's hand. This is intense, involved, unhurried stuff and therefore very un-Goldman.

The "Victims" section ends with a chapter that for no apparent reason is the only one not named after a character. It finds Edith ebullient after rebuffing Doyle. She marches into Bloomingdales and decides what to buy, engaging in cheerful banter with a sales assistant. She then lifts her arms in the air, crashes them down on a glass cabinet and—still with a happy expression on her face—twists her wrists about until they are cut to ribbons.

The first chapter in the "Trackers" section sees Eric and Haggerty arrive at the scene of the woman murdered by Billy Boy near Bloomingdales. That's right: the cop who had been instructed to scare Eric out of his policing ambitions has, in the unlikeliest coincidence, ended up all these years later as his beat partner. They make their way to the office of the Assistant Medical Examiner, a fleetingly-seen character whose thoughts about his childhood opera ambitions and his resentment at being four years older than his superior are typical of the way Goldman's bit players are these days given unrealistically tortured back stories not relevant to the plot. Eric is struck by the revelation that the murderer used not a weapon but his hands to deliver the killer blow: the damage done implies they are huge. Phoning around yields the information of a prison break in which a man-mountain named Winslow was one of the escapees.

When Trude makes his way to the fortune teller in Times Square, he has to dodge people struck by his uncanny resemblance to Henry Kissinger. This has no more significance than Haggerty's love of the Broadway shows to which he naughtily gains entrance by flashing his badge or a beer fetish on the part of Eric. That Goldman is now transparently using physical or behavioral quirks as a substitute for personality is mildly risible, even if it leads to a quite funny scene in which Haggerty, with the aid of a cooperative waiter, tricks Eric into believing he can identify any beer's nationality by taste.

In the next chapter, there features a mysterious comment from Edith, who has miraculously survived her spectacular Bloomingdales suicide attempt. "...control..." she explains to her hospital visitor Sally Levinson. "Something was in my brain beside my brain ... All my carefully built-up defenses, gone." Goldman then hits us with a switcheroo to top the reversal involved in Edith's survival (or a triple one, considering we had been led to believe she had been killed by Billy Boy): she drowns herself in the East River that night.

The path of victims and trackers bisects for the first time when Billy Boy's massive frame is spotted in the street by Eric and Haggerty, who give chase. In a scene wherein Haggerty is mercilessly slaughtered by Billy Boy for fun, Goldman sabotages most of the pathos by depicting the two cops engaged in a dialogue about films as they pursue him into a building site. Eric is naturally blind with rage over his partner and mentor's death. He uses his expertise in night-fighting to even out the odds against his gigantic and psychopathic adversary. By the end of their tussle, Billy Boy is so exhausted that his old trick of making a fist of his right hand and a club of his arm has no effect on a Zen-like Eric. At which point Billy Boy—terrified at the fact that brute force has for the first time failed him—turns and flees. Eric catches him, disables him and drags him onto the street—whereupon he is astounded to be forcibly robbed of his quarry by a team led by a man who looks like Henry Kissinger.

The first chapter of "Confrontations" sees Trude 'regress' Billy Boy, not just to childhood but beyond: to inside the head of Theodore Duncan. We have been reading, without realizing it, parallel narratives—modern-day events juxtaposed with historical ones. In contrast to the commend-able cleverness involved in that, Goldman clunkily and unnecessarily rep-resents the longueurs of the lengthy regression process via the device of separating paragraphs with central columns of dots (something else that suspiciously resembles a stratagem for filling pages).

Meanwhile, Eric is devastated to be told by his superior officer Haig that he is being sent on gardening leave and that Haggerty will not re-ceive the public police funeral traditional for an officer who died on duty. Eric is appalled when Haig insinuates that Haggerty had been drinking. The combination of knowing Haig is not powerful enough to order all this and the bizarre kidnapping of his prisoner gets his mind racing with suspicion. (It doesn't occur to him to ask, though might to some readers, that if sinister forces are sufficiently in with the authorities to get a po-lice funeral cancelled, why couldn't they also get the police department to peacefully hand over their prisoner to him?)

We are introduced to Trude's chain of command. Beulah holds his project's purse strings and is given the preternatural insight and fast quips with which Goldman often imbues such powerful types. "Never shit a shitter, son," he booms at Kilgore, Trude's line manager, when the latter uses euphemism rather than admit how unpleasant is Trude. In a meeting with Trude designed to alert him to high-up misgivings about Billy Boy, Beulah threatens to close down his whole operation when Trude pomp-ously declines to explain why Billy Boy is so valuable a subject, where-upon Trude literally grovels to Beulah. Yet a few minutes later, Trude is without censure snapping at Beulah comments like, "Quit playing with that goddam toy and pay attention to me..." Such inconsistency makes these passages seem pointless, as does the way these spooks seem indis-tinguishable in their high-handed unpleasantness. However, they provide insight into Beulah's project. "Everyone has been here before, but people like Winslow remember it all," says Kilgore. "Trude is simply trying to put a use to reincarnation." Trude gives an example of that use: "What if we found someone today who could control someone who was around Stalin? What if Stalin was disposed of as a young man?" This raises the question for the reader of why Billy Boy has been stated as knowing not just what occurred in the distant past, but what happens in the future, an ability that seems unconnected with past lives.

Beulah demands an immediate demonstration of Billy Boy's ability. Trude agrees but explains it's complicated, stating that it's best if the two parties, although separated by decades or centuries, are in the same city and are an identical nationality and that the day and time are alike. Moreover, "Contact is most easily achieved during a crisis time … When we first reached Theo he was having a crucial sex act…" This explains for the reader why Theo had been seen having an epilepsy-like fit when his relationship with Charlotte was consummated.

When Trude makes a connection with a man in 1917, Beulah is effusive: "…we can kill Trotsky—we can zap the Russian revolution before it goes anywhere … this man, well, he's a national treasure…" However, such plans are complicated by a deranged Billy Boy attempting to escape. He is brought down with stun pellets, but his obvious unhappiness at being incarcerated and regressed presents a problem: success in regression is only achieved with willing subjects. Trude, however, realizes that fear might do the track, and—courtesy of a previous discussion with him—knows that Billy Boy is hysterically afraid of the only man who has shown himself undaunted by his physical power.

Meanwhile, that man has been putting together the pieces. Eric has been directed to the Duchess's home by one of his informants, whom he had told to keep an eye out for a giant. The Duchess is missing and her ferocious dog has been butchered in a worryingly expert manner. He uncovers notes written by her, which state "Rosa Gonzales was Edith Mazursky" and "William Winslow was Theodore Duncan." He visits the address the Duchess had written for Gonzales, who the building superintendent tells him was a young girl of approximately ten who had claimed to have visions and who had been killed in a hit-and-run within the last year. Eric is amazed that he hasn't heard of this incident. It is during Eric's continuing unofficial investigations that we—and Eric—learn that Edith Mazursky died not within the eighties framework of Eric's narrative but in 1960. Eric meets up with Sally Levinson, for whom her old friend's memory is still a haunting presence. Finally, Eric visits his own sister, who had followed their father into the psychology field. After we are provided the by now usual supporting character's convincing but irrelevant backstory and life state-of-play, she imparts the information that his growing suspicion of some government involvement in psychic activities may not be nonsense. Her offer of asking around for him, however, proves unnecessary: when he gets back to his apartment he finds the same party waiting for him as had snatched Billy Boy from his custody. Goldman clearly imagines that he is ratcheting up the drama by writing that Eric is struck with the conviction that either he or the Kissinger lookalike is going to die before dawn. In fact, such meaningless portentousness detracts from it.

Billy Boy tries to escape again but the sight of Eric blocking his way reduces him to a quivering wreck. When the switcheroo comes—the escape had been set up by Trude to scare Billy Boy into a state where Trude is seen as his savior and hence someone with whom to cooperate—it is of no surprise to the reader whatsoever: the whole thing read too glibly. In exchange for the help thus rendered, Eric has been promised the custody of Billy Boy when Trude has finished with him. Eric demands to know what happened to Edith Mazursky. "Mazursky was of no special interest to us," easily admits Trude of the dead woman. "She was simply the person the Gonzales child connected with, as Billy Boy connects with Duncan. We were just using her, to see what would happen…"

With the parallel narratives revealed, Goldman is free of the obligation to be circumspect about the time period in which the narratives of W. Nelson Stewart, his wife and his wife's lover are set. Accordingly, we are furnished with details about the astronomical number of crippled horses abandoned on the streets of New York every year and told that Theo finds differentiated shoes a preposterous indulgence of the rich ("Wasteful, it always seemed to him, having a shoe curved so that it would only go over your left foot, another that would only take the right").

Having discovered his wife's affair, Stewart is prepared to be reasonable about it. He will save her from the shame of divorce by pursuing a sham marriage in which he is permanently away on business—on condition that she gives up Theo. He responds to her resistance by informing her that Theo's love poem was actually written by Tennyson. When a summoned Theo panics and denies the plagiarism, Stewart sees red. Yet in the ensuing melee, it is his wife who pushes Stewart over a balcony—a reversal, because seeds were previously planted that were intended to make the reader think Theo had caused Stewart's death.

The enjoyably well-researched journey into the past continues in the next chapter where we find "Aleck" Bell wandering a just-completed Central Park, home to the resilient homeless who survived from the original hundreds of squatting families. The narrative flashes back and forth between here, a nursing home that hosts the broken widower of Edith Mazursky, the Stewart household where Theo aggressively insists to a police officer that he is responsible for the death of Stewart and the Fifth Avenue apartment of Sally Levinson, who is contemplating suicide by gun after having had bad memories dragged up by Eric.

As he strolls, Bell is thinking about his new invention and what uses it might have for the deaf, his fiancé being of that condition. When he hears

"Bell!" called, he uncertainly raises his hand and says "Here," unaware that the young man who races his way has been told to kill him. It is Theo. After having mysteriously been stricken by another fit, he had made his hand into a fist and his arm into a club and forcibly escaped the police officer. He has been told to kill Alexander Graham Bell simply as an experiment: if the telephone is credited to Elisha Gray—a man who by fluke patented the invention on the same day as Bell (a true fact)—it will prove to Trude and co. that they can change history. When one of the limbless war wounded who then proliferated in the park comes to Bell's aid, the regressed Billy Boy repeats the words Theo hears from the crippled man. The nationality of the language of this man puts the fear of God into Trude. His appalled comment, "The Russians are back there too" amusingly and perfectly summarizes American Cold War paranoia.

Billy Boy escapes, for real this time. Eric gives chase and the two have a protracted showdown along the length of a car jam in a snow-packed New York street. Billy Boy winds up dead. So too does Trude, whom Sally tracks down and uses the gun on to exact revenge for Edith.

Eric is wounded but, it is communicated to us by a retrospective voice, not fatally so. As he lies bleeding in the snow, he has a hallucination of a visit by Edith Mazursky, who proudly shows him her "Blues" and her children. It's not an ending deserving of the book as a whole, but it's well-written, surreal and sad.

Faults in addition to the plot inconsistencies include the fact that Haggerty, Sr.'s interior dialogue is absurdly over-articulate for a bull-necked cop ("an analyst of distinction on her own"). Billy Boy's interior monologues, meanwhile, are never consistently colloquial, and it doesn't seem much of a defense for Goldman that in truth he never particularly seems to be striving for such. Much of the internal dialogue overall has a peculiarly phony quality that has unfortunately become a Goldman hallmark recently, and would continue to be so over the course of his next few novels: "Sally knew a Moment when one was at hand"; "But no one denied he was certainly a presence"; "Edith was tempted to take a cab, it was that February bitter"; "…it would unbidden come"; "Attention must be paid." People neither talk nor think like this. Nor, come to that, do they write like this. There is, however, also plenty of good dialogue—specifically New Yorkese, e.g., "*I* was the one convinced him to expand into Manhattan. Give it a shot"; "Not tailor-made or like that?"

Before the parallel narratives denouement, Goldman works hard and fairly skillfully to not alert us to the fact that the Stewart/Charlotte/Theo sections are not occurring in the present day, even if he drops hints such as Theo's lack of resistance to "epidemics" and Stewart's old-fashioned patriarchal pompousness in explaining to his two sons why they don't deserve the treats they ask him to bring them back from Boston. In places, though, the author is either cheating or simply being sloppy. Would a lady in the nineteenth century think "...he was always quick to come..."? Would a gentleman say "Shit!" or "goddam" to a woman in that period, even if his lover? Nonetheless, these parts of *Control* constitute a breakthrough for Goldman because he has finally managed the trick of writing with a mind-set other than that of a contemporary American.

Control is a good, if never literary, read. However, it was cutting-edge. Although it would not usually be disguised in this manner, *Control*'s type of parallel storytelling was soon to become very fashionable: the eighties and nineties were littered with novels pulling that historical/contemporary trick for stylistic, anthropological or political purposes. In being in on this at the beginning, *Control* saw Billy Boy Goldman steal a march on far more heavyweight writers.

4

One of the quotes in Richard Andersen's book on Goldman that have become particularly interesting in retrospect was a statement that Goldman would cease writing screenplays when "...I cut my umbilical cord by writing my nonfiction book about Hollywood and become *persona non grata* in Southern California." However, as late as the turn of the eighties, Goldman wasn't seriously contemplating such a drastic step. He told John Brady in *The Craft of the Screenwriter*, "I think it would be suicide to try and write a nonfiction book about the movie business." Goldman cited all the theatre people who continued to refuse to speak to him because of what he'd written in *The Season* a decade previously.

That non-fiction work on Hollywood appeared on March 30, 1983, by which time Goldman had become *persona non grata* in Southern California for different reasons previously explored. Ross Claiborne recalls, "He seemed to run out of stream or what, and he became much more involved in Hollywood than writing fiction." There was an upside for Claiborne to Goldman's declining interest in prose: "I got Bill to write

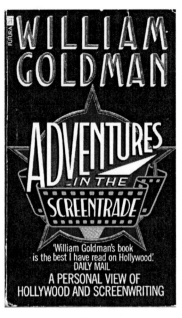

Adventures in the Screen Trade, which he dedicated to me, which was very sweet."

In fact, Adventures in the Screen Trade seems to have been written as a direct consequence of The Craft of the Screenwriter. Explains Brady, "The [Goldman chapter] was based upon hours of interviews and phone conversations with Bill in the late Seventies. On reflection, I think that his interview is the most honest in my book. Before the book was published, my agent sold magazine rights to Esquire for the interview with Bill, and the editors there removed my questions and merged Bill's answers, running the story as though it was written by William Goldman. My name was mentioned in the editor's intro to the piece, but there was no by-line 'By John Brady.' I was very annoyed.

"Of course, Bill's answers were great, and they had such narrative force, the parts held together. To Esquire's credit, the readers were served—so effectively, in fact, that I believe an editor at a publishing house got in touch with Bill and said, 'Hey, would you like to do a book about screenwriting?'" Said editor was presumably Claiborne.

Brady continues, "After Bill signed on to do the book, he called me, asking me if I wanted to serve as research assistant and interview him again, only this time all of the material would belong to him for his book-in-progress files. I was living in Cincinnati, Ohio, at the time, where I was editor-in-chief at Writer's Digest magazine. Bill offered to pay me generously, including expenses for travel to New York to spend time with him on the project. I said that I would be pleased to assist, but no payment would be necessary. He said he wanted to think that over. Then he called back and thanked me, saying he did not want to put me to the trouble of flying to New York, etc., so instead he would come to Cincinnati, which he did in early January 1982. There we sat in his hotel room and talked over a tape recorder for a couple of days, returning to many of the questions and answers that were part of our original interview for my book. At night Bill took me and my wife to the best restaurants, where we had great meals and wine (he really knows wine) and where my wife fell in love with him (only kidding, sorta). " The questions were devised by Brady. As to why Goldman didn't just write his book from memory, Brady offers, "I think he found me to be a good sounding board and that as a conversationalist I sparked him to respond, and to do follow-up on the spot. It was a conversation that became animated, not a Q-and-A style interview. When transcribed, this conversation would give him a first-draft document that he could then edit and rewrite and expand. "

In a sense, *Adventures in the Screen Trade* was a book that was the culmination of a life's work. It is sub-titled *A Personal View of Hollywood and Screenwriting* but the book is more than profession-related memoir: it's suffused with the passion and knowledge of a movie nut.

In *Adventures in the Screen Trade*, Goldman continues the writing style employed in *William Goldman's Story of A Bridge Too Far*. It is one that also featured in his other previous work of non-fiction but in less cartoon-like form—the timbre of *The Season* was relatively sober—and would characterize all his future non-fiction. An example:

> *This year's Quigley poll doesn't even list Stallone in the top twenty-five stars, much less the top ten. And what is his reward for this career in which he has demonstrated four times in his last five outings that there are no multitudes waiting out there to receive him?*
>
> *Ten—million—dollars.*
>
> *For that is the amount Stallone is being paid to write, direct, and star in Rocky III. Have you ever heard such madness? Can you believe that figure? Probably the largest amount of money ever paid a performer in the entire history of the civilized world. Isn't that insanity?*
>
> *Me, I think it's a steal.*

Conversational, exclamatory, reversal-packed, almost boggle-eyed— as well as often two things not in the above example: profane and studiedly self-deprecating—it is a style that for all its cartoonish qualities is immensely immediate, likeable, and readable. It also doesn't prohibit being very informative.

Sometimes this book's semi-colloquialism becomes an excuse for grammatical sloppiness. ("All you can be sure of is this: Does it 'work' or not?") There is also minor repetition to a degree that is a surprise even for someone we know to not be prone to revision. These, though, are small bumps in a very smooth-flowing journey.

In Part One—"Hollywood Realities"—Goldman tells us his accumulated wisdom on the movie industry, various players in it and films they have made. Goldman has done some research, such as his half-decade lists of the highest-grossing movie stars. Additionally, he interviewed studio executives, producers, directors, and stars, not so much to quote them as to acquire an insight into those parts of the movie industry to which neither a screenwriter nor a simple cinemagoer is normally privy. Much of the time, though, he employs personal anecdote and knowledge.

His analysis is not without flaw. "There's no doubt in my mind that *E.T.* will win" he asserts of the 1983 Best Picture Academy Award, which in fact went to *Gandhi*. Some of his observations now seem banal: it seems unlikely that there are many people left who don't know that studios refuse to read unsolicited original scripts from newcomers in case they're sued for plagiarism, even if, in fairness, that banality stems from the fact that there is a lot more writing about the movie industry these days, partly because of this book. Some of the films he discusses—such as *The Verdict*—were hot issues at the time but require a blowing away of the cobwebs from one's memory to recall today. However, it's only when Goldman steps outside of his comfort zone (clueless comments on rock music where Billy Joel is described as a purveyor of "bubble-gum songs" and "teenyboppers" are cited as quintessential albums, as opposed to singles, buyers) that we get the impression of anything other than an expert.

He gives us a flavor of the sometimes insane machinations that go on in Tinseltown. For example, the way a small picture that could have been a minor success was doomed when Barbra Streisand expressed a desire to be the female lead: the combination of her salary and the public's proven lack of interest in seeing her in such a dowdy role all but guaranteed failure, yet that knowledge couldn't stop the juggernaut of disaster, because all the parties cleaved to a formula that stated that the presence of such a star made the picture important and the expense of her salary ensured the studio would get properly behind the film to protect its investment.

In the section on Directors, Goldman symbolically restricts his comments to half a page, one part of which is, "There is not one whose 'philosophy' or 'world view' remotely interests me. The total amount of what they have to 'say' cannot cover the bottom of even a small teacup." A noteworthy comment to be sure, but it's the section on Studio Executives in which he proffers a line that has become famous. Julian Garvey in *Tinsel* has a philosophy about successful pictures: "Nobody knows what will work." (Goldman is quoted saying the exact same thing to John Brady in

The Craft of the Screenwriter.) Goldman has now reworked that into (the actually less eloquent), "NOBODY KNOWS ANYTHING" (capitalization his). As a consequence of the persuasiveness of the case he outlines, rare is the article on Goldman since that doesn't repeat this line. Goldman elucidates, "Not one person in the entire motion picture field *knows* for a certainty what's going to work. Every time out it's a guess—and, if you're lucky, an educated one." He gives examples of sure-fire hits that never did business, movies that shouldn't logically have succeeded but did (only to have their success dismissed by execs as a "nonrecurring phenomenon") and demonstrates how transient is the longevity of once world-bestriding icons.

Part Two—"Adventures"—finds Goldman recalling his screenwriting work on various movies, some produced, some not produced and some produced but with his screenplay rewritten either moderately or substantially. Disclosures come thick and fast, with the Nanette Newman *Stepford Wives* episode not being the half of it. He includes pages from different drafts of the screenplay of *Harper*, which reveal that the celebrated credit sequence in which the audience warms to the protagonist because of the pitifulness of his life was pure serendipity. After receiving a phone call demanding padding material, he dashed off pages of silent action whereby Harper wakes up alone in his scuzzy office-cum-apartment and realizes that if he wants his morning coffee he is going to have to fish yesterday's filter out of his garbage pail. Goldman confides that Dustin Hoffman stood arguing for hours with director John Schlesinger on the set of *Marathon Man* about whether his character would reach for a torch; Goldman felt he was worried about looking chicken. Then there is the interesting disclosure that Robert Redford pulled out of a planned movie version of *The Thing of It Is...* because "his fans" wouldn't accept him as the "kind of weak" Amos McCracken. Caustically notes Goldman—who was acquainted with Redford back when the actor was nobody—"I don't know what happens to people when it happens, but it sure happens fast." But then he has special cause to be angry with Redford, who he accuses of a "gutless betrayal" in a chapter on *All The President's Men,* wherein he recalls that the producer-star allowed a competing script cowritten by Carl Bernstein to be considered after Goldman had been slaving over his screenplay for many months. The most eyebrow-raising of the behavior Goldman relates is the incident where he was assured by agent David Begelman that Stanley Donen, his preferred director for the ultimately never-made film of *The Thing of It Is...*, was professionally finished due to a nervous breakdown—only to discover much later that there had been no breakdown and that the agent hadn't wanted the director on the project because he wasn't his client.

That the chapter on *A Bridge Too Far*, which appears in this section, is comprised almost completely of material that appeared in *William Goldman's Story of A Bridge Too Far* only serves to reinforce the impression that that earlier book served as an unconscious maquette for this one.

The book is substantial: 418 pages in its first hardcover printing. (A later version of *Adventures in the Screen Trade* was expanded to include the full script of *Butch Cassidy and the Sundance Kid.*) It could easily, therefore, have lost part three—"Da Vinci"—and this would have been a wise move as it, unfortunately, serves to undermine much of the confidence Goldman has instilled in us in the first two parts about his movie-making-related judgment. Goldman decides to show us how a work is adapted for the screen, a reasonable idea were it not for the fact of the 1960 short story he utilizes for this purpose. That 'Da Vinci' is mediocre is less important than the fact that its subject could hardly be less cinematic. A barber who is able to dispense men haircuts that literally make people gasp is a tenuous enough concept on the page but one that would implode in a visual medium. Goldman presents us the story as it originally appeared in *New World Writing*, then his thoughts on what would need to be jettisoned and amended in a film version, then his rewrite of the story in screenplay format. This is merely tedious so far, but he then ratchets up the situation to a toe-curling level by asking top figures from the movie industry—a designer, a cinematographer, an editor, a composer, and a director—to give their thoughts on how they would apply their talents to his script. Although their revelations about what their jobs consist of are interesting, their minute dissection of such a worthless artifact becomes ever more risible. As does their circumspection. Goldman states, "Of the *Da Vinci* interviews, [George Roy] Hill was alone in much of what he felt." Which is Goldman's way of saying that the director was the only one with the balls to tell him that 'Da Vinci' was a. a dog and b. unfilmable.

Just as in *The Season* Goldman made several gloomy predictions about Broadway's future that have been disproven, so to some extent he inaccurately tolls the bells of doom for cinema here. In the context of falling attendances and the wake of the colossal failures of *Heaven's Gate*, *Raise the Titanic!* and *Honky Tonk Freeway*, he states, "This book was begun at the greatest time of panic and despair in modern Hollywood history…" He does offer salvation, but his claim that it will take the form of cinema-savvy "young talent" seems less prediction than wishful think-ing and well-meaning posturing. Cinema was in fact saved by affordable pre-recorded video cassettes serving to massively increase the shelf-life of motion pictures, then bonus-packed DVDs, then new forms of dis-semination. There was no way he could have predicted all of that at a time when video versions of movies for home use retailed at around $80 and DVDs, cable and internet streaming had yet to be invented, but these phe-nomena do fall into the bracket of technical advances like CinemaScope, which he states had always saved the motion picture business before.

Adventures in the Screen Trade was a bestseller and became a hardy perennial. Ross Claiborne says he was not surprised by this: "I had great confidence in that. It's very instructive as well as being entertaining."

The book additionally had a peculiar effect on Goldman's aura. That it appeared when Goldman's Hollywood stock was in roughly the middle of an almost decade-long trough is unremarked on by (indeed, unbe-knownst to) many. So well-written, insightful and revelatory is it that it caused Goldman to be unofficially anointed World's Greatest Expert on Screenwriting. Over the next few years, he would become the go-to guy for any journalist who wanted a quote on the film industry in general or screenwriting in particular. When he did make his screenwriting come-back in 1987, he was often to be found pronouncing in print on the craft, clearly at the interviewer's prompting.

The book had another peculiar effect: William Goldman the novelist began to be forgotten. Including by him. That there would be only three more Goldman novels seems in retrospect related to the way he embraced his new status as Screenwriting Expert (which should more properly have been Screenwriting Expert Whose Golden Days Are Behind Him). In the absence of any idea on the part of Goldman himself why he abandoned the novel form, perhaps it might be suggested by an outside party that on some level the success of *Adventures in the Screen Trade* and the status it gave him made Goldman begin to think of himself for the first time as pri-marily a screenwriter, and that this is something he has never shaken off.

How many times has Goldman seen quoted his line "Nobody knows anything"? "Oh, endlessly … I mean, God knows I don't, and I know you don't, and nobody in the picture business knows what's going to work or what isn't going to work. It's an insane world. If you get a book by John Grisham it's going to sell 'x' trillion copies because there's a certain faith-fulness to the book audience, but there's no faithfulness to the movie au-dience. You can pay a fortune for Brad Pitt, who's a big star and a wonderful actor, but nobody went to see the [*Assassination of*] *Jesse James* movie. It's a totally weird world out there and there's no logic to it."

But isn't that phrase just glib? If an actor with box office appeal is given a good script and a good director, there is surely a more-than-average chance that the relevant project will reap dividends? "No. There's no logic to it. I promise you, there is no fucking logic to what movies are going to be commercial and what movies are not. The big hit movie of the last couple of months is a movie called *Juno*. Nobody had the least idea that *Juno* was going to be a tremendous money-maker. *Juno* was a gigantic success, but *No Country for Old Men* isn't. You can just go down the list of what's playing and they don't know remotely what's going to do business. If you're a studio executive and you put your money in a movie that's a flop, that nobody goes to see and it's expensive, you're probably going to get fired. They don't want you around. It's a huge deal."

Presumably, though, when he is writing a movie, he himself has some kind of faith in the project in order to be motivated to write it? "No, no, no. I have no idea. It's not my problem: is a movie going to be a commercial success? What I want to try and work right is something that moves me because—basically this sounds like I'm being a virgin—I've only done movies that I've wanted to do and the reason you want to do them is something in the source material touches you and you want whatever that was to get into the screenplay, etc. But then it's not my problem. The producer then has the huge problem of taking my script and trying to get someone to do it and that's horrible, that's something I would rather die than try and do … We live in such a crazy world now. I was talking to a movie executive the other week and he was saying that they would make low-budget movies—he meant movies less than twenty million dollars, which is inconceivable to me but that's a low-budget movie today—and they would make movies for more than seventy, because that might be a gigantic special effects movie, but they didn't want to make movies in between. Now that's total horseshit."

When he was writing *Adventures in the Screen Trade* did he worry that he might have to meet again at some point some of the people about whom he was so scathing? "No, I didn't care," says Goldman. "They were big stars and anything I wrote wasn't going to deter their career."

5

"That was the other book like *No Way to Treat a Lady*," says Goldman, by which he means that *The Silent Gondoliers*, published in October 1983, was the other novel in his career whose idea plopped fully-formed into his consciousness.

He explains, "I was in Venice with my then-wife and we were on one of the water buses, Vaporettos, and a bunch of gondoliers came rowing down the canal and they were quiet. I suddenly turned to Ilene and I said, 'I know why the gondoliers don't sing' and we got off the bus immediately and I went running back to the hotel. I wrote the story down in about five minutes on a piece of paper."

Goldman decided to make this story another fable from the pen of S. Morgenstern. He had gone to the trouble of not printing his usual photograph with his wife and daughters on the jacket of *The Princess Bride* so as not to give away the fact that the contents (in which, it will be remembered, he has a son) were fiction. By now, it was fairly open knowledge that *The Princess Bride* had not really been his distillation of an actual olden times tale. The only pretense Goldman maintained now, therefore, was a playful one, with the book carrying a preface in the form of a letter from Morgenstern to publishers Del Ray informing them that he was not deceased as had been reported by Goldman in *The Princess Bride*.

In the tradition of fables, *The Silent Gondoliers* proposes to provide an explanation for a puzzling aspect of life. In this case, a reason for the fact that the gondoliers of Venice no longer sing for their clients as they did in days of yore. It all goes back, Morgenstern/Goldman tell us, to a man named Luigi. A superb gondolier, Luigi is even able to tackle the hairs-breadth bend of SPLAT Corner with ease and to silence the scorn of his tartar of a gondolier coach John the Bastard with his natural facility with a boat. However, after graduating from gondolier school and picking up his first fare, Luigi realizes that none of his schooling is going to allow him to ply his trade: he is tone deaf. His singing is not just bad, it is objectionable. Clients complain and demand to be let off his boat. People living in homes lining his route pelt him with vegetables.

Luigi is forced to abandon his dream of being a professional gondolier and to take a job as a dishwasher in an alehouse frequented by gondoliers. He maintains a brave, cheerful face but the depth of his devastation is revealed by the fact that at night he takes out his boat and sings to the vast open spaces of the Adriatic Sea. After ten years of this, Luigi goes

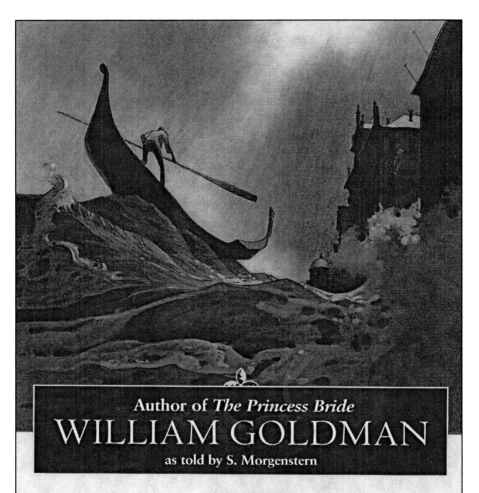

Author of *The Princess Bride*

WILLIAM GOLDMAN

as told by S. Morgenstern

THE
SILENT
GONDOLIERS

"This inventive, offbeat fable has a touch of magic about it."
— *Los Angeles Times*

off on a quest to secure a voice coach, but the coaches are so appalled by his voice that they pay him to go away. After unwillingly amassing quite a tidy sum this way, Luigi finally finds someone prepared to coach him. Bolstered by new knowledge about how to use his diaphragm to project his voice and to never allow himself to get nervous because of the negative effect it has on the singing muscles, Luigi returns to Venice to resume his career as a gondolier. However, his first attempt at singing for his clients is not the triumphant homecoming he imagined it would be: it causes people to literally fall ill. His singing coach had been deaf and, while he had instructed him in the proper techniques, had not been able to hear the result. With Luigi's old job of dishwater at the Gondoliers' Tavern now taken, he becomes the assistant dishwasher.

One terrible day, a meteorological catastrophe hits Venice. The Killer Storm—as it comes to be called—causes water levels to rise to undreamt-of levels and turns the normally placid waterways of the city into a foaming inferno. When the Church Of Souls of Those Who Died for the Sea—which resides beside the Gondoliers' Tavern—catches fire, the top gondoliers can't muster the bravery to ride to the firehouse in order to raise the alarm. (Telephone lines are down.) Without telling anyone, Luigi take his gondolier out. In doing so, he learns to do something that will later inspire the invention of a whole sport: shift his weight and position on the gondolier in order to maintain his balance, just like a surfboarder. Luigi makes his way to the firehouse, successfully raises the alarm and thus causes the Church to be saved. He is however not around to be thanked: realizing that nobody can hear and therefore object to his singing in this maelstrom, he is riding Venice's Grand Canal vocalizing at the top of his lungs, thereby fulfilling his lifelong dream.

After this, Luigi's gondolier friends—who had always adored this loveable fellow despite his failings as a singer—cannot allow him to return to the humiliating position of assistant dishwasher, or even head dishwasher, at the Gondolier's Tavern. From here on, every request for a song by a passenger on Venice's canals is met with an unbearable barrage of noise as the gondoliers sing deliberately badly. Objections are responded to with a show of guilelessness. Soon, tourists begin ceasing to request songs and instead the modern tradition of accordion accompaniment is inaugurated. Luigi is now free to return to the profession he loves.

The Silent Gondoliers is by far the shortest of Goldman's adult fiction works, 110 pages in its first hardcover edition, which count includes more than two-dozen illustrations (most full-page, some double-page) by Paul Giovanopoulos. Too short even to justify the term novella it may be, but this immediately ensures it is a vast improvement on its sort-of predecessor: unlike *The Princess Bride*, its whimsical tone doesn't get the opportunity to drag. A fable written in a wiseacre style may be destined to be nothing more than lightweight, but *The Silent Gondoliers* is also a sweet and good-natured story, rendered in a sprightly and amusing way. It's additionally another left-field entry in an already impressively varied curriculum vitae. Sales, though, seem not to have been impressive: the book took eighteen years to graduate from hardcover to paperback.

6

The Color of Light, published on April 23, 1984, is Goldman's most literary-minded (if not most literary) novel. It also sees him pull raw material from deep within his soul for possibly the very first time.

Just as *Tinsel* explored the traditions and fascination of the film industry, so *The Color of Light* focuses through the story of Charley 'Chub' Fuller on why and how people become writers and what happens to them when they do. One might imagine this to be a fundamentally less interesting proposition than the glamour-enveloped world of movie-making and that a writer's interior, sedentary regimen in no way lends itself to drama. However, the book's narrative is dynamic enough that one doesn't have to be a writer or would-be writer to find it absorbing.

Not the least of the reasons for the dramatic depth of this work is that it sees Goldman properly mining the terrible childhood he was too inhibited to as a young man. In fact, in some ways this book is Goldman's second pass at *The Temple of Gold*, with the fairly stable background of the protagonist in that pseudo-autobiographical work replaced by something closely resembling the very young Goldman's wretched domestic situation in a narrative that is in large part genuinely autobiographical. It features an alcoholic father who feels like a failure and ultimately commits suicide and a mother whose spitefulness towards her son is based on her preference for his older brother. The deeply personal vein is continued in the form of Chub's schooling at Oberlin College, references to a fondly remembered grade school teacher named Miss Roginsky and the protagonist's literary activity, which takes in a love of *Mixed Company* by

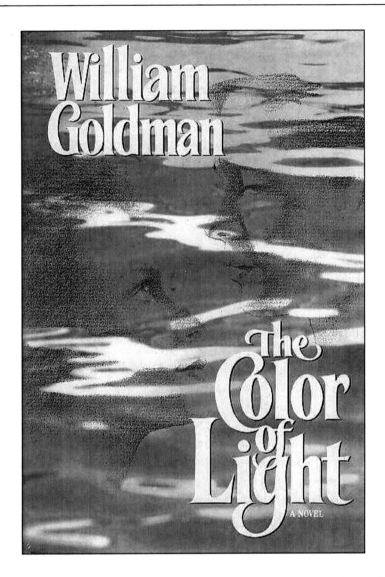

Irwin Shaw and, after initial publishing success, a writer's block similar to Goldman's own paralysis during the gestation of *Boys and Girls Together*. Even his protagonist's rare strain of pneumonia resembles the condition by which Goldman was afflicted in the mid-seventies.

The book is seen entirely through the eyes of Chub (the handle a resi-due of a childhood nickname of 'Chubby-Cheeks'). The protagonist's vin-tage is not overtly stated until past page 100, when we are told that Chub was "born with the half century." The narrative starts with twenty-year-old Chub walking on the campus of Oberlin. There, he is astonished to see B.J. Peacock—the girl of his dreams but long engaged to Chub's friend

Del—crying. Chub knows immediately that the couple's hope of going to the same college has been dashed by the selection processes. Only this is reversal-heavy Goldman-land: they have both gotten into Yale and are still together.

Details of Chub's sad childhood are fed out slowly by various devices, the main one being his writing. The fight between B.J. and Del provokes in Chub a traumatic memory. Denied sleep by it, Chub gets out of bed and puts a piece of scratch paper into his Olympia typewriter. Chub had "at least since the start of high school, held tight the secret fancy of some-day being a writer. And he had written—fragments, little ditzy stories…." He now begins banging out notes to try to make sense of the memory, which revolves around his parents. The fact that he always called them Michael and Gretchen rather than "dad" and "mom" gives a flavor of the extent of the dysfunction of their household.

The memory takes place at the home of his mother's parents, where Chub is frolicking in the house's swimming pool. Ducking under the wa-ter, "…he opened his eyes as he began to surface and was amazed at how the world altered—sizes, shapes, the color of light—everything changed when you came up from under." Everybody is overjoyed as Chub pro-ceeds to learn how to swim. Except he realizes that his parents are having a furious argument and the only way he can blot out the terrible things being said is to duck under again. It is the first of many arguments his parents are to have in his presence.

Despite his writing ambitions, Chub doesn't have the expected liter-ary heroes. Although there are numerous references that demonstrate he is familiar with the works of all the highbrow authors one would expect him to be, we are told "…he loved Ross Macdonald more than any American now writing, except for Irwin Shaw." These writers being, of course, the subjects of Goldman's two published book reviews. Shaw's *Mixed Com-pany* anthology—"the book that finally made him admit he wanted to be a writer," Chub recalls—provides one of this book's motifs: not good at thinking up names for his characters, whenever he is writing a new story, Chub pulls out Shaw's book and steals some. He does so now, turning B.J. and Del into "Chris and Louise" from 'The Eighty-Yard Run.' 'The Girl(s) of My Dreams' by Charles Fuller is the result, a story that sees "Chris" making a connection between his fight with his fiancée and his parents' fight at the swimming pool. Without the linking text to the next chapter, this opening section could have been a pretty good self-contained work in itself, an intriguingly unusual creation in being a short story about the process of creating a short story. Which itself would have been the irony of ironies for this man never able to master the short story form.

Chub takes the story to classmate Stanley Kitchel, a man he first met in the college library, where Chub is a bit of a star for his preternatural competence with the Dewey Decimal System. Kitchel is scruffy, loud, overweight and—courtesy of childhood polio—mobile only on crutches. His nickname is 'Two-Brew' due to his bailing early from a drinking contest (described in flashback at boring length by Goldman). As well as larger-than-life, Kitchel is not quite recognizable as from real life, at least in the early sections of the book, where he is apt to produce florid dialogue like, "Smartass repartee does not become your sweet visage, Fuller; plus you're not clever enough by half. Now close your hole while I explicate." In his ugliness, superior mien and unlikely eloquence, he is very reminiscent of Zock in Goldman's very first novel, another suggestion that this is *The Temple of Gold 1.1*.

Kitchel had spotted Chub's talent in the creative writing class to which he had gained entry in sophomore year. Chub had submitted a short story called 'The Men's Room,' which detailed a trip with his mother to collect his alcoholic father from a bar called Melchiorre's. Told that his father is in the establishment's male toilet, he enters, finding his father on his knees vomiting. Waiting, Chub looks around.

> *—and then the power of the room hit him.*
> *The ceiling was very low, and it wasn't the dirt or the stink that shocked him and it wasn't the urinal that flowed continuously and it wasn't the bugs that skittered across the walls—*
> *—it was the walls themselves. Because every available inch was taken up with something foul. Virulent graffiti ... hundreds of drawings, of gigantic penises dripping sperm and vaginas with spiders crawling out of them and breasts with gigantic nipples slashed off and lying nearby. Chub wanted to get the hell out but his father wasn't done yet and he stared away from the walls, up to the low ceiling, and they were up there, too, the drawings and the rest, and Chub was totally surrounded, enveloped in this putrescent cell...*

His tutor, Andrew Cheyney, is not impressed, reading the story to the class with a voice loaded with contempt and then dismissing it because it deals with "scum" rather than "glory." His contempt balloons when Chub names his favorite author, Irwin Shaw, being to Cheyney a "common popularizer." Already freaked out by the implication that his own flesh and blood is scum, Chub flees the class, never to return. We have only seen a précis of the short story (Chub's fiction is never reproduced by Goldman) but when Kitchel later tells Chub, "You have a voice, Fuller. I felt that slimy men's room…" he is echoing the reader's thoughts.

Kitchel's reaction to 'The Girl(s) of My Dreams' is "On to the next," which, after overcoming his shock at its pithiness, Chub realizes is a statement of approval. From then on he shows all his new stories to Kitchel, who proceeds to become his life-long friend.

When he accompanies Kitchel on a visit to his family home in New York, Chub is in for several shocks. One is the wealth of Two-Brew's folks (the accuracy of his mother's Southern argot is, incidentally, a welcome relief from Kitchel's implausibly eloquent speech). Another is that Kitchel's father is the head of the prestigious Sutton Press. The third is that Sutton's esteemed literary journal *Serendipity* is going to publish 'The Girl(s) of My Dreams.' "Jesus God, did that mean he was a writer?" thinks Chub. The fact that the published story is in the illustrious company of works by Cheever, Borges, Oates, Plath and Nabokov suggests that indeed it does. Although Goldman's work did occasionally keep such illustrious company when one of his short stories achieved publication, we are realizing that Chub is a writer on a higher level than his creator, who—although he has hit the artistic heights across his career—is more akin to a "common popularizer."

His father has been dead for five years but Chub proudly flies to his grandparents' home to present his mother with a copy of *Serendipity*. We learn from a flashback that his mother blames her own over-ambitiousness for her husband's spiral of descent. Gretchen—increasingly fragile and bewildered—deflates Chub with her lack of interest in his achievement. The next day, however, she engages him in conversation about it, asking him to tell her what his story is about. When Chub is partway through explaining, she screams at him in furious rage, accusing him of lying over the poolside argument, but behind her inaccurate memory is anguish about something Chub had never previously known: he had a blue-eyed, angelic-looking brother who died a crib death before he was a year old. "…he never once cried, never was trouble," his mother avers, unlike Chub who was "born to make trouble." His grandmother fills Chub in further and the pieces fall into place about something that had nagged at him throughout his formative years: his parents' complete lack of interest in him despite all his efforts not to make their lives in any way difficult—a boy scout demeanor a girlfriend would describe as "the bestest good boy in all the world."

The device of making the favored older brother dead seems to be the only place herein where Goldman does what he did consistently in *The Temple of Gold*: disguise the facts of his real home life so as not to offend. James Goldman was then still very much alive and presumably susceptible to taking offence.

Once again, Chub turns to writing therapy to sort out his feelings. However, the story he writes is itself pretty traumatic, dealing with his conviction that he was responsible for his father's death. The flashback that follows is probably the book's most powerful and pivotal passage. His father Mike is trying hard to kick the bottle and seems to be succeeding until his inability to find an item for a customer in the dime store in which both he and Chub work leads to a complete over-reaction—a furious, desperate turning out of stock drawers, culminating in Mike simply saying, "Aw, God, I'm sorry … but I just can't fight the battles any more." Chub takes his father home. Mike begins drinking the miniature bottles he has been hiding. As he does so, he tells his son, "I'm not special." This leads to a morose reminiscence about the incident that made him feel he was blessed and destined for great things. In Europe in World War II, he had been injured in such a way that, although conscious, he couldn't move or speak. He was presumed deceased in the field hospital, whose busy staff unceremoniously threw him on the 'dead pile.' Knowing that unless he did something he was doomed, Mike moved the only thing he could: his eyes. He was saved by catching a doctor's glance and following his movements. The incident had become totemic throughout his business failures:

> "I knew I was special and when it went bad I knew it was only temporary, because I was special, and all these years I knew what I was going through was only a tunnel, and I was going to come out bright and shining on the other end because I was the one that left the dead pile, I was special. But I'm not, Charley. I learned that today once and forever. I couldn't even find a tailor's thimble in a dime store."

Chub can't forgive himself for what happens next. When he leaves his father alone to work on his schoolwork, Mike takes a fatal overdose of Nembutal.

After college, Chub is at a loose end, taking menial jobs, including a distressing brief stint in a brick factory. In contrast, Kitchel is doing well at Sutton Press, having turned a manuscript from the slush pile into a phenomenal bestselling franchise. Just when Chub is at rock bottom, Kitchel presents him with a check for $17,500: Chub's combined advance from Sutton for a book of the short stories about his childhood, which he has been churning out, and a novel to be called *The Dead Pile* about how an American man's life is destroyed by his country's complicated relationship with success. "The sales meeting was today," declares Kitchel. "I told the part where your father was pitched in with the corpses and they didn't fucking *breathe*." It all seems to confirm Two-Brew's earlier declaration, "I'm going to be your Maxwell Perkins and you're going to be my star."

So ends the part titled *Under the Weather*, which is the name of that short story collection, whose favorable reviews are detailed at the start of Part II, *The Dead Pile*. Said reviews are good pastiches of the styles of the likes of *The New Yorker* and *The Sunday New York Times*. *Under the Weather*'s hardcover print run of 3,500 almost completely sells out. The paperback tops 100,000 and the book becomes part of the culture's frame of reference: "...for one brief month or so, collegians all across the country put down *Siddhartha* or *Bury My Heart at Wounded Knee* and gave *Under The Weather* a try."

Meanwhile, Chub is declining lecturing work because he needs to press on with *The Dead Pile*. We are given regular progress reports on it, at first positive ones. ("Page 380 now and counting. The rehabilitation section in England ... was, Chub thought, probably a section in need of cutting, but maybe the best thing so far.") However, it all starts going wrong when Chub gets a debilitating affliction belatedly diagnosed as a rare strain of pneumonia that attacks the nerves of the eye. Within a few pages we are two years on and *The Dead Pile* is barely further developed. Gretchen is now dead (at least, that's what Chub's grandparents claim) and Chub is now driving cabs because the money has run out.

Chub's poverty and long-term residency in a cheap New York Ninety-Eighth Street top floor tenement apartment make no sense in light of the fact of the huge sales of *Under The Weather*. (If Sutton demanded back the advance for *The Dead Pile*, it's never mentioned.) Meanwhile, Goldman never quite convinces us that Chub's pneumonia would be something that would have "taken his energy and impulse away." It all seems a contrived way to turn this from a success story into a narrative of struggle—the type of which, of course, Goldman (also published very young) never experienced.

194 • *William Goldman: The Reluctant Storyteller*

Chub accepts with some relief an offer to take over the writing class at Oberlin for a semester. A local drunk called Wallinsky turns out to have written a single book before his own decline: Chub visits him on his deathbed and babbles about how there is no shame in the one-book wonder status of Harper Lee and (at that point) Henry Roth. Chub is now convinced that Kitchel—who had the idea for both linking his short stories by making them about one character and *The Dead Pile*—is in fact the real talent.

The "life-preserver" Chub imagined the Oberlin job to be turns out to be anything but. One of his students—a self-conscious 'character' named Peter Hungerford—turns in a story that Chub recognizes as a rip-off of 'The Eighty-Yard Run' from Irwin Shaw's *Mixed Company*. Chub reports him. Hungerford successfully claims that he merely wanted to please his Shaw-loving tutor with a pastiche of his favorite writer—but looks at Chub with murder in his eyes.

Back in New York, another measure of Chub's falling stock comes when Kitchel offers him work writing a novelization of a Charles Bronson movie. ("I couldn't think of anything better to get you untracked.") His doubts about his writing talent deeper than ever, Chub decides to move into work connected with the one thing at which he had always been unequivocally good. His "EXPERT EXPERIENCED RESEARCHER" advertisement in the *Sunday New York Times* might be a bit of a comedown from the last time he appeared in the Book Review section but it garners him a lucrative, long-term client in the form of prolific crime novelist Elliott Carter, although only after an awkward beginning to the relationship. Having suggested times to call, Chub goes out for a walk, Bergman double feature and dinner. "How in the name of bleeding Jesus am I supposed to reach you between nine and five when there is no one there to answer the fucking phone between nine and five?" is Carter's laugh-out-loud opening gambit. Chub's expertise at libraries and how they work is a valuable asset for a man with burning queries like "Could you kill a man by forcing him to swallow an entire tube of toothpaste?" Carter also recommends Chub to fellow writers. Chub's invests some of the money that starts rolling in ($400 per week on occasion) in the luxury item of an answering machine. (Goldman, incidentally, almost predicts the internet phenomenon that would wipe out many researcher's jobs when he has Chub think, "It will all be computers someday.")

The return to Chub's life of B.J. Peacock occasions the cringe-worthy line of dialogue "There is no way that can be considered bad news." There are also examples of those phony Goldman colloquialisms of recent years

("Duse need not spin"; "Chub turned to the doorway and was aware, instantly, that Somebody was there") but their appearances merely remind us how the characters' speech herein is generally unshowy and naturalistic, Kitchel's spiel aside.

B.J. is now in the process of a divorce from Del. Chub falls in love with her all over again and, this time, it is reciprocated. Chub also falls in love with B.J.'s five-year-old daughter Jessica. Not only is Goldman recycling a little-girl name from his backlist, Jesse is the usual unconvincingly articulate and wise Goldman child character. Moreover, Chub's fanciful bedtime stories for her are as sigh-makingly boring as *The Princess Bride*. Nonetheless, a lot of their interaction is sweet: when Jesse is worried that her doll Big Baby might be stolen while they are away, Chub sets her mind to rest by leaving a note beside it stating "This is *not* Big Baby."

A meeting with Del, in which he claims that it was he who left B.J. rather than, as Chub had been led to believe, the other way around, is Chub's first clue that hooking up with the Girl of His Dreams is not going to be unequivocally blissful. The next comes when he realizes that B.J. is jealous of his relationship with her child. When B.J. storms off after an argument, Chub and Jesse go walking on the beach. Jesse is snatched by a wave. Chub is beside himself—actually picturing in that moment the recriminations at the funeral—until she is washed back his way, babbling, "...Daddy, Daddy, I was scared." Then in the ultimate, most horrific Goldman reversal of all, she is snatched away by another wave, never to be seen alive again.

Part III, 'The Predator and the Prey,' is essentially the story of a broken man who has come to know far more profound grief than writer's block.

In his grim 98th Street apartment, Chub has packed away the manuscript of *The Dead Pile* and with it his literary dreams.He now focuses exclusively on research. This is symptomatic of a section where writerly issues are mainly dispensed with. Instead, the book moves toward the quasi-sensationalistic milieus of *Tinsel* and *Control*, not least in the way the now slimline Kitchel becomes head of Sutton Press: the *coup d'état* Goldman describes makes the publishing industry sound like the House of Borgia.

An old face re-enters Chub's life in the form of the Irwin Shaw plagiarist Peter Hungerford, who beats him bloody before being carted off to a mental institution. (The beating happens when Chub goes to show his respects at the Dakota building on the night in 1980 when John Lennon was slain. Otherwise rock—despite being so important on so many levels to baby boomers like Chub—is absent, a betrayal of the fact that Goldman's generation have no first-hand experience of popular music as a socio-political force.) Chub makes friends—although at first it's still too soon to have sex—with Bonita 'The Bone' Kraus, a skinny, prattling, spiky ex-model turned would-be writer with a fixation on trash art and entertainment. Just when we feel there have been more than enough plot turns (in fact, that enjoyable as the book is, there is no real need to prolong it), it transpires that Goldman is keen to demonstrate that he has delved into the recently commonly-used notebook where he keeps lists of bizarre medical conditions. The Bone suffers from cluster headaches that make one side of her face droop. As with Pig's engorged breast in *Tinsel*, Goldman is way too quick to regurgitate his research on the cause and symptoms as opposed to just letting the information flow from the narrative.

A girl named Sandy, who treasures her copy of *Under The Weather*, rings Chub with the news that her boyfriend is going around impersonating him. The boyfriend has shown her the real street on which Chub grew up and a driver's license in his name. Fleeing her unhinged partner, Sandy turns up at Chub's apartment where she shocks him further by telling him that 'her' Chub told her about *The Dead Pile*. Unfortunately, Goldman never informs us how anyone outside of the Sutton Press would know the title of his unfinished novel.

Chub enters into a sexual relationship with Sandy, whose literary worship and curiosity about his childhood fires his muse again. He goes to his typewriter and hammers out a story. The Bone likes it. For the first time, they have sex. The relationship with Sandy continues, though, despite the fact that she is clearly disturbed: Chub has to coax her away from his window as she babbles about suicide.

The plot twists now really began to pile up, a series of dramatic occurrence and coincidence so rapid as to be absurd but intoxicating for that very implausibility and breathlessness. When Sandy is found dead at the bottom of his building, Chub at first assumes the obvious. But an insulting message from Peter Hungerford on his answering machine sends him off to Hungerford's parents in a red haze. Hungerford is indeed free and has indeed killed today. Not Sandy, though, but a man from whom he had hitched a ride. Reeling, Chub goes back to his apartment. There he receives a call from "Charles Fuller" and his bewilderment changes to clarity. Chub arranges to meet the fake him in Central Park, taking a gun he hastily buys on the street. Fake Fuller is Ben Werner, an unhappily married teacher deflected from his writing dreams by his lack of talent and his girlfriend's pregnancy. When he had pretended in a bar to be a writer he admired, the results were so invigorating that he kept it up. That, though, is the worst of his crimes. When Fuller begs Chub to persuade Sandy to come back to him, Chub realizes he has made a terrible mistake.

Going home, he is at his lowest-ever ebb:

> *All his life, all he had ever tried to do was please. Be good, be better, be the bestest good boy in all the land.*
> *And now Sandy was dead and dear Jesse was dead and his father was dead and his mother, if she was dead, didn't even want him at her funeral, and always in the air now, always a step and a year ahead of him, always laughing and triumphant, was his perfect brother with his perfect blue eyes.*

Chub goes to his Olympia and hammers out the framework for *The Predator and the Prey*, a thriller loosely based on Sandy's murder. Kitchel is very impressed. The writer's block is clearly over. Chub realizes *The Dead Pile* had been a dead end but that "life is material … you just have to be able to live long enough to see how to use it."

An elated Chub goes to the Bone's apartment and tells her all about Sandy and his plan for a book about a man who refuses to accept her death is suicide. When Bonita asks why the character won't accept the suicide verdict, Chub explains that the real Sandy was a game show freak and he could no more imagine her killing herself when they were being broadcast than the fictional him can of the fictional Sandy. "Oh, that's right," says The Bone. "The TV was on." Which leaves a stunned Chub trying to console himself with the fact that everything is material.

It's certainly a shocker of a finale but—leaving aside the fact that Bonita has no knowledge of Sandy and that she never visits the Ninety-Eighth Street apartment—it also underlines the third section's betrayal of the novel's writerly premise and of its mostly naturalistic tenor. Those final few chapters—so cluttered with contrived, horrifying reversals as to be neither Hitchcockian nor Goldman-esque but a parody of both—spoil what could have been a relatively 'pure' book focused on slow-burning truth instead of slam-bang sensation and, moreover, one that addressed environs dedicated to one of life's more refined endeavors: the quest to fill a page truthfully and poetically.

That Mike's dad had to help secure a bridge in Holland in September 1944 is a clear reference to Arnhem and an obvious legacy of Goldman's work on *A Bridge Too Far*. That type of echo from previous works is pretty harmless, but an exchange between Chub and Sandy—"Do you want to go to bed with me?"/ "I'm *in* bed with you"—is hackneyed: it feels in some not-quite-definable way like an overfamiliar Goldman-esque exchange.

The Dead Pile is a book that one would genuinely like to see written. (Goldman: "Well I'm not going to write it, what can I tell you? It ain't going to happen.") Ditto *Under The Weather*. Even a couple of plots that Chub devises as *Dead Pile* displacement activity sound intriguing: one about an obituary writer who checks facts with the ailing and is thrown into the middle of intrigue because his latest subject has been poisoned by his family; the other about a man who finds the stardom that has eluded him in his acting career via a string of robberies.

It's a little curious that the coming-of-age section doesn't deal in any significant way with that most important of growing pains: sex. Chub seems to smoothly segue from childhood to the status of dating adult. On the other hand, a fairly lengthy sex scene between Chub and B.J. feels real in precisely the way most novels' sex scenes don't.

As usual for Goldman, there is little evocation of place (the Melchiorre's men's room excepted), the emphasis being on narrative momentum, perfunctory description and reversals. However, there is a greater feeling of substance than normal of late for Goldman. Part of the impression of weight is literal: the book was over 355 pages in its first hardcover edition. However, in addition, it seems more considered than most Goldman novels. Whereas many of his books read like they were devised on the hoof, *The Color of Light* is peppered with references to incidents that only make sense later in the narrative.

Throughout, Goldman shows a sensibility for the literary—its precepts and its world—rarely suggested by his own populist prose. It's not just the sprinkling in of names like Kafka, Poe, and Salinger. He captures the way a writer sees life as a series of potential story plots, mantras like "This is going to be material, you'll write about this someday" popping into his protagonist's head and consoling him in moments of crisis or distress. The book title that the swimming pool incident creates is quintessential literary novel territory. Yet despite all that, this book never feels like a literary novel. Rather, it reads like the work of a bestseller writer tackling the milieu of the literary world. As Goldman once wrote unequivocally literary novels in the shape of *The Temple of Gold* and *Soldier in the Rain*, it would seem that he has lost either the ability or the inclination to produce such a thing.

There again, there is no denying that the description of the Melchiorre's men's room is one of the finest things Goldman has ever written, a skin-crawling immersion into despair and depravity. Moreover, the scene where Mike tells his son the story of the dead pile does indeed possess such seismic pathos and poetry as to be worthy of spinning off that Great American Novel that Chub never got around to completing. There are some other very good pieces of writing, such as Goldman's adroitly casual dropping in of Chub's ageing *wunderkind* status: "He hated the chair. Like all the other Salvation Army shit that was growing old along with him." Additionally, when in the middle of his writer's block Chub sends Kitchel a couple of new short stories and his friend's critiques are waffling and ambiguous, both Chub and the reader know without it being stated that the lack of a simple "On to the next" response is confirmation of Chub's artistic deterioration. The book also veritably zips along, brimming over with life. It is that not-so-common beast: something that you look forward to reading.

We now know that the days of Goldman writing novels were coming to an end. Because it is a loving exploration of the writer's muse and a reflective delve into Goldman's own past, as well as simply a good read, *The Color of Light* would have made a fine valedictory. Goldman, though, had to go and ruin it.

7

Asked if *Heat*, published on May 20, 1985, was his homage to Elmore Leonard, Goldman says, "No, it really wasn't, but I understand why you can say that." He explains, "I had that main character and I had that opening sequence and I'd been in Vegas a lot, and it's such a terrible place to be a compulsive gambler and try to earn a living there."

The title of *Heat* is a reference to a feeling experienced by protagonist Nick Escalante when his Reptile Brain takes over. All humans have a Reptile Brain buried deep down, we are told, but that pitiless state takes over Escalante's mind more than it does most and "...he seemed most alive when pain was in the air." During that state, he finds "the heat in his groin increased..." (A title with less unsavory allusions was given the book in the United Kingdom, where it is known as *Edged Weapons* after the instruments over which it is stated Escalante is "master.") The first two chapters feature female perspectives. Chapter one sees a character called Holly trying to pull herself together after a vicious rape and battery, calling out the name "Mex." While Holly will later be pivotal, chapter two is the protracted point of view of a woman who will never be seen in the narrative again. Multiple divorcee D.D. is sitting in a Las Vegas bar waiting for her boyfriend Os-

good to show up for a meeting that she knows will result in her declining to travel with him to his new job in Atlantic City. When D.D. thinks, "She couldn't help being *zoftig*, goddamnit. They started sprouting when she was eleven, so go blame God," it feels fairly natural. However, when Goldman then has her mulling, "She had planned her life as much as possible to avoid the cold," he is once again succumbing to his unhealthy habit of putting a stylized spin on human impetuses, thereby rendering the common unrealistic.

D.D. tries to dissuade a drunk from buying her a drink, even though she is attracted to him. For the first time (outside of the match amongst friends in *Tinsel*), Goldman's sports references encompass the game of tennis: "...he had the same kind of killer looks Pancho Gonzales had when he was pushing forty."

Osgood arrives but the drunk's behavior drives them out of the bar. A fight ensues on the street. A succession of quintessential Goldman reversals then occurs, with the author feinting with and manipulating the reader all the way. ("D.D. cried out but there was no need. [New paragraph.] Because the Mex did nothing.") The battle seesaws bloodily but ultimately results in timid, bewigged Osgood revealing himself to be more of a man than D.D. had ever imagined—something that physically arouses her, not to mention changes her mind about the move to Atlantic City.

The real switcheroo comes in the next chapter, when Osgood meets the Mex—whom we now know is named Nick Escalante—at his hangout-cum-base of the coffee shop of the Silver Spoon Casino Hotel. Osgood give Escalante his fee for the staged fight. As ever, a Goldman big reveal creates a frisson of pleasure at an unexpectedness that is the result of a layering in what preceded it that, on closer examination, makes the plot turn implausible: nobody is so good at play-acting as to be able to take in a woman to the extent that she is both terrified and aroused.

Escalante is not a private detective. Rather, he styles himself a "chaperone," i.e., he specializes in personal security work. However, he has all the trappings of a literary gumshoe: he is solitary, spiritually exhausted by his job, laconic, observant to the point of uncanniness, well-known around town and owed favors by a large number of people, which he duly calls in when he is on a job or in trouble. Only the absence of an adoring secretary who fetches him a morning Danish and coffee and lambasts him for neglecting himself is missing from the litany of private dick archetypes. That and guns, which Escalante shuns despite being a Vietnam vet. However, according to a description of him in a magazine feature, he is "in a situation that did not involve firearms, from twenty feet on … the most lethal man alive."

The rest of *Heat* is devoted to the next two tumultuous days in Escalante's life. Nick usually takes refuge from his unhappiness by fantasizing about exotic travel. Today, he needs that refuge more than most times, for he is miserably aware that this is his 5,000th day in the city he hates. (Nobody in real life, of course, measures out their life in days, but presumably "13.69 years" was felt to not sound so poetic.) His dream is to somehow accumulate a hundred thousand dollars, which is what he estimates it would cost to travel the world for five years. At the moment, his net worth is about three hundred dollars.

Escalante is contacted by a man called Cyrus Kinnick who wants him to be his bodyguard when he visits a casino. He is also contacted by Holly, who it turns out is an old friend/flame. When Holly tells Escalante how she came to go through her ordeal, it feels chillingly real: three strange men persuaded her into a room at the Croesus Hotel on the pretext of revelry; when she found the room empty and asked, "Where's the party?" one of them responded, "You're it."

She wants Escalante to find out the identities of her rapists. Escalante doesn't believe her claim that her aim is to "sue" but agrees to talk to a contact he has at the hotel. This is Millicent, of whom we are told, "She'd gone through a bad time a few years back but Escalante had done her something then to ease her through"—a line not so much straight out of Elmore Leonard but a parody of him. This is a recurring phenomenon. When we are later told of a character, "He had done her something once, a few years back, but she was in good shape now..." what was cliché is now snort-inducing. By the time Escalante says of another character, "I did him something once, several times," it's simply laughable, and that's not even the final example. Goldman, of course, is aware of this, but fails to see that conforming to genre style isn't just a matter of boiling it down to its base formula.

Also laughable is the cryptic telephone message left for Escalante: "The Reverend says please." This message is from a man named Paxton, a television evangelist and bestselling author. Escalante had provided protection for him and his wife Ashley several years back. He was told by Paxton at the time, "You ever get a message from me that says 'The Reverend says please' you'll know I'm afraid." Of course, Paxton could have simply called and explicitly told Escalante that someone has sent him a virulent ransom demand, but something so mundane would be another thing lacking a tinge of the poetic.

It would also be too mundane for Escalante, having been apprised of the identities of Holly's defilers—DeMarco, spoiled heir apparent to one of the town's biggest gangsters, and his two bodyguards—to accost them on the street or in a doorway. Goldman, therefore, gives him a flimsy rationale for bluffing his way into their hotel suite: "...he wanted to talk to them first, not just barge in swinging. It always helped—at least it always helped him—to dislike the enemy." The dialogue between DeMarco and Escalante—artfully playing a pimp who is angling for financial recompense for the maltreatment of one of his hookers—is convincing and well-written. Yet it then segues into comic book violence complete with double-bluffing psychological gibberish ("...everyone knew that the worst place to be was between your enemies so if you went there, intentionally put yourself in jeopardy, there would be a gift given back to you, a respite in the enemies' concentration...") In the literary equivalent of slow motion (perhaps Reptile Time), Goldman takes several pages in type smaller than the rest of the book to relate the carnage Escalante wreaks in the space of only eighteen seconds with his metal-heeled boots, old credit cards whittled to razor sharpness, a heavy, octagonal piece of jewelry and his fists. With the three men rendered helpless, he lets Holly in to make DeMarco grovel, sob, and ultimately pass out at her threat of an unspeakable revenge. He and Holly also relieve DeMarco of $20,000, which they divide.

While Holly leaves town, Nick decides to go to a casino to gamble his share at the blackjack tables. Goldman takes us on a roller-coaster ride as Escalante reaches the magic, life-changing $100,000 mark and abruptly realizes that it's not enough: he won't be able to bear returning to mundane life when the money runs out, and that itself will spoil his five years of freedom. He decides he needs "fuck you money," which amounts to $250,000. He goes for it—and loses all. He passes out at the bar.

He wakes up in the apartment of his client Kinnick, who had watched him crash and burn at the tables. The latter earned $20 million in computer chips before he was twenty-eight but isn't happy. He wants to learn Escalante's physical self-confidence. He also says he can help Escalante with the obsessive gambling problem the Mex swears he doesn't have.

Nick is picked up by Baby, the incongruously named man who controls the 'Combination' in most of Nevada. Baby is, like just about everybody else in town, fond of Escalante. However, he has a grave errand: adjudicating on an allegation that Escalante cold-bloodedly killed DeMarco's two trussed bodyguards. Escalante knows that DeMarco probably murdered the bodyguards himself to prevent them snitching about his blubbing in the face of Holly's revenge threat, but he can barely be bothered defending himself because it has glumly dawned on him that he is indeed a compulsive gambler. However, he extricates himself from his situation by pointing out that he knows of an intimate scar on DeMarco's body—inflicted by Holly, who had been left out of DeMarco's recounting of events.

A human finger has now been sent to Paxton in furtherance of a ransom demand that, because he has no children, makes little sense. Nick's doctor friend Froggie says the absence of an epidermis makes it untraceable. Now Paxton admits to Escalante that he may indeed have children, not by his sterile wife but by either of two women with whom he long ago slept in Los Angeles. Escalante flies to LA, the city in which he grew up, to check them out. One of them turns out to be an ex-girlfriend of his. The other is the ex-wife of a man who may conceivably be sending the notes out of revenge and financial desperation.

Meanwhile, an assassin has been hired by DeMarco's father from an area of Nevada beyond the control of Baby. Naturally, he has a myth-draped nickname: the Glider. Naturally he has preternatural abilities, being not just the stylish operator his name implies but "the monarch of handguns." And naturally, he is fond of Escalante because of unspecified favors rendered in the past. However, the Glider's wife is ill and he has accepted the hit job because he needs money for hospital fees. For old times' sake, he gives Escalante advance notice of his imminent death, which will be in Las Vegas. Despite this, Escalante continues to look into the mystery Paxton needs solving.

Back in Vegas, Kinnick meets Nick off the plane, Escalante having exploited his adoration to get him to chase financial information on his prime suspect in the kidnapping (which he knows is a phony one because, although there are children of logical age in each woman's case, both are accounted for). Kinnick comes to his place—where he is shot through the window. Stripping off the wounded Kinnick's shirt, Escalante comes upon scars that are tell-tale signs that Kinnick was once a woman.

Knowing that The Glider wouldn't have missed by that much, Escalante takes Kinnick—strapped up by Froggie—to the location of the real would-be assassin: the Paxton home. Various clues have led the Mex to realize that Kinnick is the real Paxton daughter—given up for adoption because of their religious shame at their youthful desires. Kinnick complains he had been scorned by the pair when he tried to make contact after noticing a physical resemblance when they appeared on television. He has been hounding the Paxtons ever since, the phony ransom note being an example.

Leaving the Paxtons to sort out their own issues, Escalante departs. The Glider calls Escalante at the Silver Spoon to tell him he has turned down the hit job because his wife refused treatment and decided to die at home. He also warns him that DeMarco's men are coming for him. Escalante realizes they are already in the restaurant and runs. Hiding on an overhang, he shakes himself out of his death wish and his fantasizing over exotic climes. The heat starts in his groin and the reptile brain begins to take over. The narrative ends on an unresolved (although not unsatisfactory) note as he leaps on his five pursuers.

Heat is quite a short book, 244 pages in its original US hardcover edition, something in keeping with its pared-down, hardboiled style. As with much of Goldman's writing since *Marathon Man*, its naturalism and procedural material sits awkwardly with the comic book/self-mythologizing violence. In fact, Escalante's preternatural skill with edged weapons against overwhelming odds—only the central theme—is probably *Heat's* most substantial flaw: it just doesn't ring true.

Some of the writing is sloppy and pulpy ("He had no way of knowing, of course, that a great deal of blood would be lost before he slept again. [New paragraph.] Only some of it his"). Most of it, though, is nimble and fast-clipped. Some of the dialogue—verbal and interior—is impossibly eloquent and/or straight from the mouths of movie characters ("Every so often I try and remember the existence of logic"). There is also a fair few instances of an awkward combination of poetry and street talk ("If you were involved with the Combination, that sort of chickenshit behavior was not much esteemed"). Much of the dialogue, though, is very good in its naturalism, for instance Kinnick's response when asked by Escalante if his start-up money came from his adopted parents: "– my folks?—are you serious—I told you what they were, the scum they were—shit, if they'd had it they'd have thrown it away before they gave a cent of it to me…"

There is also some deft writing. When a whining DeMarco denies Escalante's allegations against him and indicates to Baby his Mex-inflicted wounds with a "See?" the line, isolated for effect, "Baby said he did" provides an acutely judged tinge of mockery.

Additionally, it can't be denied that the preposterousness of the movie-style repartee and private eye stereotypes becomes a virtue simply because it's so stylishly done: the tale rolls smoothly along, sweeping the reader up in its adherence to comfortingly familiar gumshoe tradition. Plus, sprinkled in amongst the angst and violence, there are some funny jokes. Additionally, in its panoply of characters and the interaction thereof, *Heat* – like so much of Goldman's fiction – veritably pulses with life.

Yet although a good book, there is something awry here, a fundamental disorder occasionally glimpsed through the more threadbare parts of the edifice. Escalante's obsession with travel is convincing but only just, and his adoration of the Liberace Museum—the single place that "provided salvation" when he was at rock bottom—not at all. The impression left is that Goldman is beginning to run out of credible examples of the quirks he has taken to giving his protagonists in lieu of personality. The condition he gives Ashley—blepharospasm, a locking of the eyelids—shows he has yet again resorted to scanning the weird ailments sections of medical textbooks to beef up the interest level. He also throws in a lot of extraneous detail, which suggests he had trouble filling up even this meager number of pages, whether it be subsidiary character D.D.'s extended mulling on her luck with men, the recitation of another subsidiary character's legal scam involving false allegations of plagiarism or the descriptions of the twinkling exhibits in the Liberace Museum. Moreover, he continues his recent lazy habit of conveying characters' appearances by comparing them to a celebrity: Gonzales, Fred Astaire, Ed Asner…

It's like seeing a comedian telling jokes that are in his inimitable style but at the same time not quite as funny as they once were, or a sportsman throwing the same shapes of yore but to less spectacular effect. *Heat* reveals Goldman the novelist beginning to creak at the seams.

8

Says Goldman, "I'd written one sequel before, which was *Father's Day,* and I had this notion that Doc wasn't dead and I thought, 'Shit, I'll bring him back and see what happens.'" What happened was the publication on February 11, 1986 of *Brothers*, Goldman's worst novel, a book which not only besmirched *Marathon Man* but provided a pitiful—but, for the same reason, merciful—farewell from Goldman to the form. "And then after that it all ended," says Goldman. "I never thought when I was writing *Brothers* that that would be the end of my novel career."

Brothers opens on a desert island where Doc/Scylla is recovering from, erm, his death in *Marathon Man*. His Lazarus turn is explained in disconnected memories, one of which is a speech to him by his Division superior and friend Perkins: "You were essentially dead, we brought you this far back … the doctors don't think we can bring you any further than where you are unless radical techniques are attempted … I have an idea … if we can bring you back, you have one tremendous advantage—everyone knows you're dead … I want to change you—your prints, your face, voice, state-of-the-art surgery…" And with that *Six Million Dollar Man* scenario, the absurd tone of *Brothers* is set. This is separate from the fact that the revelation of Doc/Scylla's survival cheapens the pathos of both his murder and his brother Babe's vengeance in its predecessor.

The book switches to the quiet English village of Tring where two schoolboys are spending birthday money. The reason for the British element of the plot is related to a conviction of the chief villain Beverage that, due to their historical civility and sophistication, the British are the people who should take over the world after the holocaust he is planning. (He clearly hasn't visited Newcastle City Centre of a Friday night.) The children are assassinated by a mysterious man named The Blond. This

potentially intriguing development is somewhat undermined, at least for British readers, by Goldman's poor observance of the English vernacular. Although he at least correctly writes "sweet shop" rather than "candy store," he gets lots of things wrong in just a few pages: the phrases "half a pound," "allowance," and "bug" are not in the British child's vocabulary; "50p," "pocket money," and "creepy crawlie" are.

Two villains are then introduced in successive chapters. Standish is a camp and sadistic individual who has invented a concoction—which he dispenses through an atomizer—that makes people completely pliant. He uses it on a low-life couple, turning the tables on them after they had been about to ensnare him in a habitual trap whereby the female takes a male stranger to a back alley ostensibly for a quickie and then watches, enraptured, as her boyfriend beats the man to a pulp. Before the introduction of Standish, we are shown the couple doing just this in a scene that is truly distasteful ("I'm so wet Arnold, and I need it," breathes the girl as she takes in the violence).

The second villain is named Arky, a man who has invented a formula that makes people almost instantly and overpoweringly despairing. He is introduced in a section showing the visit of a basketball prodigy to a rundown set of courts that is a Mecca for lovers of his sport because it is where some of the legends of the game cut their chops. After triumphing there, the young man goes home aglow to his girlfriend—and commits suicide with her, courtesy of Arky's chemical formula. The basketball court scene is actually the most vibrant and interesting of the entire book, Goldman's love of the sport shining through and lending the section not only a verisimilitude that the book's espionage elements (virtually all the rest of the novel) don't possess but also giving it a humanity and warmth otherwise absent from *Brothers*. This section is simply too good for what surrounds it and would (with the tragic ending lopped off) have made for that elusive of Goldman-penned beasts, a great short story. The book's only other flash of greatness comes when Scylla, summoned back into civilization by Perkins for an important job after a six-year absence, is bewildered by an advertisement for a VCR.

The assassinated children turn out to be key. They are part of an army under the control of a group called the Bloodies, high-connected warmongers in opposition to the dove-like Godists. Standish and Arky are people whom Perkins has identified as Bloodies. The trigger for the global conflict desired by the Bloodies is imminent. The Blond also turns out to be working for the Bloodies.

The *modus operandi* of the various Division operatives is detailed and elaborate—trips to bus station lockers in order to open boxes that merely contain keys to other lockers and the like. The preposterous nadir of this sustained hokum comes when Scylla seeks information on the Blond's weakness from an informant who is an apparently mute pavement artist who works for any side that will pay him and who conveys the required intelligence via plus and minus chalk signs on the sidewalk on which he is working.

The plot possesses labyrinthine reversals and twists but, unlike the switcheroos in *Marathon Man*, they are in no way stimulating. Almost the opposite: sometimes the reader has to resist the temptation to sigh at another matter-of-factly presented rug-puller. Not only does one grow weary of the relentless intrigue but also of the baton-passing of murder: one operative is disposed of by another after having fulfilled his task of killing an operative deemed superfluous (usually because he has seen Scylla's new face), before being disposed of himself. Such unremitting and stylized bloodshed would be distressing if it weren't so ludicrous.

Because these people take human life so coldly and casually, we care about none of them, including Perkins, who dies in agonizing circumstances. Only Scylla's little brother is likable. Although he still runs for pleasure and fitness, Babe is now a professor of history at Columbia University and happily married for four years to a woman named Melissa. However, his role in the book represents a cameo, something not mitigated by the fact that, in a contrived final-page shock revelation, it transpires that, in her capacity as a speech expert, his wife has been unwittingly used by the Bloodies in their schemes.

The cast of characters is large and Goldman is almost obsessive in his determination to give them each a chapter from their own point of view, even if their presence in the novel is fleeting and, in several cases, ended by sudden death. A similar approach worked reasonably well in *Marathon Man* but fails here, partly because almost none of the characters have a real personality. Goldman's attempts to make them something more than ciphers by portraying them variously thinking about favorite novels, movies, foods, and shopping techniques is both transparent and qualitatively indistinct from his habit in recent novels of implying personality via medical condition, behavioral quirk or physical resemblance to a celebrity.

The verbal dialogue ranges from mediocre to poor. The interior dialogue plumbs depths beneath the floorboards ("except what The Stick had done to him wasn't quite 'not going well' unless you were the kind who considered King Kong to be just a tyke"). When Melissa is attacked by an intruder, she thinks to herself, "Such a mistake, oh, such a one." The first three words of that piece of internal dialogue would have been sufficient and naturalistic—by adding the last four, Goldman turns it into something florid and unbelievable.

Only on the last page is it dismayingly confirmed to readers that we are correct in an assumption about the army of children that the author has been inviting us to make but which we don't want to because it is so idiotic:they are robots.

Essentially, *Brothers* is elaborate and overwrought junk not fit to be mentioned in the same breath as the comparatively classy *Marathon Man*. Goldman should have known better. After all, when Doc takes in a movie herein, it is stated, "They really should pass a law, he thought, as he sat there: No Movie Sequels. Ever."

Goldman makes several mentions of Irwin Shaw in this book, including one involving, once again, *Mixed Company*. He also works in a reference to his own novel *Soldier in the Rain*, as well as to Tom Horn. He even has a character say, "May I make a sports analogy?", a comment that is presumably self-awareness on Goldman's part. (For the record, the analogy is about boxing.) This probably being Goldman's last-ever novel, you could half-plausibly extrapolate from those facts that the book constitutes something of a conscious farewell. However, leaving aside the fact that, from what Goldman says, it was not intended as such, Goldman would have done profoundly better for a parting shot to produce a novel that merely displayed his manifold writing gifts.

"My whole career is kind of different now," says Goldman of life after his literary swansong. "All of a sudden I stopped and if you said why did you stop, I have no fucking idea."

That Goldman abandoned short stories is no real surprise: he was neither good at them nor successful in selling them. That he should have abandoned novels in favor of screenwriting and non-fiction is very much a surprise, not just because he has written several good-to-great ones nor even because he had a public receptive to them, but because they were the examples of his writing that appeared to provide him the closest thing to professional fulfillment.

Ross Claiborne says, "Bill regarded screenplays, he said, 'Oh, it's not an art. It's just a craft.' He felt that writing novels was a lot more satisfying." Asked if he imagined Goldman would end up as a screenwriter, Richard

Seff says, "No, not at all. And I think he thinks of himself as a novelist. He always did. Even during the *Family Affair* days, he thought he was a novelist who was kind of slumming writing a musical."

In his published non-fiction writings, Goldman himself has repeatedly, explicitly stated that, as a writer, the novel is the only form of fiction in which he is interested. In *Adventures in the Screen Trade*, he wrote, "I truly believe that if *all* you do with your life is write screenplays, it ultimately has to denigrate the soul. You may get lucky and get rich, but you sure won't get happy." He has also written, "…as a screenwriter, the amounts you are paid are so staggering, compared to *real writing*, that it's bound to make you uneasy." (This author's italics.) And, "Screenwriting is basically shitwork. It's only noticed if it's bad. And the reality is, enough of that erodes the soul." In the mid-seventies, he told Richard Andersen, "On my tombstone, I don't want somebody to write 'screenwriter.' Whatever I am, if it's of any interest, it's expressed in my novels … I keep that part of my life as pure as possible." He also said to this writer about screenwriting, "You don't have the power that a novelist has. I mean, if it's a novel it's your baby all the way." It doesn't appear that he simply changed his mind about his professional priorities, either. In the twenty-fifth anniversary edition of *The Princess Bride* (1998), he wrote, "I haven't written a novel [in the last dozen years], and please remember that that's painful for me because in my heart that's what I am, a novelist, a novelist who happens to write screenplays."

All of which means that in writing screenplays to the exclusion of book-length prose fiction, Goldman was settling for a profession he finds less interesting, fulfilling and worthwhile. Which simply begs the question: why?

Claiborne feels he spotted Goldman's increasing lack of interest fairly early: "*The Color of Light* was very much a step down for Bill. I think it was becoming more difficult for him. The novels weren't coming easily anymore. His latter books for us were not up to his earlier standard by any means." Claiborne's feelings on this were all the more acute in light of the fact that, when he left Delacorte for Warners, Claiborne brought Goldman with him, only for the author to deliver what he considered a sub-standard trio of works.

Those who might be inclined to allege at this juncture that Goldman abandoned the novel because he realized that his craft was declining might have a point. There again, maybe he also apprehended that his oft-repeated claim that he considered himself a novelist who happened to write screenplays was somewhat more nuanced than he had always believed. After all, he has now written five books about the motion picture industry but no non-fiction about literature or publishing.

Goldman says he did not start the writing of any further novels after *Brothers*. "It was one of those funny things," he says. "It just ended. It came as a shock to me. I don't know what happened. My wife left me the next year and that certainly was a change … When I was a novelist—those thirty years—something comes along and hits you and you think, 'Oh my God, that might be interesting,' but I haven't had an idea for that for twenty years now. If I started writing a novel tomorrow it wouldn't shock me because, as we all know, it's all instinctive."

Told of Claiborne's mid-eighties perception of a flagging energy for novels on his part, Goldman concedes, "I think that's true. I think you write them and write them and then you think, 'Jesus. I've done this already.' It's tricky. I just think it's, can you do something that you think in your head is going to be wonderful? 'Cause it's hard, writing. If you could say, would you like to have a novel finished tomorrow, yes, I would like that. Is it liable to happen? I doubt it."

Richard Seff offers an interesting observation: "Well, you get burned out. I think some of the great writers should have stopped earlier than they did. Even in my field of musical theatre, it's a shame that Richard Rodgers and Julie Styne and Alan Lerner went on and on and on until they really were writing very badly. They should know when it's time to leave the party, like E.M. Forster."

PART V

An Ambiguous Comeback

1

One wonders whether Goldman would have abandoned novels had it not been for the fact that his final one roughly coincided with the ending of his almost decade-long exile from Hollywood.

"I am, at this point in the movie business, as hot as I'm ever going to be, and I want to get out before they get me out … I expect to uninvolve myself. I don't expect to make a new movie job that isn't something of mine … These are 1976 quotes from Andersen. With 1987 seeing the release of both the movie version of *Heat* and a motion picture adaptation of *The Princess Bride*, Goldman was back on a ladder he had once publicly disdained. If he still no more loved writing screenplays than he did back in his heyday, there remained several benefits to it that were undeniable. His first wife was always of the conviction that Goldman enjoyed the socializing that went with screenwriting. Moreover, as discussed previously, screenwriting put him in the not unpleasant state of being "wanted." One wonders whether there was now an additional psychological bonus for him in the sense of, as Joni Mitchell once put it, "You don't know what you've got 'til it's gone." Finally, screenwriting must have provided a reasonably enjoyable distraction in light of having fallen out of love on some level with producing prose. In other circumstances—the complete failure of the *Princess Bride* movie, perhaps, or his return to Hollywood not leading to further screenwriting opportunities—Goldman might have been forced to properly contemplate a follow-up to *Brothers*, but such was not to be.

Not that his comeback film was much to write home about. That *Heat*, released on March 13, 1987, is the first Goldman adaptation of his own work to suffer in the transition to another medium becomes apparent from the moment Escalantes is paid by Osgood for the phony fight. In the book, there had been a $200 bonus on offer if D.D. came to Atlantic City with Osgood because the fight made her realize she loved him. Remembering the woman's unnatural level of interest in him, Escalantes refuses to take it. Such hard-boiled nuance is absent throughout. On a similar note, Goldman feels compelled to convey Mex's long-term desolation—entirely spiritual in the book—via physical depletion: he is regularly shown taking a handful of unspecified white pills.

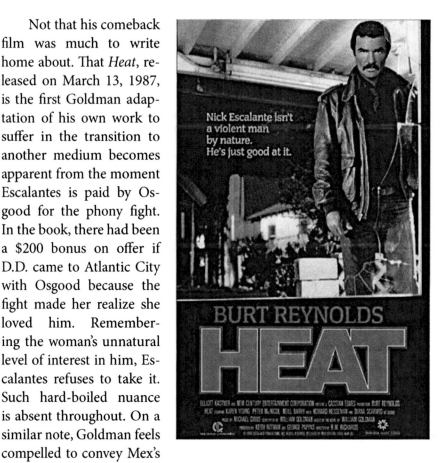

Escalantes shares an office with his lawyer friend Mel, a decision clearly made only for purposes of exposition and character population. Kinnick is present far more in this narrative. Goldman has stripped out the plot strand about the blackmailing of the Reverend and his wife, and hence Kinnick's grudge against them, and hence Kinnick's past as a woman. Also gone is hitman the Glider. The loss of the Liberace Museum is an unmourned one, but in general the de-layering of the narrative robs it of both richness and capacity for drama and reversals.

Escalantes agrees to teach Kinnick self-defense, which ultimately leads to them getting relatively close. Kinnick urges that Escalantes flee DeMarco and his goons. To this purpose, he offers him a one-way ticket to Venice (which has replaced the world as a whole as Mex's fantasy travel destination) and $20,000 cashable only in that Italian city. It is at that moment that DeMarco and his men burst in. Kinnick dies as he offers unsolicited help fighting them off.

In a medium predicated on the explosive resolution, it's inevitable that the non-ending of the book is dispensed with. It's replaced by a chase in which DeMarco's men are one-by-one picked off by an Escalantes using his ability to make lethal weapons of everyday objects: a pile of bricks, a pole, petrol, plus of course his fists and reflexes. He then confronts De-Marco in his hotel suite in a scene rather reminiscent of that absurd part of the *Marathon Man* book wherein Scylla is able to taunt an opponent while remaining un-locatable in a darkened room. Just as risibly, it goes with a complete change of Escalantes's character, even if it is a change more from the book Mex than the movie one: he is not only now a man prepared to kill, but even sadistically tells DeMarco that it will take him days to die. Rather than take the chance of missing the Mex with his one remaining bullet, DeMarco turns the gun on himself.

The final scene finds a blissful Escalantes sailing down a canal on a gondola in Venice, but this is possibly his deathbed fantasy: we had seen him sustain a gun wound to the abdomen in the confrontation with DeMarco.

To no clear purpose, the *Heat* movie storyline has a Christmas backdrop. More perplexingly, Escalantes volunteers his real name to DeMarco when he arrives at his suite to help Holly exact revenge. The soundtrack features an awful, elongated caterwauling saxophone theme.

That Burt Reynolds plays Escalantes is a fairly big deal—he was the biggest movie star in the world for five consecutive years in the late seventies and early eighties, even if, by '87, people were already bewildered that he had ever achieved that plateau. He looks the right age to play the Mex, although has hair unconvincingly dark for someone with such a multi-creased forehead. He conveys quite well Escalantes's perennial poise, but it's rather difficult to assess his performance without the baggage that comes with his movie star persona getting in the way, something encapsulated by the fact that he insists on sticking to his trademark bushy moustache, the one familiar from *The Cannonball Run, Smokey and the Bandit*, and other lightweight blockbusters. The diminutive, almost feminine Peter MacNicol is well-cast as the permanently terrified Kinnick. Neill Barry as DeMarco makes a convincing spoiled pretty boy rapist. Karen Young as Holly is less easy to call. She's clearly a talented actress but something about her grates over and above her thick Southern accent.

It's difficult to apportion blame for the direction: according to Goldman there were six directors involved in *Heat*'s thirty-six-day shoot (two—Dick Richards and Jerry Jameson—are formally credited). Whoever is the culprit, the directing work is clunky, naïve and crass. That the scene in the hotel suite where Escalantes takes care of DeMarco and his men with edged weapons is in slow-motion is consistent with the 'Reptile Time' in the book, but do horn blasts need to accompany punches like something from the sixties Adam West *Batman* series and do *Six Million Dollar Man*-type wrenching sound effects have to accompanying leaps? A later fall by Escalantes through a sugar-glass window is groan-inducingly formulaic.

Heat is not a terrible film but is rather stiff and staid. The bad smell hanging over it through its production troubles, its lackluster quality and its poor box office reception made it a very shaky start to Goldman's cinema comeback, but, luckily for him, *The Princess Bride* was just around the corner.

Goldman doesn't have much to say about how well the *Heat* movie turned out: "I don't think very well, did it? Jesus, we had six directors didn't we? Did you see it? How is it? We had troubles, what can I tell you?"

Further underlining the fact that 1987 constituted something of a Goldman comeback, on June 12 that year, a musical version of *No Way to Treat a Lady* received its world premiere at Hudson Guild Theatre, New York City. Underlining, as well, how ambivalent his comeback was, the off-Broadway adaptation had nothing to do with Goldman but was written and scored by the upcoming Douglas J. Cohen. Despite the bill poster credit "Based Upon the Novel by William Goldman," the play in reality also had a minimal amount to do with Goldman's book, instead taking its cue from the single-murderer/happy ending motion picture variant.

The play—at least judging by the edition published by Samuel French in 1999 after it had gone through several other productions and doubtless multiple revisions—is pretty good. Cohen is skillfully unobtrusive with exposition, fact-planting and dovetailing of songlines and dialogue. There are some funny pieces of dialogue (Moe's mother sternly admonishes him, "Oh, that sicko strangler again. I'm warning you, Morris, the less you have to do with that man, the better. He's not well") and Cohen even makes clear, in a way that neither the book nor the movie ever quite did, the joke involved in someone with a surname like Brummel being given the pet name "Moe." Cohen even provides a greater depth to some characters and relationships.

Plot and presentation changes include killer Kit being obsessed with securing a headline specifically in the *New York Times*, the appearance as a ghostly apparition of Kit's mother, Kit being unable to perform one particular murder, the lipstick trademark left on Kit's victims' foreheads being a compensation for all the kisses his mother never gave him, Kit securing himself a job in Sarah's workplace, and a denouement in which Kit tricks Moe into killing him.

Puzzling notes are struck by Kit managing to get jobs at every food outlet visited by Moe and Sarah, even when the couple hadn't known where they were about to visit themselves, and Kit's statement in a lyric that the telephone is an old-fashioned form of communication (the play is stated as occurring in 1970). Otherwise, though, Cohen does a sterling job in continuing the process started by the *No Way to Treat a Lady* movie in turning a flimsy and quasi-distasteful piece of material into something that could almost be passed off as substantial.

A cast recording was released of this production.

This was, incidentally, not the only attempt made to bring the project to the stage: Seymour Krenzer and Miles McGee wrote a play version of *No Way to Treat a Lady*, which was not produced.

2

"That's the movie I care about most," says Goldman of *The Princess Bride*, released on September 25, 1987.

The genesis of the *Princess Bride* movie had been about a third longer than Goldman's lengthy Hollywood exile itself. "It kept almost getting made and then not," he explains. "It was one of those things where a lot of people have always liked *Princess Bride* and various studio guys said, 'We're going to make it' and they'd then get fired. I never thought it was going to happen. I wrote the book in '72, it came out in '73, I went to meet with [originally slated director] Richard Lester in London in '73 or '4 and the movie came out in '87. It's a long time."

The second 1987 movie adaptation by Goldman of one of his works was a somewhat happier affair than *Heat*. The author retained a degree of control over the project, the film was touched with an originality of vision in which the very generic *Heat* was completely lacking, and it was

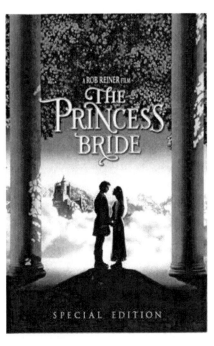

received well by both the critics and the public.

The proceedings in the movie are simplified. The book's sub-plot about the narrator hunting down a copy of Morgenstern's *The Princess Bride* as a present for his son, who transpires to be unimpressed, is completely jettisoned in favor of "The Grandfather" (as he is credited) turning up to read the book to "The Grandson," who—despite initial skepticism—enjoys it. The grandfather's readings give way to fairytale settings from which we are occasionally wrenched back to reality by gripes and questions on the part of the boy. The proceedings are also mildly updated: the grandson is shown at the beginning entertaining himself on his sickbed with computer games not in existence during Goldman's childhood, let alone 1973.

Considering the deletion of waffle and flab the transition from prose to screenplay necessarily entails, it's surprising how talky and static is the *Princess Bride* movie. It takes quite a while for the film to pick up after a slow start that has us huffing alongside the grandson at all the kissy stuff. Meanwhile, a seasoned screenwriter like Goldman should know that the murder of Inigo's father by the six-fingered man is a classic example of the need to obey the dramatic maxim, "Show, Don't Tell."

The hair-raising drop faced by those scaling the Cliffs of Insanity can finally be appreciated when seen on screen, but otherwise the film's surprisingly perfunctory special effects and landscapes are a waste of the potential of the visual medium, even if the suspicion is that director Rob Reiner is being ironic: the patently papier-mâché rocks and painted backdrops would seem to be some sort of commentary on the post-modernist flavor of this particular fairytale. The only feature halfway toward a water cooler moment is the Rodents of Unusual Size by which Westley and Buttercup are threatened. We never feel our heroes are in any danger, giant rats or no: how can we when Buttercup keeps trilling the drama-deflating mantra, "My Westley will save me"?

That English accents abound in the fairytale parts makes a sort of sense, although where Miracle Max's Brooklynese fits into this is anybody's guess.

It's interesting that the waffle about Buttercup's beauty is dispensed with here, because Robin Wright is a peculiar piece of casting as the Princess Bride. Although she's perfectly attractive, her face has the sort of flaws—a couple of large freckles, an asymmetrical nose—which certainly wouldn't put her in the running for most beautiful woman in the world.

Most of the leads are merely okay: the blandly beautiful Cary Elwes as Westley; the only mildly villainous Chris Sarandon as Prince Humperdinck; the sometimes difficult to understand French wrestler André the Giant as Fezzick; an over-mannered Peter Falk as the crotchety Grandpa; Fred Savage as a not-quite-endearing Grandson. The stand-out actors are Wallace Shawn as a weaselly Vizzini; Billy Crystal as a motor-mouthed, sardonic Miracle Max; and Christopher Guest as Humperdinck's smoothly slimy crony Count Tyrone Rugen. Best of all is Mandy Patinkin as Inigo Montoya, who is allowed to steal the show from Westley with his dignity, humanity, swordsmanship, charisma and, most importantly, full consciousness (Westley staggers around recovering from torture for most of the film's back-end). Inigo's revenge on the six-fingered man is the film's only really powerful moment.

The novel's ambivalent, complicated ending doesn't feature, replaced by the grandfather closing the book on an unequivocally happy final page. The boy suggests his grandpa comes back the next day to read it again—to which the grandfather replies, "As you wish." This tidy echoing of Westley's mantra as a farmboy doesn't appear in the novel, one of the few impressive facets of a movie of which the best thing that can be said is that it's a bit less boring than the book on which it's based.

3

After a working lifetime of contriving means to include sports in his writing, with *Wait Till Next Year*, published on December 1, 1988, William Goldman got to help put together an entire book on the subject.

Wait Till Next Year is not fiction but a series of essays on the American sports season of 1987 written in collaboration with New York *Daily*

News sports writer Mike Lupica. "It was his idea," explains Goldman. "Mike is the leading sports writer in America. He's got a television show and everything and he's a leading sports columnist. We've been friends for thirty years and he got the notion that we should try and write a book together, from my point of view and from his point of view.

"I wanted to be a sport columnist when I was a kid, and then I learned more about what they did for a living and I decided I didn't want to do it. You have to go to see all that shit. It's fun to go to a ball game occasionally. What was great, the year I did the book with Lupica, was I had press passes so I could go sit with all those people whose columns I read and watch a baseball game or a football game or a basketball game. It was wonderful, but I wouldn't want to do it now.

"I can't imagine anything worse than covering a tennis tournament. It's one thing if Federer is playing or whatever, but most of the time it's just all of these guys slamming the ball and grunting and all that shit, and occasionally it's exciting but most of the time it isn't. I decided I didn't want to do that."

In terms of the physical writing of the book, Goldman explains, "We did alternate chapters and I would eventually show him what I had and he would show me what he had but, for the most part, we kept away from each other. We'd talk all the time."

"It was an interesting idea," he summarizes of the project. "It was a total flop—it didn't work commercially—but it was a wonderful time for me."

Although *Wait Till Next Year* is cowritten , Goldman is not just along for the ride: his contributions constitute forty percent of the book. Moreover, it being the case that the book was 363 pages in its first hardcover edition, Goldman's chapters would have made for a tome in themselves. It's also remarkable that someone who doesn't report on sports professionally seems to know history and statistics in as much detail as Lupica. As with Broadway and movies, it strikes one that Goldman doesn't so much take an interest in the subject as utterly immerse himself in it.

The book is divided into sections on baseball, basketball, and football. It's a small pity that the authors didn't choose to cover sports like boxing or tennis. Because games with international appeal are spurned, the book has little appeal to those outside the United States' borders, not least because—like the American sports scene itself—it suffers from an almost comical insularity. An example comes as early as the introduction, where the authors declare, "We knew this book had to be written

"Read the book Steinbrenner and a host of other sports notables will want to burn. It's a beauty." —Elmore Leonard

WAIT TILL NEXT YEAR

The Story of a Season When What Should've Happened Didn't and What Could've Gone Wrong Did

WILLIAM GOLDMAN
Lunatic Fan and Author of Butch Cassidy and the Sundance Kid
AND MIKE LUPICA
New York Daily News and Esquire Sports Columnist

about the 1987 year in New York sports (and by extension, sports in general) simply because for the first time in many too many years, we had two world champions prowling for repeats." What they mean by that, of course, is two national champions in sports in which most of the rest of the world is not interested. This is all particularly galling for Britons because so many American sports, and particularly the three examined in this book, are simply cartoon versions of UK games, American football being a beefed up form of rugby, basketball a dramatized variant of netball and baseball constituting rounders with knobs on. It's worth noting (if not to an American athlete's face) that for all the macho posturing surrounding American sports, netball, and rounders are predominately played by young girls in their country of origin. This is all compounded by a ridiculous vocabulary that dictates that a provincial baseball tournament be named the World Series, field positions have the smack of something from a Carry On movie ("tight end") and a game in which hands are used is called football.

Not only is the book littered with terms only familiar to American sports fans, it is scattered with then-topical references and is in places obscurely colloquial. Those inclined to check out the book simply because they have enjoyed Goldman's other works are advised that this sometimes leads to passages incomprehensible to the uninitiated and non-American, like this from a Goldman chapter: "Super, if you've got Cliff Branch chasing his tail across the Greensward and Stabler or Plunkett uncorking. But if you try and do that without the personnel, you end up where Oakland is now: Irwindale." The text's relentless self-referentialism and self-absorption means that even the explanations need to be looked up ("[Nagurski] was the Bambino of Football").

Goldman's books about motion pictures appeal to both cineastes and general readers because every purchaser will, to some extent, have interest in and knowledge of the artform even if not the specific movies discussed. Because *Wait Till Next Year* is of no deep relevance to anyone who is not a devotee of the sports debated, the statistics, results, terminology, and match précis are often eye-glazing, while the passion the two men invest in what they are discussing has a patina of the absurd. It is, however, often well-written enough to make the reader temporarily interested in these specialized—and now long historical—matches, intrigues, and disputes.

Just as Goldman got lucky in the fact of the theatre world being in upheaval when he wrote *The Season*, the authors of *Wait Till Next Year* were assisted by the season they chose to tackle transpiring to be far more eventful than even the drama implicit in the scenario of "two world champions prowling for repeats." They end up reporting on a failed drug test and open warfare at baseball's New York Mets, heart-breaking decline in the performances of basketball's New York Knicks, and a players' strike for freedom of contract in football that naturally impacted on the 'repeat' Super Bowl Championship aspirations of the New York Giants. This ratchets up the human interest level considerably.

Lupica's chapters are given the umbrella title "The Reporter's Notebook" and are generally recitation of event. His style sometimes seems very similar to Goldman's, whether it be the device of individual lines annexed for purposes of drama or a general profane laconicness.

Most of Goldman's alternating chapters—"A Fan's Notes"—tend more toward opinion piece. They are written in a first-person, exclamatory, reversal-packed style similar to that in his books on movies. In one, he goes to see the worst college football team in the country and enjoys himself. Although the reader does too, the chapter lacks a concluding point or moral to give it resonance. His relaying of his disgust with the makeshift Yankees team cobbled together in response to the strike is also entertaining, although a bad taste is left in the mouth by his terminology. As he states that he considers strikes to be wrong and something that should be statutorily replaced by arbitration, why reach for the emotive and insulting term "scab football," which buys unequivocally into their validity? A chapter in which he goes to farcical lengths not to jinx the New York Mets by learning the result of their game is not quite believable precisely because it is so reminiscent of scenarios involving hapless, frenetic, and eccentric protagonists from his novels.

Chapters in which Goldman dispenses with his usual style to interview sports players, presenters, and statisticians constitute impressively professional and objective reportage. (It's rather puzzling if not contemptible, though, that when meeting presenter Bob Costas he snitches on his ownership of an apparently stolen library book, even going so far as to print its number. Perhaps it was an in-joke between the two men.)

Ironically, now that he has finally gotten to write at length about sports, Goldman ends up shoehorning in movie references, citing a scene in *Shane* to convey the skill of baseball pitcher Sandy Koufax, mentioning favorable reviews for *The Princess Bride* as a possible good omen for the performance of the Mets, and rendering one chapter in the format of a film script that depicts two producers discussing a putative sports movie (and which is as much a critique of movie producers as what it nominally addresses). Lupica himself invokes by name *Adventures in the Screen Trade* in his concluding chapter, co-opting the phrase "Nobody knows anything" to apply it to everybody in sports (including reporters). (Earlier on, Goldman uses a new spin: "No one knows.")

Despite the "wonderful time" Goldman claims to have had indulging his passion for sports over an extended length, it's remarkable how little joy this book suggests he gets out of sports. He bellyaches endlessly about clueless managers, interfering owners, sub-standard players, waffling presenters, and deteriorating values. His spectating seems akin to Obsessive Compulsive Disorder: activity that has long lost a purpose in and of itself and become more a matter of doing it because its familiarity is comforting.

4

Hype & Glory—published on April 25, 1990—is a book like no other. It is, as its first edition cover précis states, "A true account by the only person to have been a judge at both the Cannes Film Festival and the Miss America Pageant—in the same year—and lived to tell about it!"

It's a little more than that, though. A thread running through the book—and in some ways the cause of the author immersing himself in the aforementioned activities—is the break-up of Goldman's marriage to his wife Ilene. Although their split was civil, the fact that the marriage had lasted twenty-seven years and produced two daughters naturally made it quite traumatic. "I didn't know that I was going to write the damn thing," recalls Goldman. "My wife had left me. I got the Cannes Film Festival invitation while we were still together and then she left and then Rob Reiner said, 'I am on a personal campaign to get you accepted on the Miss America contest.' I began keeping notes because I thought it was something that could be an interesting little book."

He adds, "Twenty, thirty years ago, the biggest television shows in America were the Academy Awards and the Miss America contest. Now the Miss America contest is no longer televised by a major network. It's disappeared entirely. You can find it on some small network. It's not a big deal anymore. Public taste, for whatever reason, has changed, and I don't know if the public wants to watch the Oscars next year. I don't watch a lot

of television but I'm stunned at the fact that the Miss America contest has disappeared as a piece of popular culture. It just shocks me."

Also not stated in *Hype & Glory*'s breathless strapline is the fact that in some places it is in effect that thing that Goldman has technically not published since 1986: a novel. In a decidedly discursive narrative, there are flashbacks to childhood, juxtapositions of unrelated scenes for dramatic effect, use of sports events as metaphor, dialogue sections far too long to have been remembered from reality, comedic interludes far too heightened to be quite truthful (Goldman's fantasizing about a female check-in staff member at the airport handily encompasses much exposition about his marital situation), details of medical problems, intrigues surrounding rivalries between favorite restaurants, a melancholy imagining of Marilyn Monroe's darkest days, and even a scene wherein our hero—sorry, author—is humiliated by petty officialdom's labyrinthine, pompous procedures that is reminiscent of several such Kafkaesque occurrences in Goldman fiction (the lost property attendant in *The Thing of It Is...* immediately comes to mind). What with the fact that many novels are at least semi-autobiographical, one wonders why Goldman didn't just go the whole hog and make this fiction.

There is, in fact, a passage where the author's daydreams lead him to start thinking up the plot to a new novel. Thankfully, he never fleshed out his idea for another sequel to *Marathon Man*. It sounds just as ludicrous as *Brothers*.

Naturally the Cannes jury process enables Goldman to pronounce on films and filmmaking, as well as reminisce: many occurrences act like Proust's madeleines, triggering memories that, in his case, often involve world-famous celebrities, sometimes behaving badly.

His experiences in Cannes—where he successfully roots for *Pelle the Conqueror* for the Palme d'Or—are inevitably more interesting than his work on the Miss America Pageant, where he gets to be a more good-natured version of Eustis Clay, his girl-grader from *Soldier in the Rain*. Some of his comments are interesting and witty, for instance his observation that the more calculating and coquettish of the entrants know how to parade:

> *...some of them, the best actresses of the bunch, had a slow drumbeat coming from somewhere, keeping them company as they came closer and closer, all the time whispering ...*
> *'I want you ...*

... oh Daddy yes...
... so bad...
... oh Daddy yes ...
... just you, Daddy ...
... please ...
... take me, Daddy ...
... take me all the way ...
... d

   o

    w

     n ...'

Some, comments, however, are neither interesting nor witty, and the official pageant profiles of his favorite contestants that he includes are of no interest to any human being alive, including the once sashed girls. Luckily for him there is a minor disaster at the final count, which creates something resembling an interesting denouement.

Goldman casually litters his text with first-name references to American celebrities, which one imagines will even puzzle some Americans, let alone non-US citizens. There are long quotes included from Arnold Schwarzenegger and Clint Eastwood, which seem to be provided specifically for this book, even if this is not actually stated.

Like most of Goldman's non-fiction, *Hype and Glory* is full of sharp observation, witty comment, and studied self-deprecation delivered in a likeable, conversational, and often profane style. Also like most of Goldman's non-fiction, it's essentially a variant of *Adventures in the Screen Trade*, if a particularly idiosyncratic one. There is even an attempt to create a new movie industry-related catchphrase. Unfortunately, "He didn't fucking know" is not quite in the same league as "Nobody knows anything."

"No it was not my attempt to woo back my wife," says Goldman of *Hype & Glory*'s chief autobiographical strand. "She was wonderful and we're still friends and talk all the time." He adds, "Nobody in my family ever said, 'God, how could you have trivialized your divorce or your marriage by writing that book?'"

5

For the rest of the nineties, Goldman put all forms of prose aside and concentrated on screenplays. With his next, *Misery*—released November 30, 1990—he returned to adapting to the screen the work of another writer.

Stephen King stories that aren't strictly (or even remotely) within the author's preferred horror genre often seem to make for better movies than his spooky fare (e.g., 'The Body'/*Stand By Me*, 'Rita Hayworth and Shawshank Redemption'/*The Shawshank Redemption*, *The Green Mile*). Although flawed, *Misery* (published in 1987) is another example.

Paul Sheldon is an author of romantic fiction only reluctantly, despite his vast success. He decides to kill off Misery Chastain, the curiously named lead character in his franchise. As is his custom while working on a manuscript, he is staying at a hotel in Silver Creek, Colorado. He takes his completed manuscript and drives off in very snowy conditions to deliver it to his New York agent Marcia Sindell (played in a "Special Appearance" by old-time move legend Lauren Bacall). The terrible conditions cause his car to veer off the road and tumble into a valley. Sheldon loses consciousness. He is rescued—possibly from death—by Annie Wilkes (Kathy Bates), an overweight spinster and Sheldon superfan who has followed him, concerned that he is driving in such adverse conditions. Wilkes—a nurse by profession—takes Sheldon back to her isolated house and mends his broken legs and arm. When he regains consciousness, Wilkes explains to Sheldon that the phone lines are down and the road through to the hospital snowbound, so his removal to a professional place of care will be slightly delayed. Wilkes also mentions in passing that she has noticed the

manuscript in his briefcase and politely asks if she might read it. Sheldon—naturally grateful to her—agrees.

Things start going awry, however, when Wilkes is forty pages into the book. She tentatively takes issue with Sheldon over the profanities. When Sheldon suggests that everybody swears, Wilkes reacts with disproportionate fury. Her hysterical reaction is the first glimmer for Sheldon that his guest is not the sweet-natured guardian angel he had assumed. However, if that reaction to something of which she disapproves in his book is bad, when she reaches the end and finds that her heroine has been killed off, Wilkes's response is cataclysmic. At first, she pleads with Sheldon to reconsider. Sheldon tries to humor her but is as unyielding as might be expected of a man who was relieved at getting rid of the millstone around his neck that Misery constituted. Wilkes now becomes unyielding herself. As a fan steeped in the lore of Sheldon, she knows that for reasons of superstition he only creates one copy of his manuscripts. A measure of her sadism is the fact that instead of just destroying the manuscript herself, she brings barbecue apparatus into the room where Sheldon is bed-bound and insists he sets the manuscript alight. When Sheldon demurs, she starts spraying the lighter fluid onto the bedsheets. With the implication obvious, Sheldon does as he's told.

Things get even worse. Sheldon manages to get out of the locked room with a hairpin when Wilkes is not around, but finds the phone lines are cut and all exits are barred. He has to humor Wilkes as she demands that he write a new Misery Chastain novel, this one with a narrative of which she approves. On one of Sheldon's sorties from his room, he discovers, to his horror, a scrapbook that seems to indicate that Wilkes is the murderer of several people—some of them infants. He hides a kitchen knife under his mattress. When Wilkes discovers that he has been out of the room, she ties him to the bed and—in a wince-making scene—breaks both of his ankles with a mallet.

Fortunately for Sheldon, there are people looking for him. Buster, the sheriff of Silver Creek (played by Richard Farnsworth), may seem a simpleton but is in fact a canny old geezer. He realizes that the missing-presumed-dead Sheldon may be secreted in Wilkes's home when he reads the new Sheldon book and sees in it a quote that he remembers Wilkes spouting once at a trial.

That Buster's scenes are interpolations, designed to open out the original book, are a measure of the material's shortcomings. An effective two-hander with a single setting is the hallmark of a stage play. The movie's smallness counts against it. In order to feel substantial, a film must either be cinematic or else incredibly rich in spite of its paucity of characters and settings. While *Misery* is undoubtedly well-acted (Caan is good and Bates won an Oscar for her role) and there are some memorable scenes (the moment when Buster discovers Sheldon only to then be unexpectedly blown away with a shotgun blast by Wilkes is stunning), the film is only diverting entertainment rather than great (or even very good) art. One wonders whether it would actually have benefited from being more faithful to its source in one way: the "hobbling" scene was even more horrific in the book, where King had Wilkes cut off her captive's feet. This would have turned a mere thriller into something altogether more macabre.

One could argue, incidentally, that King only has himself to blame if, like Sheldon, he feels hemmed in by success. The good box office of the movie adaptations of naturalistic stories like this one show that there is an audience for his non-fantastical writing that he has never properly exploited.

6

Nineteen-ninety-two was a year in which Goldman had no fewer than three new movies in the theatres.

One was a mediocre adaptation of a fine book, one a commercial—and to some extent aesthetic—catastrophe, and one an interesting biography of an icon to which Goldman's contribution was a draft or two. No matter. He was undeniably once again a player.

In Goldman's 1984 novel *The Color of Light,* his protagonist Chub mused on one-hit literary wonders Harper Lee and Henry Roth. Three years later, a new name entered the literary landscape that ultimately could also be added to that list: H. F. Saint. His novel *Memoirs of an Invisible Man* was not just a stunning debut but a brilliant book *per se.* To date, he has not followed it up, reputedly a victim of his own success: after the book earned him vast amounts of money through bestsellerdom and ancillary rights, he saw no need to ever type another word.

One of those ancillary rights was, of course, a movie sale. Goldman shares billing with Robert Collector & Dana Olsen for the screenplay of the film version of *Memoirs of an Invisible Man,* released on February 28, 1992. In the credits, the Collector & Olsen team (their collaboration signified by the ampersand) appears before Goldman (and after an "and" signifying Goldman's was a separate draft). Yet Goldman's detailing of the creative process in *Which Lie Did I Tell?* reveals that it was he who worked on the script first. He lost the gig when he refused to go along with the desires of Chevy Chase—who was playing the lead role—to address the loneliness of invisibility. Perhaps billing matters became confused by Chase's attempts to get Goldman back on board after the Collector & Olsen version was considered unsatisfactory.

It's understandable that Chase wanted to explore the loneliness issue: it was a central theme of the original novel, which most certainly did not portray invisibility as a jolly wheeze. Goldman, however, didn't think this light comic actor had the acting chops to bring it off. Sure enough, although Chase is quite good in the movie, shedding his previous buffoonish mien hasn't made him a heavyweight. Daryl Hannah as his girlfriend Alice Munroe is unspectacular in all respects bar her heavy-lipped beauty. A reptilian Sam Neill as ruthless CIA man David Jenkins is the acting highlight.

That John Carpenter—responsible for well-regarded and edgy material like *Dark Star, Assault on Precinct 13, Halloween*, and *Escape from New York*—was chosen as director suggests that the ambition to capture the paranoid, glum flavor of Saint's book survived Goldman's departure and the rewrite. However, it was a striving doomed to failure, Chevy Chase or no. The book is written in the first person and is lengthy (396 pages in its first hardcover edition). This leisurely, subjective narration was the ideal method for exploring the melancholy and dread experienced by Nicholas Halloway when a scientific accident leaves him the world's only transparent human being. Naturally, that governmental agencies want to capture him for their own selfish purposes is a worry, but far more so is the crushing realization that never again will he be able to properly interact with humanity. Film, though, does not lend itself to such ruminative narration, whether it be because the visual medium creates a pressure for spectacle or because cinema audiences are, on balance, less likely than readers to be satisfied by something approaching intellectual. It is also an omniscient medium, hence the fact that, despite the retention of Halloway's authorial voice via the device of the narration of a video tape detailing his plight, the movie has, amongst other new digressions, a sub-plot detailing the internal divisions of the government department hunting Halloway. The film also dispenses with the book's relatively unresolved ending, wrapping things up in the tidy and climactic manner preferred by moviegoers. When Halloway manipulates events so that he is presumed dead, leading to the governmental agency calling off its search, he goes and lives a secluded but happy life with Alice, the only person to whom he has confided his predicament.

Naturally, the film gets as much visual mileage as possible out of the un-usual state of its protagonist. Unfortunately, it was made just before comput-er-generated imagery had developed sufficiently to do justice to the concept. It's fairly impressive in this regard nonetheless, starting from the moment that an unseen Halloway unwraps some gum, chews it, and blows a bubble.

What we ultimately have here is a special effects-orientated chase picture. For every halfway intriguing exploration of the problems of in-visibility—the unsightly phenomenon of food digesting in the gut, for instance—there is a phalanx of helicopters and chorus of police sirens. The movie is fairly enjoyable but in no way feels like what the book did: a subversion of a genre.

With *Year of the Comet,* released on April 24, 1992, Goldman finally pro-duced another fully original screenplay to follow up *Butch Cassidy and the Sundance Kid.* It wasn't, unfortunately, worth the nigh quarter-century wait.

Year of the Comet is a screwball comedy about a valuable bottle of wine and a couple entrusted with its care. As in the long tradition of screwball comedies—they go back to the 1930s—the central couple are a chalk-and-cheese pair who are destined to be together despite initially despising one another.

Maggie (Penelope Ann Miller) is the daughter of a man who sells rare wines to wealthy clients. Frustrated at never being allowed to catalogue wine cellars, she is finally given her chance by her father after threatening to resign. She arrives at an old castle whose owner has recently died, where she begins noting down the contents of the cellar. Her arrival throws a gang of villains resident in the castle into panic. The gang is there to find a chemical formula, which supposedly gives the secret of eternal youth. Maggie finds an impossibly rare (and extremely large) bottle of wine featuring the crest of none other than Napoleon. It dates from 1811, the titu-lar Year of the Comet. She takes it away in the company of Oliver (Tim Daly), who is acting as agent for a buyer who has parted with $1 million. When the villains mistak-enly come to the conclusion that the eternal youth formula is written on the wine casket (they later realize it is, in fact, behind the la-bel on the bottle), they give chase.

"Don't be surprised" says a villain at one point as Maggie finds a hand being placed over her mouth. We're not. The incessant transference of property of the wine and the wine casket amidst chases, fisticuffs and clamor quickly becomes wearisome. Amongst the people in the convoy of cars, helicopters, and motorbikes in this pursuit is a group wrongly promised the right to buy the wine by Maggie's hated, patronizing half-brother and who think Maggie and Oliver are thieves.

Daly's character is an oaf, or at least seems like one for the first nine-tenths of the movie. However, the attraction to him felt by Maggie (which she admits to when the pair are plunging to what seems certain death in a helicopter) is not implausible because he is ridiculously handsome, right down to a moustache evocative of the original era of the screwball and one of its biggest stars, Errol Flynn. Miller, on the other hand, doesn't make one nod one's head in understanding of Oliver's side of the attraction, for although she is pretty, she just doesn't have the type of charisma and ditsy charm possessed by an actress like *When Harry Met Sally* star Meg Ryan—and it has to be said that that and other romcoms (the modern-day successor to screwballs) seem to have been at the forefront of at least the producers' minds when making this movie.

Moreover, Goldman's inexperience with out-and-out screen comedy shows in the fact that there aren't any actual laughs. Not only does he fail to transfer over to full-length comedy his knack for funny scenes in serious films (e.g., *Harper, Butch Cassidy and the Sundance Kid*), there is more than one scene that induces a wince: Goldman depicts solid objects impacting with heads and groins as though he is writing a Looney Toons cartoon. Another fault is that setting part of it in the Highlands betrays the fact that Goldman's grasp of the Scottish vernacular is almost as bad as his English argot.

Year of the Comet is spiritually good-natured and reasonably life-affirming but artistically flat.

Rounding out Goldman's superficially momentous 1992 was *Chaplin*, released on December 25 (creating symmetry with Chaplin's death on Christmas Day, 1977).

Goldman's role on *Chaplin* seems to sit halfway between screenwriter and script doctor. Although the writing credits for the film read "Screenplay by William Boyd and Bryan Forbes and William Goldman," the "ands" instead of ampersands give away the fact that this did not involve collaboration. Goldman was brought in by director Richard Attenborough who—

according to Goldman—felt the existing script needed a 'declunk' job. Goldman has stated that his major contribution was to get rid of stilted exposition, his solution a device whereby Chaplin is shown discussing with an editor elements of the first draft of his autobiography.

Nonetheless, one suspects that a lot of the work of Britons Boyd and Forbes remain. (In fact, the last draft may be Forbes's.) Either that, or Attenborough kept a steady hand on the tiller: that the dialogue of the many English characters is authentic cannot be down to Goldman, whose record of writing speech for English people ranges from clichéd (Euripides's fusty stepfather in *The Temple of Gold*) to execrable (the robot children in *Brothers*). (To add to the problem with accreditation, incidentally, Diana Hawkins is credited with "Story," and this isn't even to mention that everything is based on two books, *My Autobiography* by Chaplin and *Chaplin: His Life and Art* by David Robinson.)

Charlie Chaplin, of course, became famous for skills that are almost a foreign language to today's world. Sophisticated modern audiences are left stone-faced by slapstick, pratfalls, winsome nose-twitching, and other comedic techniques rooted in overcoming the barrier created by a lack of sound. While there is no getting around this fact, the filmmakers make no apologies for authentically recreating Chaplin-esque audition pieces and film scenes. Music hall (called vaudeville here) skits and dinner party clowning are also conjured up without agonizing over the fact that their once hilarious qualities have been washed away by time. There is even an attempt to incorporate into the narrative a flavor of the freneticism and mugging of silent shorts in an undercranked sequence in which Chaplin and cohorts whisk film canisters across state lines to stop the star's grasping estranged wife claiming them as an asset. It works reasonably well.

The period detail is good too. Who knew that motion pictures in the artform's earliest day were colloquially referred to by the British as the "flickers"?

While the film captures Chaplin's talents (which also encompassed directing and scoring) and humanity (he always felt compassion for the underprivileged), its recognition of his faults only goes so far. His weakness for jailbait is covered (it could hardly be ignored, considering its prevalence) but not his well-documented ruthlessness and authoritarianism.

Despite the vast scope of the narrative, the picture explores at satis-fying length most of the important keystones of Chaplin's life and career, and it does so in a way that is surprisingly well-paced.

The movie ends with Chaplin's visit to the Oscar ceremony in 1972 to collect his Honorary Academy Award twenty years after having been banished from the US as part of J. Edgar Hoover's anti-leftist drive. As the now wheelchair-bound Chaplin watches, the audience is shown some of his greatest hits—which are clips from real Chaplin movies. It means that for fully five minutes before the closing credits roll, there is no dialogue—and perhaps there is a moral in the fact that this in no way prevents the finale from being genuinely stirring. As a pleasing final touch, the closing acting credits are accompanied by captions giving us the answers to all the questions buzzing in our heads about what happened to the people we have just seen portrayed.

Paul Rhys impresses as Sydney Chaplin, Charlie's brother, particu-larly in the way he effects an accent journey from cockney to mid-Atlan-tic. Dan Aykroyd makes a good fist of the role of bombastic silent movie production king Mack Sennett. Kevin Kline is suitably dashing as swash-buckling icon Douglas Fairbanks. Kevin Dunn is quiveringly menacing as the FBI head J. Edgar Hoover. For added poignancy, Geraldine Chaplin plays her own grandmother, turning in a creditable performance while enduring what must have been the unnerving experience of playing op-posite a man portraying, and uncannily resembling, her late father.

That Robert Downey, Jr. in the lead role is rarely unpersuasive as he makes a gradual transition from teenager to octogenarian is clearly partly down to the brilliant efforts of Wally Schneiderman, Jill Rockow, and John Caglione, Jr. in the Makeup and Hair department. However, it is also clearly partly down to the fact that the actor is in possession of skills that are colossal. This Londoner can find little fault with Downey, Jr.'s accent, which itself morphs expertly into the Received Pronunciation Chaplin affected as he got older. While Downey, Jr.'s adoption of the Little Tramp's iconic bow-legged, cane-twirling traits is a relatively simple pro-cess of mimicry, he also had to learn the body comedy of both Chaplin and the silent era in general, an artform in itself. Looks-wise, Downey, Jr. both resembles Chaplin and has his own magnetism, the type appropriate when portraying the first human being to become world famous by sight.

Chaplin is absorbing and informative. That it was a box office fail-ure may be understandable—absorbing and informative is not the recipe for bums on seats anymore, if it ever was—but it remains a mystery that

Downey, Jr. didn't win Best Actor at that year's Academy Awards. That prize went instead to Al Pacino for his role in *Scent of a Woman*. For Goldman, this was no mystery. He predicted Pacino's win and, before it occurred, publicly wrote of it: "Pacino plays a blind man. The Academy loves that kind of thing—they think it's hard to play drunks or autistics. But it's the easiest thing in the world for a skilled actor."

That Bryan Forbes—with whom he had, of course, clashed over *The Stepford Wives*—may have doctored Goldman's work on *Chaplin* is not the end of the ironies. In September 1991, Forbes had the job of presenting Goldman the Writers Guild of Great Britain's 1990 Special Award for Contribution to Writing, now known as the Lifetime Achievement Award.

7

Maverick—released on May 20, 1994—was Goldman's first movie Western since *Butch Cassidy and the Sundance Kid* in 1969. Included in it is an apparently deliberate nod to the bicycle motif of *Butch*. However, whereas that earlier film rejected and subverted Western traditions, this one embraces them.

Maverick was a 1950s US television series about a family of dashing Old West card players, one of whom was played by James Garner. Phrases like "Shitty week" and a sex scene reveal this film version to be made in a different age to the small screen template. However, the blandness of fifties TV is still present in spirit: except for the last few minutes, it is full of blood-free gunplay and stylized brawls.

The film is a comedy-drama that follows the escapades of Bret Maverick as he attempts to raise the $25,000 entry fee to a celebrated poker tournament set to take place aboard a paddleship steamer. In a stagecoach travelling to the steamer, he finds himself in the company of ostensibly dainty lady gambler Annabelle Bransford and Marshal Zane Cooper, who will be the security at the competition.

One of several adventures and mishaps with which Maverick gets involved on the way underlines the difference between him and "Mrs." Bransford (there is no Mr. Bransford "and thar never wee-all be, thank you very much"). Whereas Maverick ultimately refuses to take his reward

from missionaries after risking his life to re-trieve their stolen fortune, Bransford is less good-natured than the man to whom she is otherwise a female counterpart: she robs any-body and everybody, including Maverick.

Maverick is a quicksilver draw, superb shot, and demon card player. However, all those attributes are things he keeps hidden until absolutely necessary. One thing he can't keep hidden is his devastating handsome-ness, or at least actor Mel Gibson can't. Jodie Foster as Annabelle Bransford is, like Gibson, beautiful and, also like Gibson, an effortlessly fine thespian. James Gar-ner is cast as Cooper and reveals no melancholy about being displaced as the franchise's handsome young lead as he inhabits whole-heartedly the role of the pompous, middle-aged lawman. The glowering Alfred Molina makes a fine adversary for Maverick in the shape of Angel.

Those excellent actors are delivering mediocre material. Everything here is pat. It's the kind of movie where the hero shoots at an object to cause it to fall on an assailant's head or who, when looking for somebody with whom he is angry, goes to the window and finds the object of his an-ger within bawling-out distance. The grand sense of convenience extends to phony nail-biters: Maverick does not technically return from a break in the climactic card game by the stroke of five o'clock as the rules state, yet he doesn't get disqualified. In said set-piece game, Maverick bets his all on a card that he has not even turned over but which transpires to be the ace he needs for a royal flush.

Where it's not pat, the film is generic. The jolly, banjo-flecked score feels creakingly over-familiar. The script is full of formula repartee, even if it is impressively period-correct—or what we imagine to be period-correct after having watched so many Westerns. Indeed, this is often the saving grace of a picture that skirts tedium: it is so knowledgeable about Western traditions that it feels comfortingly familiar, making the clichés seem a virtue. Richard Donner's sumptuous direction—full of gorgeous vistas—doesn't hurt either.

The plot is chockfull of crosses, double-crosses, counter-crosses, and switcheroos. Many take place in the final few minutes. Marshal Cooper turns out to be less than virtuous: he holds up the paddle streamer at gun-point and makes off with the half-million-dollar prize money. He is then double-crossed by the Commodore, a losing entrant who had been in on the robbery. Then Maverick appears and retrieves his loot, leaving the two to fight it out between themselves. It is then revealed that Cooper is Maverick's father and Maverick knew all along that he was going to steal the money. Then Mrs. Bransford appears and robs the father-and-son schemers of their loot. Or, rather, half of it, as Maverick had hidden half. ("It'll be lots of fun getting it back.")

Although the revelation of the familial connection makes Garner's casting even more touchingly sentimental, the plot turn doesn't make sense: why would Maverick have engineered the boat hold-up when he had already won the money fair and square? It's an example of the sort of pointless, mindless reversal whose propensity in films in the 1990s Goldman would lament in his book *The Big Picture*. It underlines that while *Maverick* is sometimes good fun in its formula way, it is essentially an exercise in slick emptiness.

8

If the release schedules of 1992 gave the impression of it being a hectic year for Goldman, October 11, 1996, had the appearance of a busy *day*.

In one of the freak occurrences in movie history, his next two motion pictures—*The Chamber* and *The Ghost and The Darkness*—were released simultaneously. Not that Goldman cared. He says, "I probably knew which other flicks were opening but I didn't give a shit … In those years I cared only about whatever I wrote. Screw the other guys."

That Goldman was once again a hot property in Hollywood is demonstrated by the fact that with *The Chamber* he was given the job of adapting a novel by one of the world's biggest-selling authors. Yet that his first drafts were handed over for improvement to Phil Alden Robinson—whose work as "Chris Reese" was sufficiently extensive to garner him a co-credit—confirmed yet again that no screenwriter is so elevated as to be immune to replacement.

Based on a John Grisham novel, *The Chamber* explores the legacy of the civil rights battles in the Deep South in the 1960s. The movie starts shockingly: a Jewish civil rights lawyer gets up and takes his children into work. As the kids hang out of the windows, calling to each other in high spirits, the building explodes.

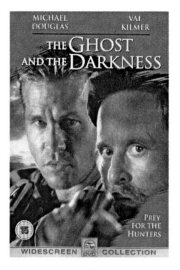

This is the crime of which Ku Klux Klansman Sam Cayhall (Gene Hackman) has been convicted and for which—after sixteen years on Death Row—he is due to be executed. A young lawyer named Adam Hall (Chris O'Donnell) volunteers to take on his case after Cayhall fires his attorney a month before his execution date. As a metropolitan liberal, Hall is hardly the obvious candidate for the job, his predictable opposition to capital punishment notwithstanding. It transpires that Hall has a particular, if perverse, interest: he is Cayhall's grandson. He has never met Cayhall, however: his own father had dissociated himself from him.

When Hall flies in to town and starts digging around, he discovers that Cayhall is guilty of a murder that he was never convicted of. However, it also begins to emerge that Cayhall may not have been guilty of the crime for which he is due to go to the gas chamber. The bomb that blew up the lawyer's office was more sophisticated than the ones he had previously planted, all without casualties. Cayhall seems to be keeping quiet about the real murderer out of misplaced loyalty to the Klan. A race against time ensues to both persuade Cayhall to sign a document that will compel the state governor to unlock files that may reveal the identity of the real killer and to persuade the governor—who won election to office partly by campaigning to punish Cayhall—to grant clemency.

The usual powerful performance of Gene Hackman and a surprisingly good one from O'Donnell, plus a twist in the tale—the governor arranges the arrest of the real killer even as he refuses clemency for Hackman—are just a few of the reasons that *The Chamber* makes for a superb motion picture. Verisimilitude in all areas—the legal briefings and meetings, the prison visits, the gas chamber—are another. However, and ironically considering the traumas that seem to have been involved in its composition, Goldman and Reese's script is the main one. The film veritably glides through its nigh two-hour running time, challenging the viewer's opinions from both angles on the death penalty (Hackman's character is hard to feel sympathy for, but his final moments as the lethal gas causes foam to come from his mouth are horrific) and on racism (Hackman gets inside his grandson's head, invoking a "jungle bunny" cutting up his car with deafening music blasting from his speakers).

It should be noted that this writer's opinion of *The Chamber*'s excellence is a minority view. Goldman himself wrote that it was "… a total wipeout disaster … a terrible experience … I never saw the movie." In *Entertainment Weekly*, Grisham publicly savaged it. ("It could not have been handled worse by those involved, including me. I made a fundamental error when I sold the film rights before I finished writing the book. It was a dreadful movie. Gene Hackman was the only good thing in it.") Critics dismissed it, while the public stayed away.

The Man-Eaters of Tsavo by John Henry Patterson (1907) was the sort of shaggy dog story common in Britain in the age of Empire. It involved an intrepid hero who, whilst helping expand the dominion of the King across the Dark Continent, supposedly encountered lions with unusual man-eating dietary habits, totally uncharacteristic hunting patterns, degrees of cognitive powers unknown in the animal kingdom, and anthropomorphic levels of malice. Yet Goldman believes in all this stuff implicitly. In explaining his decision to script a film based on it, *The Ghost and the Darkness*, he described the story Patterson and others recounted as one of only two "great pieces of material" he'd ever come across as a professional writer. (The raw data on *Butch Cassidy and the Sundance Kid* was the other.)

Val Kilmer initially seems miscast as engineer and colonial veteran Patterson, his toothy, pouting-lipped beauty out of place in such a rugged landscape and his Irish accent only just passable. However, he puts in a sufficiently committed performance that one comes to accept him, something assisted by his initially slicked hair growing out to something less overly groomed.

If it seems a bit uncharitable to attribute the beautiful photography to the naturally awe-inspiring wildlife and spectacular landscapes of Africa rather than Stephen Hopkins, it should be noted that the director is consistently maladroit. When we are presented with the sight of the point over the River Tsavo in what is now Kenya where Henry has been instructed to build a railway bridge and are asked to understand what a fiendish task this is, we are left thinking, "Doesn't look that difficult." Hopkins is also unable to make intelligible much of the dialogue of the character Abdullah (Om Puri).

The Tsavo campsite is besieged by a trio of lions. Patterson manages to kill one, but within three months of his arrival, the remaining duo has killed thirty people. So canny do the animals seem in dodging guards, barriers, and traps to drag men to a terrible fate, that the Indian and African workers are convinced the devil has come to the region. They tag one of the lions "The Ghost," the other "The Darkness." (A conceit of Goldman's to differentiate the animals, it proves futile as they are indistinguishable from one another.) By the time famous stalking expert Charles Remington arrives, their tally is around forty. Remington is your standard grizzled, blunt-natured, plain-speaking hunter. Possibly in the spirit of such archetypicalism, Michael Douglas plays him with pretty much the same attitude, hair, and hat he adopted for the role of Jack T. Colton in *Romancing the Stone.*

After failing to kill more lions by the method of sitting in a tree with a rifle, Patterson resorts to a more elaborate scheme, constructing a cage where the animals, once lured, will trip a wire and be at the mercy of gunmen behind a screen of wooden bars. Even if we are to believe the real Patterson's story that, by a combination of surprise and fluke, three men failed to hit a cornered lion at virtually point-blank range before it escaped the trap, the passage depicting this scenario is ludicrous. Once again, Hopkins is at fault: the scene goes on for such an absurdly long time, and the action is so obscured by fast-cuts, that the impression is left only of a scene designed as a contrived way to prolong the story.

The lions' apparent invulnerability continues. Remington orders that a new camp hospital be built because the smell of blood in the existing one attracts the beasts. The lions attack the new hospital as Patterson and Remington lie in wait with cattle as bait at the old one. When they pursue the cats into the wild, Patterson's rifle misfires with one of them in his sights. At this point, all work on the bridge ceases because the workers flee. Patterson ignores a skeptical Remington to lie in wait atop a peculiarly narrow platform over the plains. Despite falling from it when startled by an owl, he takes out another of the lions—naturally when it is leaping directly at him rather than in undramatic repose.

In a celebratory interlude, Patterson, Remington, and their native ally Samuel (John Kani) engage in some banter around a campfire while sharing a drink. The scene is very reminiscent—possibly a deliberate homage to—that in *Jaws* wherein the three shark hunters get drunk and bawdy on the boat at night-time. The jubilation doesn't last long: Remington's empty, disordered tent reveals he has become yet another man dragged away with a lion's jaws around his leg. Almost mindless with rage, Patterson goes off in pursuit. He loses his weapon, flees up a tree, finds the lion scrabbling up the trunk in pursuit, falls to the ground, frantically retrieves his gun, and fires just on the point of the pursuing lion being about to sink its teeth into his flesh. In this genuinely exciting dénouement, and in other scenes involving close-ups of lions, Hopkins does at least distinguish himself: we feel the cats' deep growls vibrating in their chests, see the muscles rippling in their flanks, hear their teeth grinding on human bone, and are chilled under their yellow, dead stares. However, this is not enough to make *The Ghost and the Darkness* anything other than a passable movie.

The main problem is that while they may be fearsome-looking and their activities horrifying, lions are simply inadequate to their assigned function of villain. Even if we are to believe Remington's apalled comment when he encounters these cats' bone-strewn lair, "They're doing it for the pleasure," they are at the end of the day merely creatures that know no better. We are not disgusted by them in the way that we are sentient human beings who cause people to suffer through greed or sadism.

The picture's other major in-built fault is its antediluvian air, by which is not meant its nineteenth-century setting. It feels very old-fashioned because a movie about white men in peril in colonial-era Africa is a throwback to a long-passed cinematic era when exotic backdrops and foreign predatory animals were sufficient to satisfy audiences largely devoid of the relative worldliness of even the least cultured moviegoer today.

That an old hand like Goldman thought so highly of the potential of the source material is befuddling. The film is essentially what he should have known it would be prior to sitting down to write it: a Jungle Jim flick.

9

Released on February 14, 1997, *Absolute Power* was adapted by Goldman from the debut novel by David Baldacci.

Director Clint Eastwood is Luther Whitney, a cat burglar past his sell-by date. When robbing a wealthy socialite's mansion, he is disturbed by the arrival of a couple intent on carnal relations. Hidden in a vault located behind a two-way mirror designed for voyeuristic purposes, Whitney is astonished to realize that the male half of the couple is no less than the President of the United States (Gene Hackman). After the President gets a little too rough, the female slaps him. He retaliates, which prompts the girl to reach for a knife. Just as she is about to plunge it into the President's chest, his secret service guards arrive and shoot her dead.

A cover-up—involving the two secret service men and the President's loyal aide Gloria Russell (Judy Davis)—is immediately put into operation. However, it quickly begins unraveling as the police and the security men realize that a burglar was present in the house on the night of the murder. Socialite Walter Sullivan (E.G. Marshall), grieving husband of the slain woman, also apprehends this and hires a hit-man to kill Whitney, for—like everyone else—Sullivan is under the impression that Whitney is the murderer. Whitney had initially decided to go on the run but changed his mind after being disgusted by the sight on television of the President comforting Sullivan. Armed with the murder weapon and its attendant bloodstains and fingerprints, he sets out in the teeth of the apparatus of the state to reveal the President's true character.

A sub-plot involves Eastwood's adult daughter Kate (Laura Linney), who is resentful of the fact that he missed her childhood because he was languishing in prison cells. That he keeps a protective, watchful eye over Kate is unbeknownst to her, for Whitney's cat burglary skills are so adept as to approach comic book levels: not only does he gain entrance undetected to his daughter's apartment to check out the healthiness of her diet he is also able to startle Seth Frank (Ed Harris), a cop who suspects he had something to do with the slaying, by silently effecting entry to his home when he is brushing his teeth. Similarly fantastical is a scene in which Whitney makes his escape from a police sting, leaving his overcoat and hat behind him. Strangely, another sub-plot, in which it emerges that one of the secret service men involved in the cover-up has surreptitiously taped a confession from the President, is left dangling.

Curiously, what undermines this so-so film more than any fault in craftsmanship is the feeling of *déjà vu* induced by the casting of Gene Hackman. In the 1987 movie *No Way Out*, in which he costarred with Kevin Costner, Hackman played a very similar role: a powerful man (in this instance, the head of the Navy) who tries to cover up a lover's death in which he is complicit. It's rather difficult to get over the way that picture keeps flashing into the memory as this one unfolds—not least because *No Way Out* is by far the better picture.

10

November 17, 1998, saw the publication of a twenty-fifth anniversary edition of *The Princess Bride*. It was only really made possible by the success of the movie version (whose own twenty-fifth anniversary would be marked by the coffee table book *The Princess Bride: A Celebration*, containing photographs, script pages, production designs and reminiscence from cast and crew). That Goldman added a new introduction to his own *Princess Bride* for its anniversary edition didn't make it notable, but that he also provided a chapter of a putative sequel titled *Buttercup's Baby* did.

On one level, the format of *Buttercup's Baby* is the same as before: long preamble to the supposed edited highlights of the Morgenstern book, themselves interleaved with Goldman's own asides to the reader. On another level, it's very different. This is quite a tortuous little piece of writing, much of which is taken up with events from the timeframe of *The Princess Bride*, such as Inigo's training to take on the murderer of his father.

It's also full of stuff that doesn't make sense, such as rhymes that suggest Goldman has forgotten his conceit of this being a translation from Florinese. Or perhaps blithely ignoring the fact that these rhymes couldn't possibly have existed in the 'original' is as much a part of the post-modernism as anachronisms like "time out" and mentions of America?

The writing is as self-consciously delightful as in the precursor book—which is to say, full of itself and tedious. There is also some clunky writing ("The whirlpool knew from the first it had them, it had not lost a battle in centuries"), although the text is also speckled with a few mildly amusing lines ("…perhaps not the most brilliant of fellows but certainly the most devoted bringer-up of any rears you might mention…") Generally, Goldman successfully puts himself back in the mindset that he adopted a quarter-century previously. Although he does a fair pastiche of

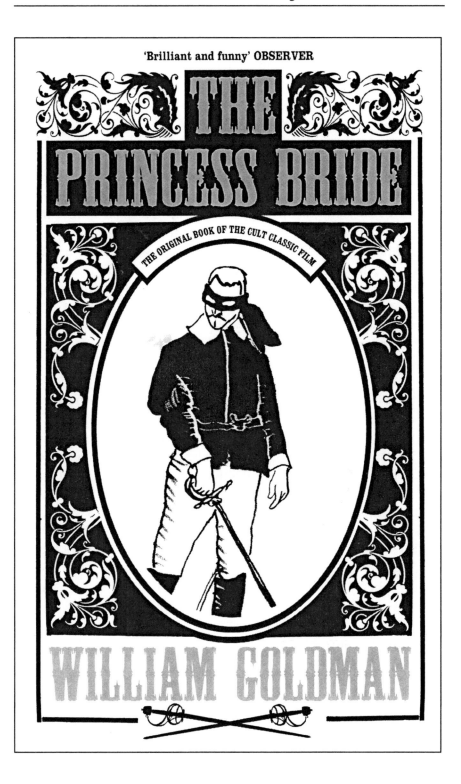

the original book's style, a major difference is the fact that there is a passage in which Westley and Buttercup discuss making love. Not even postmodernism would have justified talk of sex in a fairytale in 1973.

Those who think *The Princess Bride* unspeakably droll will probably adore *Buttercup's Baby*. Those who think *The Princess Bride* overrated and insufferably self-satisfied will find themselves just as impatient as they were previously. The Goldman scholar, however, will find one aspect very interesting. In the preamble, Goldman 'reveals' that events have moved on in his fictional life, him now the proud grandfather of a boy who—unlike his own son—likes *The Princess Bride* and wants to read the sequel, not yet published in the States. Only it turns out that Goldman is in competition to adapt *Buttercup's Baby* with no less a figure than Stephen King. The latter is the preferred choice of the estate of the now-deceased S. Morgenstern not simply because he is arguably the world's most popular author. "He wasn't always called King," Goldman is told by a lawyer representing Morgenstern's estate. "He has ancestors who lived in Florin City way back when. He still visits in the summertime." A confrontation between Goldman and King himself occurs.

This would all be remarkable enough, but Goldman makes part of the conceit a desperation on his part to secure the abridgement job because of the lack of fulfillment engendered by his recent cessation of novel writing. "...I would be a *real* writer once more," he muses. At the end of his confrontation with King, he ponders on his rival author, "...what would he do if he ever lost it, his power, storytelling, as I'd lost mine, and how would he like to spend the rest of his life writing perfect parts for perfectly horrible people who happen to be movie stars this week..." This is astounding stuff, whether it be fictional (in which case, Goldman is gleefully portraying himself as the lost soul he isn't) or non-fictional (Goldman is revealing that the nonchalance he displays in interview about abandoning novel-writing is superlative acting).

And how in this mix does Goldman's failure to follow-up the first chapter of *Buttercup's Baby* fit? "I have been desperate to write a sequel to *Princess Bride* for years," he says. "I published about an eighty page start to the second book and that's all I've got and I'd love to write a sequel to it but it's not something that's working for me ... I don't think it's on the cards."

11

Released on June 18, 1999, *The General's Daughter* is an adaptation of a novel by Nelson DeMille. Christopher Bertolini wrote the first draft of the screenplay, at which point Goldman was brought in, the "and" between their names denoting separated contributions. Although those are the only two writers credited, according to DeMille, Goldman's doctoring was itself doctored: in a 2008 reprint of his book, he wrote of "a final excellent polish by Scott Rosenberg."

The General's Daughter sees John Travolta take on the role of Paul Brenner, a warrant officer in the Criminal Investigation Division, which probes allegations of crime in the army. Brenner is called in when a female officer in a camp's Psychological Operations Unit is murdered. Arriving at the crime scene, Brenner finds a dead, naked woman spread-eagled, her limbs fastened to the earth with tent pegs. He is horrified to find that said victim is a beautiful if blunt captain named Elizabeth Campbell (Leslie Stefanson) with whom he had been flirting (somewhat unsuccessfully) shortly before. He is almost as horrified to find his very much ex-girlfriend Sara Sunhill (Madeline Stowe), a rape counselor, on the scene. The two are forced to work together as they seek to unravel the mystery of the fact that Campbell has, in fact, not been raped.

There is more dismay for Brenner when it is revealed that the woman is the daughter of the same camp's General Joe Campbell (James Cromwell), who is soon to retire, with a career in politics beckoning. The general orders Brenner to investigate and close the case quickly so as to create the minimum of fuss in the three-week interim before the FBI will be called in, pointing out that Brenner is a soldier first and a police officer second.

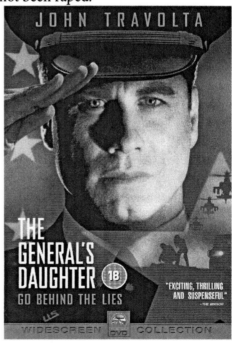

Searching Elizabeth's house, the pair find a secret room containing sadomasochistic costumes and sex aids and a cache of video tapes showing Elizabeth sexually dominating male partners. Brenner insists they conceal this evidence, worried about her posthumous reputation. However, the two begin questioning the men to be discerned on the tapes, one of whom is Colonel Moore (James Woods). Moore becomes their main suspect but he is a red herring. A visit to Elizabeth's former analyst reveals the fact that she was raped on army maneuvers seven years before. The crime had never been reported because her father had concluded that its revelation would do damage to the role of women in the army. The mystery of how Elizabeth died begins to unravel: she had become extremely bitter over her rapists' lack of punishment and had responded by flaunting in her father's face her sexual dalliances with superior officers. When her father had given her an ultimatum to stop, Elizabeth's response was to arrange for a friend to tie her naked to tent pegs and then call her father out to see the sight so as to communicate to him the depth of his betrayal. Her father left her there. Enter Colonel William Kent, a soldier in love with Elizabeth. When she spurned his affection and spat in his face, he strangled her in a rage.

Kent has realized Brenner is on to him and responds by calling him out to a booby trapped field, where he proceeds to blow himself up, although Brenner manages to save himself and Sunhill from the same fate. The movie ends with Brenner confronting General Campbell as he is preparing to take his daughter's remains home to be buried. Brenner promises him he will be court-martialed. A caption tells us that this is indeed what happened to the General.

Although it is well-made and watchable, it is difficult to like *The General's Daughter*. The characters played by both Travolta and Stowe are unpleasant and one can't accept the movie's invitation to find General Campbell as evil rather than misguided. Meanwhile, the movie's pious closing caption stating that all areas of the army are projected to be inhabited by women before long verges on the offensive, seeming to imply that anybody who might dispute that this is a good thing is *ipso facto* in favor of rape.

12

After a period spanning a decade in which Goldman issued no books, in the first quarter of the year 2000, two bearing his name were published within six weeks. *The Big Picture: Who Killed Hollywood? and Other Essays*, issued by Applause on February 1, 2000, is a collection of Goldman's film-related journalism from the 1990s. The nature of *Which Lie Did I Tell?*, released by Pantheon on March 13, 2000, is explained by its sub-title *More Adventures In The Screen Trade*. The close proximity of the two new books to each other was fortunate on one level—serving to make a big deal of Goldman's return to the page, with some outlets inevitably reviewing them together—but not on another: although inconsistent, *Which Lie Did I Tell?* is a substantial piece of work, while *The Big Picture* is, in many ways, embarrassing.

The Big Picture features material that originally appeared in the pages of *Premiere*, *The Daily News*, *New York*, and *Los Angeles Magazine*, thirty-four articles in all, most of them a couple shy of ten pages. The articles are reproduced as-is: Goldman did not go back and revise his often wrong predictions or even correct his grammatical and factual errors. The only new component is an introduction in which he seems to be admitting he only began accepting these commissions to take his mind off his divorce. Said introduction overall feels rather confused: his enthusing over the press passes he received for sports games creates the peculiar impression that he thinks he is writing the intro to *Wait Till Next Year*. As might be expected from the *Who Killed Hollywood?* sub-title, Goldman avers in the introduction that the sequentially presented articles became "a chronicle of the worst decade in movie history." In one of the articles/essays, he claims that quality movies are no longer being made by Hollywood because they "wouldn't appeal to the young men in southeast Asia."

Despite this suggestion of a thesis, this is a rather bitty and repetitive book, much of which is an exercise in pointlessness. In several essays, we are told Goldman's and anonymous industry insiders' thoughts on and predictions for that year's Oscar wins, Christmas hits, and opening grosses. Not only is this a recipe for instant datedness but the format is replicated to *Groundhog Day*-like effect. This is where Goldman's likeable, wiseacre writing personality comes into its own: it keeps you reading despite the marginal differentiation between chapters—even, remarkably, looking forward to reading.

The exceptions to the format are inevitably the better chapters: a fond obituary for *Princess Bride* actor André the Giant (even if a revisit to a passage of *Hype and Glory*); a thoughtful analysis (or as thoughtful as his colloquial, button-holing, would-ya-believe-it? style can be) of the blockbuster movie phenomenon started by *Jaws* in which he observes that even

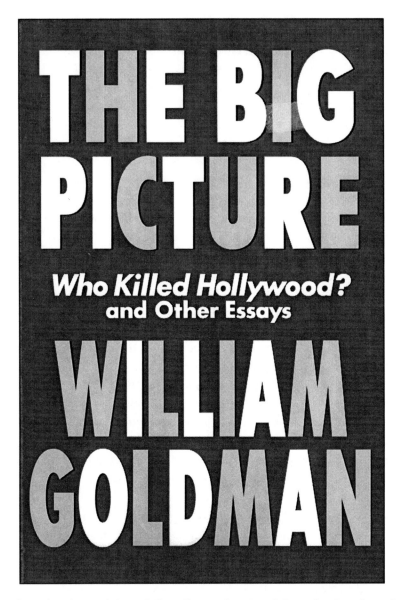

that form has been debased (he alleges that *Jaws*'s lengthy drunken, late-night boat conversation would never make it into a blockbuster movie today); an examination of how being granted an Academy Award measurably diminishes an artist's output (although the fact that his frequent post-1970 excellence seems to make him an exception is not explored).

While he states his case well on occasion, he also sometimes states it more than once, such as his theory about why stars secretly hate commercial films and his philosophy on the difference between independent films and Hollywood movies (itself almost exactly how he described the difference between Popular Theatre and what he called the Third Theatre in *The Season*). Moreover, his conclusions are sometimes surprisingly wrong-headed. While his assessment that *Saving Private Ryan* proves the deterioration of Spielberg's directorial and structural judgment is reasonably persuasive, he seems to lose sight of what a breathtaking piece of cinema it nevertheless remains. He seems oblivious to the possibility that whatever *Schindler's List*'s merits, its Oscar success was partly dictated by the disproportionately Jewish make-up of the membership of the Acad-

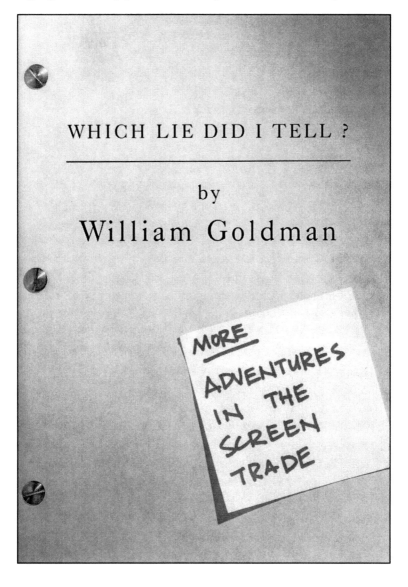

emy of Motion Pictures Arts and Sciences. If he felt that the script of the 1997 film *Good Will Hunting* was "wonderful" rather than psychologically phony and a repository of cinematic cliché, it makes one wonder how he ever managed to write so many good scripts himself. And as for his confident statement in a 1996 article that "Hollywood is headed straight off a cliff; the crash will occur in the next eighteen months, and very painful it will be"—it seems safe to say that, if this had happened, we would have heard about it by now. But then, by his own admission, predictions are impossible in this business: in *The Big Picture*, Goldman becomes one of those many people who have quoted the "Nobody knows anything" line ("In the movie business, as it's often been said, nobody knows anything, so don't search for an answer here").

Perhaps, in any case, this book is above criticism: as with all Goldman titles published by Applause—several of his screenplays have been issued by the theatre and cinema publishing imprint—100 percent of the author's royalties are donated to the Motion Picture and Television Fund. Moreover, *The Big Picture* works as much as it can work considering it is comprised of examples of journalism from various sources that were never meant to be read within a short span in one place.

That, though, doesn't excuse the shockingly amateurish presentation by his publishers. The chaotic interior makes a nonsense of the handsome hardcover casing to which Applause treated the book. There is much hamfisted bulking (it's one of the few books ever issued with both indents—oversized themselves—and blank lines between paragraphs), many instances of words incorrectly given a possessive apostrophe, several uncorrected spelling mistakes, some orphaned quote marks, and barely an apostrophe that hasn't been erroneously software-reversed to become an inverted comma.

Although *Which Lie Did I Tell?* sees Goldman relating more of the sort of tales from Tinseltown featured in *Adventures In The Screen Trade*, it is more overtly instructional than his earlier book.

Goldman uses a similar conversational, point-emphasizing style to that in *Adventures in The Screen Trade*. One example is, "Understand this about stars: *they do not want to appear in commercial films*. Oh, some will put up with them..." That's right—the same point he has just made in *The Big Picture*, and that's not the only common passage. Others include a recitation of the difference between independent films and Hollywood movies, and André the Giant anecdotes. While one can excuse the repetition insofar as the material in *The Big Picture* was not intended for a book at the point at which it was written, that some of the anecdotes related herein also appeared in *Adventures in the Screen Trade* suggests once again that Goldman's claim that he doesn't re-read his work is true.

Another example of his conversational, exclamatory style is, "But here is what you must know about [lions], and I mean this- [New paragraph] –**they are scary.**" The style is by definition entertaining and amusing but also sometimes tiring. Occasionally he pitches over from conversational into banal ("[Stephen] King, in case anyone is interested, is amazingly unpretentious. And real smart"). He recalls historical conversations in unlikely depth.

Part one, "More Adventures," deals with the period in the late seventies and first half of the eighties when Goldman's run of successful films came to such a rude halt that he considered himself to be a Hollywood "leper." He then details the writing and making of most of the movies he scripted when he hauled himself back into contention. Part two, "Heffalumps!!!," sees him analytically praising key scenes in movies scripted by others. Part three, "Stories," examines ideas for narratives and why they will or won't work on screen. All are intriguing and absorbing. Scattered throughout is fascinating autobiographical material from both childhood and adulthood.

Part four, "The Big A," is devoted to an original Goldman screenplay and its deficiencies as analyzed by the author and—separately—luminaries in the industry. It being the case that Goldman is hardly going to pen a high-quality script and then throw it away in a book, we are in territory similar to that excruciating part of *Adventures in the Screen Trade* devoted to Goldman's short story 'Da Vinci' wherein Goldman embarrassed fellow industry figures by having them critique garbage. The dismaying difference is that this time the process takes fully a hundred pages. Just as did the 'Da Vinci' part of *Adventures in the Screen Trade*, it actually serves to undermine the book's implicit contention that Goldman is a screenwriter of significance.

13

His two movie-related books in 2000 must have suggested to some that Goldman's screen-related career was set to continue apace. In fact, it turned out to be winding to a quiet close. There would be just two further movies before he drifted into an unannounced semi-retirement. Curiously, both saw him adapting books by Stephen King.

King's interconnected short story collection *Hearts in Atlantis* was published in 1999. In Goldman's movie adaptation, released on September 28, 2001, Anthony Hopkins takes on the role of a man named Ted Brautigan who it gradually transpires has psychic powers that make him a figure of interest to Hoover's FBI. Brautigan becomes friends with Bobby (Anton Yelchin), the eleven-year-old son of the family who live in the apartment below his. When Bobby shakes Brautigan when he is in a trance one day, the boy finds himself imbued with the power to read people's minds, although this only lasts long enough for him to tell Brautigan where his misplaced cigarettes are and to beat a sleazy fairground three-card trickster at his own game. There are sub-plots about the bullying of Bobby's sort-of girlfriend Carol and the assault of his mother by her boss.

Although a perfectly enjoyable hour-and-a-half, *Hearts in Atlantis* is a movie with pretensions beyond its size. Goldman is constantly attempting to inject portentousness into the proceedings. He is also contriving to convey a journey to manhood engendered by Bobby's experiences. The coming-of-age element feels underserved: neither setting about the local bully with a baseball bat nor seeing Brautigan whisked away to his doom in the back of a Fed car are particularly character-forming stuff or, if they are, the script doesn't convey their life-altering properties sufficiently. The other problem is that the picture feels peculiarly like it has been adapted from a play. The crucial settings—Bobby's family's apartment, Brautigan's apartment, Bobby's mother's workplace—are all interior and the script is leisurely and dialogue-heavy. Such a constricted timbre sits oddly with the larger-than-life elements.

Yelchin is merely adequate as Bobby. Hopkins is Hopkins, pleasant enough company for the cinemagoer but one whose acting style feels overfamiliar and limited. Goldman is not responsible for this, of course. Nor should we blame him too much for the insubstantiality of the story. Goldman has probably done the best he can with the classic/overfamiliar King milieu (all-American fifties childhood) and theme (kids possessing an insight into life denied adults no longer in possession of a sense of wonder).

An interesting footnote is provided by the fact that the mysteriously gifted lodger and his relationship with the young boy of the house-

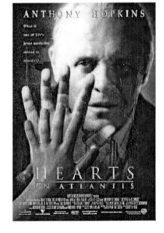

hold is by coincidence reminiscent of the set-up in Goldman's 1960 short story 'Da Vinci.' The start of *Dream-catcher*—released on March 21, 2003—sees a group of American small town kids rescue a retarded boy named 'Duddits' Cavell (Don-nie Wahlberg) from a bullying older group. They realize that there is more to this kid than meets the eye, when their brush with him leaves them with extra-sensory powers. Said powers help them find a missing girl, but also cause them a small amount of unease and/

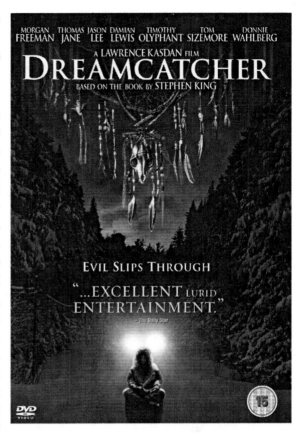

MORGAN THOMAS JASON DAMIAN TIMOTHY TOM DONNIE
FREEMAN JANE LEE LEWIS OLYPHANT SIZEMORE WAHLBERG

A LAWRENCE KASDAN FILM

DREAMCATCHER

BASED ON THE BOOK BY STEPHEN KING

EVIL SLIPS THROUGH

"...EXCELLENT LURID ENTERTAINMENT."
—The Daily Star

or trauma when they go out to find their place in the adult world.

Many years later, Duddits appears to one of them in a vision, warning of unspecified dangers. Those dangers materialize when the group goes on a hunting trip, where they encounter aliens who are trying to stage an invasion of earth by hatching inside humans and exiting from their back passages. The government is aware of the problem and has quarantined the entire area. Unfortunately, Colonel Abraham Curtis (Morgan Free-man), a man sent insane by a quarter-century of hunting down extra-terrestrials, is determined to slaughter anybody whom he even suspects of being infected by the aliens.

Director Lawrence Kasdan is co-credited as screenwriter (no amper-sand). He came aboard the project at a point after Goldman had start-ed working on the script. In the April/May 2003 edition of *Screenwriter* magazine, Kasdan said, "There was an understanding between us when I came on. We would do a draft together that was him taking notes from me based on his first one and then he was going to step away and I'd write the shooting script ... adding aspects from the book that Bill was pessimistic about getting into the movie that I thought we could." Kasdan came out with similar comments in the book *Dreamcatcher: The Shooting Script* and, as Goldman contributed avuncular comments to the same book that were written at a point after he'd seen the finished movie, it would seem to suggest this account is true.

Dreamcatcher is a far bigger, bolder, more cinematic experience than *Hearts in Atlantis*, even if that can't much help the seen-it-all-before impression it generates: a group of kids who come together as adults to deal with a threat that only they understand is a ridiculously well-worn Stephen King motif. This, though, is one of the better adaptations of a King novel, classily written, well directed (a scene in which squirrels, bears, rabbits, and deer all flee the aliens through snow is dazzling) and greatly assisted by recent advances in technology (the aliens are impressively vile).

However, the film is let down right at the death by the lack of internal logic that has always been a weakness in King's writing. Revealing at the climax that Duddits is in fact an alien who is cognizant of the plans of Mr. Gray, the alien mastermind behind the invasion plans, is a ludicrous cop-out: why would an alien hinder his mobility and ability to communicate by hiding himself in the body of a mental defective who has acquired a debilitating disease? It also provokes other questions. Why is the bad alien called Mr. Gray? Who is he? Why does he speak with an English accent (or what Americans imagine is an English accent)? Why does Duddits employ such an oblique method of warning of the terrors to come when logic dictates that if he can plant himself in people's minds, he could just tell them explicitly? All these questions and more go unanswered. It means that despite the great spectacle and entertaining two-hour diversion offered, one is left with a nagging feeling of emptiness.

14

On November 24, 2012, a stage version of Stephen King's novel *Misery* premiered at the Bucks County Playhouse in New Hope, Pennsylvania, and was performed eleven times up to December 8. Directed by Will Frears, it featured Daniel Gerroll and Johanna Day in the lead roles. Goldman was given the job of adapting the work for the theatre. The produc-

tion was unrelated to an earlier British stage adaptation by Simon Moore, but that it had been
done before is clearly indicative of the fact that
such a location-constricted work was in some
senses tailor-made for the boards.

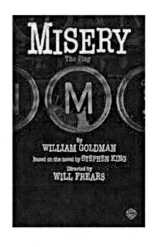

It seems a rather strange project to serve
as Goldman's return to the public eye after nine
years without a screen credit or a published
book. Goldman: "Some people wanted to do
it and they still may do it. We've had a couple
of productions, summer stock kind of things.
The producers like it and I'm, when I hang up
from you, going back to rewriting it some more.
Whether it happens or not, I don't know. It's a small cast and there was a
famous book and the movie worked and we know the Kathy Bates part
is a terrific part if I don't fuck it up, and we'll see. I would love it if it happens, but I'm not counting on it." Any major differences to his film script?
"Well, some. It's a play and you can't do much." This writer hasn't been
able to evaluate the stage *Misery* as it is currently unpublished and Goldman says, "*Misery* is in a state of flux and I don't want it being seen at the
moment."

Goldman says, "It'd be lovely," to get *Misery* on Broadway. So how
does this fit in with his earlier statement, "I would never go back to Broadway"? "Because I've already done it."

15

It being the case that it's difficult to adjudge where to discuss in this text
Goldman's uncredited work, it may as well be here.

Goldman came surprisingly late to motion picture script doctoring. Although he gained early experience in theatre script doctoring, and
his work on the movie *Masquerade* can be posited as doctoring, in the
1981-published *The Craft of the Screenwriter*, he was lamenting, "I have
always wanted to do script doctoring, though I have never done any." He
stated as his reason for this desire the fact that the scriptwriter was "always the villain" with regard to perceived faults in a screenplay, whereas

the attitude toward a script doctor brought in to rectify faults was, "They *love* you!" Soon, Goldman got the chance to find out whether his conjecture about the way script doctors were seen by producers and directors was true.

It's impossible to critique Goldman's, or anyone's screenplay doctoring work, let alone movie consultancy work, because it is by definition anonymous—unless, of course, it so happens that his work on it is deemed to exceed the Writers Guild of America minimum credit percentage levels. For the same reason, it is impossible to compile a definitive catalogue of his doctoring work. Below is an alphabetical list of motion pictures on which we at least know Goldman has worked uncredited simply because he has written or spoken about it:

> *A Few Good Men*
> *Butch & Sundance: The Early Days*
> *Dolores Claiborne*
> *Extreme Measures*
> *Fierce Creatures*
> *Good Will Hunting*
> *Indecent Proposal*
> *The Last Action Hero*
> *Malice*
> *Mission Impossible 2*
> *Point of Impact*
> *Twins*

The amount of the work he did on all these projects is obviously below thirty-three percent (not for the WGA a matter of counting lines or pages, incidentally, but assessing dramatic construction, original and different scenes, characterization or character relationships, and dialogue) but, even within this list, his input has varied. In *Which Lie Did I Tell?* he stated that his most important contributions to *Twins*—on which he worked for four weeks—were an insistence that the mother the twins are seeking out was alive and a credit sequence wherein one of the twins is tormenting the other in the crib. He was "involved" in *Dolores Claiborne* and "was around" *Extreme Measures*. His contribution to *Good Will Hunting* was spending a day spitballing with the two screenwriters/stars, Ben Affleck and Matt Damon, spitballing being a process he has defined in print as "two or more people trying to find a story."

Apart from what he has written or said, or what third parties have written or said, the only other way to determine the detail of Goldman's doctoring contributions is to guess. For instance, in *The Last Action Hero*, the smug reaction of the moviegoing boy to his screen hero being in peril ("He's okay. Minor wound. Both cops dead") is suspiciously similar to Buttercup's complacent "My Westley will save me" mantra in *The Princess Bride*. Then again, it could just be coincidence.

Asked what he feels about doctoring, Goldman says, "It depends if you've got anything else that you're doing when you're offered it. Is it something you think you can make play? Can you make something better in your head?" Noteworthy is the fact that this list doesn't include how he might feel about the bruised emotions of the original writers whom he would be replacing—or even, in their view, traducing the work of. Having said that, there is no other way to look at it. A screenplay deemed unsatisfactory by a studio, producer or director is going to get doctored regardless of Goldman or anyone else declining to come aboard. Moreover, Goldman has mostly stoically accepted being doctored himself.

PART VI

Goldman In Perspective

William Goldman's career effectively ended with *Dreamcatcher*.

Up to the time of writing—February 2014—no motion picture bearing his screenplay credit has appeared in cinemas since. From 2000 onwards, Goldman's published writing has been restricted to introductions to new editions of his books and to his commercially released screenplays, plus small contributions to the 2009 publication *The Book of Basketball: The NBA According to The Sports Guy* that credited author Bill Simmons describes as a "crucial cameo."

Even the new version of the movie *Heat* projected for release in 2014 is not all it seems. A remake of this mediocrity would seem to be the most unlikely way to herald his return to screenwriting, but would be poetically symmetrical, as his previous decade in the Hollywood wilderness was ended by the release of the first version. However, such discussion is rendered moot by Goldman's summary of his involvement in it: "Probably no more than you." He explains, "It's the same as the old. It's the identical script. I haven't seen it. They decided to make it again and I don't know anything about it."

Goldman's low visibility would seem to be a matter of choice. "The movies are not as important to me," he says. "I used to go to movies all the time but I don't anymore." Asked if he has been submitting scripts in that period, he says, "No, but I have a musical of *Princess Bride* that I wrote which may come to Broadway next year [2014], I have *Misery* which may come to Broadway next year. Shit is going on. I wouldn't count on either of them, but things are happening." A musical version of one of his novels and a play version of another man's novel—both of which he has already adapted for the screen—may constitute "shit" that is "going on" but are hardly indicative of an active writer. Does he sit down and write at his desk every day? "Sort of. Not like I used to when I was younger, but I'm still fiddling." His explanation for his lack of screenwriting output is, "I haven't seen anything I really honest to God wanted to write."

The thought occurs that there remain areas Goldman could address in his prose writing. The Nagurski chapter in *Magic* and the basketball chapter in *Brothers* both suggest that he is capable of producing a very enjoyable sports-related novel. It's also a cause for regret that he has never brought his powers of observation and wit to two subjects about which he is passionate: food and wine.

It's not a matter for regret to Goldman, though. In becoming semi-retired by any other name, he has rescued himself from what he always termed "my pit"—that period of the day in which for four-plus decades he grimly sat down to earn his living, whether in a rented apartment or his home office. Of course, as far back as the late sixties he was financially successful enough to, if not stop, then at least slow down, but he has written that what kept him going—working studiously to a semblance of office hours—was the terror that, if he did take his foot off the pedal, he would end up doing absolutely nothing for the rest of his days. For whatever reason—his children being old enough to no longer be dependent on him, divorce, remarriage, a feeling of having proven whatever he needed to or could, declining enthusiasm, changed priorities, a belief that old age should go hand-in-hand with reduced professional activity, or a combination of some or all of those things—he absented himself from the field and doesn't seem sorry that he did.

Even if in the unlikely event that he could muster the interest and energy to make a fully-fledged return to writing, the fact that he is now in his eighties rather limits what more he can realistically accomplish. For all those reasons, it is reasonable to make here an assessment of Goldman's career and abilities.

"I've never had a real job," Goldman said earlier in this text. "I've only been a writer." He elaborated on this lament in *Hype & Glory*: "…it's unnatural, spending most of one's waking hours going into a room alone … college, the army, grad school, and at twenty-four, my first novel got taken. I have had a theory for years and it's this: the trouble with novels is that they're all written by writers … we're not exactly a broad spectrum of any society you'd want to belong to… Writers tend, by the nature of their profession, to be private people; we spend a lot of time alone. All we really have is our imagination, steadily weakening as we age, and whatever pipeline we can keep open to our childhood."

By the age of twenty-six, Goldman had graduated from status of wealthy man's son to published author. By twenty-eight, he had had three novels published. By the age of thirty-four, he had a $100,000 advance and a paperback million-seller. It's a small miracle that this hinterland of cossetted privilege, absence of struggle (whatever his childhood difficulties and rocky early literary adventures), and lack of proximity to raw material related to the concerns of the majority—humdrum existence and financial exigency—did not hollow out Goldman as a writer, particularly a writer who often depicts the milieu of the working man or the underprivileged. Yet he managed to avoid that artistic bankruptcy. Goldman is no Jane Austen, writing about the minute details of a sheltered existence. His writing has always pulsated with life in its fullest range, populated by a convincingly drawn panoply of humanity. It is one of his greatest triumphs that, if he hadn't spoken and written about it, nobody would know that he has never really lived what is, to most, ordinary life.

Goldman started his career when he was too young to have much knowledge about life other than youth. This shows as early as his second novel. In *Your Turn To Curtsy, My Turn To Bow*, in the absence of his willingness to write honestly about his upbringing, he has pretty much exhausted all he has to say about not being an adult. Ironically, he may have benefitted from this situation in his third book, his lack of raw material forcing him, with *Soldier in the Rain*, to zoom in rewardingly on a set of circumstances that more seasoned writers might have assumed did not merit such intense scrutiny. He then proceeded to grow up in public—a little uncertainly in the case of *Boys and Girls Together*, a work whose ambition he had neither the chops nor the life-knowledge to fulfill.

The Thing of It Is..., *Father's Day*, *The Princess Bride*, and *Wigger* is a quartet in which he mined his marriage (the latter two works inspired by his children if not depicting them). A pinch of his Broadway experience was mixed in to the first two. From *Marathon Man* onwards, he became a different kind of novelist, one geared toward research and flights of fancy rather than milieus he had observed or heard about, even if personal knowledge still occasionally informed his fiction (e.g., *Tinsel*). The delve into his past that was *The Color of Light* was the anomaly, and even that was ultimately suborned to the action thriller requisites that were now his stock-in-trade. He maintained quality despite this mass market-oriented reinvention: his sixteen works of fiction divide down the middle in terms of what we might call populism, but, on balance, there is not a greater number of substantial works in one half of the table than the other.

Of course, he is no Jane Austen in another sense. Nobody, least of all Goldman, has claimed that he can stitch together a page of prose as exquisite as her. Nor indeed a page on the level of his literary heroes Irwin Shaw, F. Scott Fitzgerald, and Graham Greene. Goldman told Richard Andersen that he was proud of the last line of *Your Turn to Curtsy, My Turn to Bow*: "And so it's your turn to curtsy, my turn to bow, your turn to curtsy, now mine, you, now me, on and on, until one of the dancers falls, I suppose, or until the dance is ended..." Said Goldman, "I don't write that well, and if I get a good sentence, I remember it. I love that one." However, even this line doesn't approach the lyricism of a famous final sentence with which Goldman will be very familiar, Fitzgerald's conclusion to *The Great Gatsby*, "So we beat on, boats against the current, borne back ceaselessly into the past."

The approach to his own writing that Goldman sums up as "to try and keep you going, keep you going," may be the result of—the compensatory response to—his lack of refined literary skills. Alternatively, it might be the cause of them: the process involved in hammering out a narrative that keeps the reader turning the page (breathlessness of action is often intertwined with feverishness in the act of writing) leaves little opportunity for considered phraseology. Additionally, Goldman told John Brady, "One of the reasons I write so fast is that, since I don't really like what I am writing, one of the pleasures is *getting done* with it..."

Another reason for his just-the-facts-ma'am technique might be that Goldman has, for whatever reason, no elevated facility for language, something obvious from the quotes by him in this text. He is clearly not an unintelligent person, but he has never developed the verbal eloquence common among writers. In fact, it would be fair to say that—listening to the unedited transcripts of his interviews—he is not even always particularly articulate.

Thrown into this mix is Goldman's agonized disinclination to examine his own work—whether it be his refusal to do more than the most cursory reading back as he is preparing a manuscript or to consider an interviewer's questions on anything more than a superficial level—which itself would seem to be a function of that inferiority complex that leaves him afraid of being "found out" on the quality of his writing. One suspects that that lack of introspection and the presence of an inferiority complex are to some extent pretensions—until one comes across a passage in one of the essays he provided for the book *Five Screenplays* in which he recalls a director lambasting him over a scene in his script for *Heat*. (Different medium, but the point remains valid.) Goldman's startled, paralyzed reaction seems genuine: "I was too scared to write anything then ... *I was afraid that he was right* ... if what he was demanding was valid, then *storytelling had changed*. And I had not been able to sense what was in the air and change with it." Notwithstanding that writers understand they are always learning, and screenwriters understand that part of their job involves keeping an eye on shifting techniques and tastes, it's astounding that a two-times Oscar winner should be reduced to being suspicious of his own adequacy by a director who is not named by him but was clearly in no way notable.

By that point, Goldman had long proven that whatever his stylistic limitations, he knew how to tell a story in both novels and films. If the fact that his books are page-turners sounds like a whoop-de-doo achievement, it should be noted how many published books (many of them far more celebrated than any of Goldman's) leave the reader sighing at the thought of continuing and prepared to do so only because of the time and money already invested. Moreover, he keeps people turning pages that contain worthy material. There are plenty of exploitative thrillers, trashy chick-lit works, and vacuous romances that have satisfied an audience because that audience is essentially undemanding. Goldman pleases his readers without pandering to them. With odd exceptions (which themselves are increasingly rare after *Marathon Man*), Goldman can't quite be described as a literary novelist. However, he has never become a genre writer—in the pejorative sense of that term—either.

Goldman's loss of interest in novels is a shame insofar as it meant that he has never really addressed in his prose late-middle age, let alone old age, except as seen through the eyes of the young.

For all his acclaim as a screenwriter, Goldman has in fact a meager tally of three original produced screenplays to his name: *Butch Cassidy and the Sundance Kid*, *The Year of the Comet*, and *The Ghost and the Darkness*. One could add that he has written a further six screenplays that might be termed qualified originals, either because they are adaptations of his own source material (*Marathon Man, Magic, Heat, The Princess Bride*), work that is essentially his despite assistance in vision (*The Great Waldo Pepper*) or work that is essentially his despite employing other parties' characters and set-ups (*Maverick*). That still leaves close to sixty percent of his credited twenty-three cinematic releases up to 2003 as adaptations (the doctoring work of *Masquerade* is included in this adaptation tally). Not only that, but both *Butch Cassidy and the Sundance Kid* and *The Ghost and the Darkness* did not spring fully-formed from his conscious but were based on real-life stories.

Some will therefore have a problem bracketing Goldman as a great screenwriter with contemporaries whose movies were usually comprised of material they devised completely. That argument holds up until one looks down the list of his credited films. Can any writer be dismissed as not being a major talent when he is responsible for, to a greater or lesser degree, *Butch Cassidy and the Sundance Kid*, *The Stepford Wives*, *All the President's Men*, *Marathon Man*, *Magic*, *Chaplin*, and *The Chamber*? That this list doesn't even include works that have been acclaimed and/or massively popular but that don't speak to this particular author's taste (*Harper*, *The Hot Rock*, *The Great Waldo Pepper*, *A Bridge Too Far*, *The Princess Bride*, *Misery*, *Maverick*, *Absolute Power*) further demonstrates that this is a writer of note. As, of course, does the fact that the esteem in which his writing chops are held in Hollywood means that he has worked so often as a script doctor or consultant.

It is in the field of non-fiction wherein lies Goldman's greatest triumph. His seven non-fiction works without exception are enjoyable, sometimes thoroughly so. Two of them—*The Season* and *Adventures in the Screen Trade*—are quite simply among the twentieth century's finest and most noteworthy pieces of journalism about the entertainment industry.

Unfortunately, there comes a point with a writer who is not just long-serving but prolific where it becomes difficult to maintain perspective on his output. William Goldman is just such a figure. Goldman doesn't particularly have a reputation as a great writer (except perhaps a slightly underserved position of Grand Old Man of Screenwriting, which overlooks a latter-day decline). Yet, imagine for a moment that his entire oeuvre consisted of a mere eleven works:

The Temple of Gold
Soldier in the Rain
Blood, Sweat and Stanley Poole
Butch Cassidy and the Sundance Kid
The Season
Father's Day
Marathon Man (novel)

All the President's Men
Adventures in the Screen Trade
The Color of Light
Wait Till Next Year

Not all of those works are necessarily great (although several indubi-
tably are) but any writer who left merely that legacy would be perceived as
possessed of skill both rare and astoundingly broad: a writer of absorbing
literary novels who could also handle a comedy and a thriller, a screenwriter able to turn his hand to both rip-roaring populist fare and sober,
intellectual cinema, a journalist who knew theatre, cinema, *and* sports in-
side-out, and to cap it all—proving he could operate in yet another field—
a competent playwright. It should additionally be noted that many will be
spitting feathers that the list doesn't include *Boys and Girls Together*, *The
Princess Bride* (book or film), *Magic* (book or film), and various others.

Goldman is, of course, all of those superlatives listed in the paragraph above—his backlist proves it. Yet the reaction to this suggestion
from the average college professor or literary section editor would probably be amusement. This is because the above eleven great, very good or at
least notable works are only around a fifth of Goldman's (credited) work.
Although little of the remainder of his output is mediocre and almost
none of it poor, this abundance serves to dwarf and obscure his achievements. Additionally, a large catalogue of varied work is less the stuff of
mystique than a small catalogue of remarkable work. He has simply put
out too much product to qualify for status of Great Man of American
Letters.

This is in addition to the fact that great chunks of his oeuvre are
unashamedly populist or located in a mainstream medium, never a plus-
point for the average serious critic.

Are we to hang Goldman, though, for being a working writer? He
could conceivably have left behind a corpus similar to those eleven works
listed above had he been a college professor who wrote as an adjunct
of teaching others how to write. He chose not to follow that common
path and wound up instead right in the center of the post-World War II
American entertainment industry, happy to meet a massive demand for
his craft.

It would also seem unfair to hang Goldman when he has done precisely that to himself throughout his career, and continues to do so. "It's
a fluke that I'm here," says Goldman. "I've been doing this for more than

fifty years. It's just incredible. I'm thrilled, you know, but it's not anything that I thought was going to happen …The truth is I don't really think of myself as being a success now. I've gotten through it." Despite his refreshing humility, it's rather a shame that Goldman has never had the pleasure of basking in his abilities, never been guilty of the sin of pride. He appears to have been so damaged by, firstly, his loveless home life as a child and, secondly, his stinging litany of rejections when originally trying to make his way as a writer that he simply cannot embrace the fact of his obvious talent.

However, those who relish the thoughtful pleasure he has provided millions can at least take a little comfort from the fact that he occasionally betrays a scintilla or two of, if not joy, then satisfaction about the way he has spent half his waking hours during most of his adult life. "When I look at what I've written, it's a lot of stuff and I'm pleased with that," William Goldman concedes. He also says, "I think I've had a fluke life and I can't bitch about any of it."

Appendix

William Goldman
List of Works

Major Works

This section lists in order of appearance published books, produced and released films, produced and broadcast teleplays and produced stage shows whose authorship is formally credited or co-credited to Goldman.

Note: list does not include new introductions or addendums in new editions of previously published works.

Oct. 14th, 1957	Novel *The Temple of Gold*
Sep. 4th, 1958	Novel *Your Turn to Curtsy, My Turn to Bow*
Winter 1959-60	Short story "The Ice Cream Eat"
Jul. 14, 1960	Novel *Soldier in the Rain*
1960	Short story "Da Vinci"
Oct. 5, 1961	Stage show *Blood, Sweat, and Stanley Poole* (with James Goldman)
Winter 1961	Short story "Till the Right Girls Come Along"
Jan. 27, 1962	Stage show *A Family Affair* (with James Goldman and John Kander)
Apr. 1963	Short story "Something Blue"
Mar. 2, 1964	Novel *No Way to Treat a Lady* (as Harry Longbaugh)
1964	Novel *Boys and Girls Together*
Apr. 1965	Screenplay *Masquerade* (with Michael Relph)
Feb. 23, 1966	Screenplay *Harper*
Apr. 5, 1967	Novel *The Thing of It Is...*
Sep. 10, 1969	Non-fiction *The Season: A Candid Look at Broadway*

269

Oct. 24, 1969	Screenplay *Butch Cassidy and the Sundance Kid*
Jan. 1971	Novel *Father's Day*
Jan. 1972	Screenplay *The Hot Rock*
Sep. 12, 1973	Novel *The Princess Bride*
Sep. 18, 1974	Novel for children *Wigger*
Oct. 1, 1974	Novel *Marathon Man*
Autumn-Winter 1974	Short story "The Simple Pleasures of the Rich"
Feb. 12, 1975	Screenplay *The Stepford Wives*
Mar. 13, 1975	Screenplay *The Great Waldo Pepper*
Apr. 9, 1976	Screenplay *All the President's Men*
Sep. 1st, 1976	Novel *Magic*
Oct. 8, 1976	Screenplay *Marathon Man*
Jun. 15, 1977	Screenplay *A Bridge Too Far*
Jul. 1, 1977	Non-fiction *William Goldman's Story of A Bridge Too Far*
Nov. 8, 1978	Screenplay *Magic*
Feb. 1st—3rd 1979	Teleplay *Mr. Horn*
Aug. 11, 1979	Novel *Tinsel*
Mar. 29, 1982	Novel *Control*
Mar. 30, 1983	Non-fiction *Adventures in the Screen Trade: A Personal View of Hollywood and Screenwriting*
Oct. 1983	Novel *The Silent Gondoliers*
Apr. 23, 1984	Novel *The Color of Light*
May 20, 1985	Novel *Heat*
Feb. 11, 1986	Novel *Brothers*
Mar. 13, 1987	Screenplay *Heat*
Sep. 25, 1987	Screenplay *The Princess Bride*
Dec. 1, 1988	Non-fiction *Wait Till Next Year* (with Mike Lupica)
Apr. 25, 1990	Non-fiction *Hype & Glory*
Nov. 30, 1990	Screenplay *Misery*
Feb. 28, 1992	Screenplay *Memoirs of an Invisible Man* (with Robert Collector & Dana Olsen)
Apr. 24, 1992	Screenplay *Year of the Comet*
Dec. 25, 1992	Screenplay *Chaplin* (with William Boyd and Bryan Forbes)
May 20, 1994	Screenplay *Maverick*

Oct. 11 1996	Screenplay *The Chamber* (with Chris Reese)
Oct. 11 1996	Screenplay *The Ghost and the Darkness*
Feb. 14, 1997	Screenplay *Absolute Power*
Jun. 18 1999	Screenplay *The General's Daughter* (with Christopher Bertolini)
Feb 1, 2000	Non-fiction *The Big Picture: Who Killed Hollywood? and Other Essays*
Mar. 13, 2000	Non-fiction *Which Lie Did I Tell? (More Adventures in the Screen Trade)*
Sep. 28, 2001	Screenplay *Hearts in Atlantis*
Mar. 21, 2003	Screenplay *Dreamcatcher* (with Lawrence Kasdan)
Nov. 24, 2012, Aug. 7, 2014	Stage show *Misery*
(Scheduled)	Screenplay *Heat*

Published screenplays
Goldman screenplays published in book form

1969	*Butch Cassidy and the Sundance Kid* (Bantam)
1975	*The Great Waldo Pepper* (Dell)
1995	*Four Screenplays: Marathon Man/Butch Cassidy and the Sundance Kid/The Princess Bride/Misery* (Applause)
1996	*Five Screenplays: All the President's Men/Magic/Harper/Maverick/The Great Waldo Pepper* (Applause).
2000 (Feb)	*The Ghost and the Darkness* (Applause)
2000 (Apr)	*Absolute Power* (Applause)
2003	*Dreamcatcher: The Shooting Script* (Newmarket Press)

Reviews
1969	Review of novel *The Goodbye Look* by Ross Macdonald; *The New York Times Book Review*, June 1, 1969

1978   "Rich and Poor, Bums and Barons": Review of *Irwin Shaw Short Stories: Five Decades* by Irwin Shaw; *The New York Times Book Review,* November 12, 1978

Other Journalism

Film journalism published in *Premiere, The Daily News, New York* and *Los Angeles Magazine* in the 1990s as collected in *The Big Picture: Who Killed Hollywood? and Other Essays*

Miscellaneous

1979   *Butch & Sundance: The Early Days* (Goldman cited as coproducer)

1998   *The Princess Bride 25th Anniversary Edition* (contains opening of putative sequel, *Buttercup's Baby*)

2001   *The Temple of Gold* (Ballantine paperback edition contains an additional chapter)

Movie adaptations of Goldman novels by third parties

1963   *Soldier in the Rain*

1968   *No Way to Treat a Lady*

Stage musical adaptation of Goldman book by third party

1987   *No Way to Treat a Lady*

Selected Awards

Mystery Writers of America's Edgar Allan Poe Award for Best Motion Picture, 1967: *Harper*

Mystery Writers of America's Edgar Allan Poe Award for Best Motion Picture, 1979: *Magic*

British Academy of Film and Television Arts Screenplay Award, 1970: *Butch Cassidy and the Sundance Kid*

Academy of Motion Pictures Arts and Sciences Story Award for Screenplay based on material not previously published or produced, 1970: *Butch Cassidy and the Sundance Kid*

Academy of Motion Pictures Arts and Sciences Award for Screenplay Based On Material From Another Medium, 1977: *All the President's Men*:

Writers Guild of America Best Original Drama Award, 1970: *Butch Cassidy and the Sundance Kid*

Writers Guild of America Best Adapted Drama, 1977: *All the President's Men*

Writers Guild of America Laurel Award for Screenwriting Achievement, 1985

Writers' Guild of Great Britain Special Award for Contribution to Writing, 1991

National Board of Review Awards, Best Screenplay—Career Achievement, 1995

(Note: years stated are those in which award was presented.)

Acknowledgements

The author wishes to thank the following for granting interviews:

William Goldman (two in 2007, one in 2013)
Richard Seff (2010)
Ross Claiborne (2011)

Additional thanks are extended to the following for query answering
and miscellaneous help:

John Brady
Kate Broughton
Tara C. Craig of the Rare Book & Manuscript Library,
    Columbia University
Ellie Peers of the Writers' Guild of Great Britain

Cover photographs © John Brady, 1981

Selected Bibliography

Note: editions stated are the ones author personally made use of.

WORKS BY WILLIAM GOLDMAN

The Temple of Gold, 1965 (Corgi)
The Temple Of Gold, 2001 (Ballantine)
Your Turn to Curtsy, My Turn to Bow, 1966 (Corgi)
Soldier in the Rain, 1960 (Eyre & Spottiswoode)
No Way to Treat a Lady, 1964 (Fawcett Gold Medal)
Boys and Girls Together, 1965 (Michael Joseph)
Boys and Girls Together, 1966 (Corgi)
The Thing of It Is..., 1967 (Michael Joseph)
The Season: A Candid Look at Broadway, 1984 (Limelight Editions)
Butch Cassidy and the Sundance Kid, 1969 (Corgi)
Father's Day, 1973 (Corgi)
The Princess Bride, 1976 (Macmillan)
The Princess Bride, 1999 (Bloomsbury)
Wigger, 1977 (Dell)
The Great Waldo Pepper, 1975 (Dell)
Marathon Man, 1976 (Macmillan)
Magic, 1978 (Macmillan)

William Goldman's Story of A Bridge Too Far, 1977 (Coronet)
Tinsel, 1979 (Macmillan)
Control, 1983 (New English Library)
Adventures in the Screen Trade: A Personal View of Hollywood, 1985
   (Futura)
The Silent Gondoliers, 2001 (Del Rey)
The Colour of Light, 1984 (HarperCollins)
Edged Weapons, 1987 (Grafton)
Brothers, 1987 (Warner)
Hype & Glory, 1990 (Villard)
William Goldman: Four Screenplays, 1997 (Applause)
Five Screenplays: With Essays, 1999 (Applause)
The Big Picture: Who Killed Hollywood? and Other Essays, 2000 (Ap-
   plause)
Which Lie Did I Tell?: More Adventures in the Screen Trade, 2000
   (Bloomsbury)
The Ghost and the Darkness: The Screenplay, 2000 (Applause)
Absolute Power: The Screenplay, 2000 (Applause)
Dreamcatcher: The Shooting Script, 2003 (Newmarket)
Blood, Sweat and Stanley Poole, 2001 (Dramatists Play Service Inc.)
Wait Till Next Year, 1989 (Bantam)

'The Ice Cream Eat,' 1959 (*Transatlantic Review* No. 2)
'Da Vinci,' 1960 (*New World Writing* No. 17)
'Till the Right Girls Come Along,' 1961 (*Transatlantic Review* No. 8)
'Something Blue,' 1963 (*Rogue* v 8 # 4)
'The Simple Pleasures of the Rich,' 1974 (*Transatlantic Review* No. 50)

A Family Affair—Final Production Version, Undated (Unpublished)
A Family Affair—Revisions, 1960 (Unpublished)

WORKS BY OTHERS

Andersen, Richard, *William Goldman* (*Twayne's United States Authors Series*), 1979 (Twayne)
Brady, John, *The Craft Of The Screenwriter,* 1982 (Touchstone)
Cohen, Douglas J., *No Way to Treat A Lady: A Musical,* 1999 (Samuel French)

Mandelbaum, Ken, *Not Since Carrie: Forty Years of Broadway Musical Flops*, 1992 (St. Martin's Griffin)

Shaw, Irwin, *Mixed Company*, 1977 (New English Library)

Wasko, Janet, *Hollywood in the Information Age: Beyond the Silver Screen*, 1995 (University of Texas Press)

WEBSITES

www.ibdb.com

www.kirkusreviews.com

variety.com

www.ew.com

boxofficemojo.com

www.wga.org

Index

Also by Sean Egan from
BearManor Media

Ponies & Rainbows:
The Life of James Kirkwood

James Kirkwood is the forgotten man of American letters.

In 1975, he had two shows playing on Broadway, while his latest novel *Some Kind of Hero* saw reviewers comparing him to Saul Bellow and Joseph Heller. One of those shows – *A Chorus Line* – won him a Pulitzer Prize for his co-writing contribution and went on to become the biggest stage phenomenon in history. Yet today his work is largely out of print and his name rarely mentioned.

Kirkwood led a life that was as gripping as any of his novels or plays. The son of silent screen stars, he grew up in Hollywood surrounded by celebrities and opulence before his parents went broke. His childhood was littered with trauma, including finding the dead body of his mother's fiancé when he was twelve. Before writing, his professional life encompassed the coast guard, stand-up comedy and soap opera acting. His private life was equally varied, involving loving sexual relationships with both men and women.

Sean Egan – author or editor of two-dozen books – took over seven years to write this definitive biography, interviewing more than sixty of Kirkwood's family, lovers, colleagues, friends and adversaries in the process. In a sweeping narrative that takes in Hollywood in the Twenties, the boom era of New York nightclubs in the Forties and the Eighties AIDS holocaust, *Ponies & Rainbows* both details a remarkable life and seeks to re-establish an even more remarkable talent.

Interviewees include: Gary Beach, Vasili Bogazianos, Ahmet Ertegun, Bill Gile, Milton Katselas, Terence Kilburn, Larry Kramer, Arthur Laurents, Baayork Lee, Jim Marrs, Vivian Matalon, Donna McKechnie, Terrence McNally, Donald Oliver, Richard Seff, Zachary Sklar, Liz Smith, David Spencer, Elaine Stritch and Robert C. Wilson.

Paperback: 576 pages
ISBN: 978-1593936808

CPSIA information can be obtained at www.ICGtesting.com
Printed in the USA
BVOW05s1845100814

362360BV00015B/370/P